CRITICAL INSIGHTS

Cultural Encounters

CRITICAL INSIGHTS

Cultural Encounters

Editor
Nicholas Birns
Eugene Lang College

SALEM PRESS
A Division of EBSCO Publishing
Ipswich, Massachusetts

Editor's text © 2013 by Nicholas Birns

Library of Congress Cataloging-in-Publication Data

Cultural encounters / editor, Nicholas Birns.
   p. cm. -- (Critical insights)
 Includes bibliographical references and index.
 ISBN 978-1-4298-3732-3 (hardcover)
 1. Postcolonialism in literature. I. Birns, Nicholas.
 PN56.P555C85 2012
 809'.93358--dc23
                   2012007783

PRINTED IN THE UNITED STATES OF AMERICA

Contents_____

About This Volume, Nicholas Birns vii

On Cultural Encounters, Nicholas Birns 1

Critical Contexts

Postcolonialism: Origins, Methodologies, Receptions, Shaobo Xie 19
Postcolonialism: Social and Historical Contexts, John Scheckter 37
A Thousand Splendid Suns: Sanctuary and Resistance, Rebecca Stuhr 53
Identity and Popular Culture in Toni Morrison's The Bluest Eye and
 Junot Díaz's *The Brief Wondrous Life of Oscar Wao*, Ferentz Lafargue 69

Critical Readings

Island Noises: Sound Imprints of the Cultural Encounters in
 Shakespeare's *The Tempest,* Kirilka Stavreva 89
Crusoe's Empire, Gerd Bayer 107
American or Postcolonial Studies?: *The Last of the Mohicans* on
 the Frontiers of Nation, Colony, and Empire, Craig White 121
A Passage to India, National Identity, and Forster's "Others",
 Nicole duPlessis 140
The Formal Artistry of Richard Wright's *Native Son,* Robert Butler 158
Cultural Contact, Modernization, and Imperialism in *One Hundred
 Years of Solitude,* Juan E. De Castro 180
In the Shadow of Yeats: Tradition, Reaction, and Renewal, Jon Curley 197
Derek Walcott and the Idea of Postcolonial Globalization, Maik Nwosu 216
Representing the Self: Ntozake Shange's *for colored girls who have
 considered suicide / when the rainbow is enuf,* Frank P. Fury 231
The Limits of Culture and Community in Monica Ali's *Brick Lane,*
 Dave Gunning 247
Obscured by History: Language, Culture, and Conflict in
 Chinua Achebe's *Things Fall Apart* and Chimamanda Ngozi
 Adichie's *Half of a Yellow Sun,* Jonathan Highfield 262

Resources

Additional Works on Cultural Encounters   283
Bibliography   286

About the Editor   293
Contributors   295
Index   299

About This Volume

Nicholas Birns

This volume contains an opening essay by the editor followed by fifteen essays by various contributors. The first four essays explain the history and critical reception of ideas of cultural encounter in modern literary discussion, while the two essays that immediately follow compare different texts from different traditions and time periods and spotlight the similarities and differences between the two. The remaining essays examine specific texts, authors, or literary traditions as they relate to cultural encounter in literature. The essays aim to give a basic grasp of the book or books discussed, outlining plot, major characters, and most important themes. They also, though, seek to situate the texts within the critical dialogues that have surrounded and attended them. This volume can be useful for those wishing to bolster their sense of a specific text and also for those who desire an understanding of how literary study is conducted in the twenty-first century, why it has concentrated so much more than in previous generations on historical and political connections, and how it has established links with kindred disciplines such as sociology and anthropology. A list of works cited accompanies each essay, and the volume concludes with a list of suggested further primary readings and a bibliography of relevant secondary sources.

This volume addresses the theme of cultural encounters in literature through a diverse set of texts and through multiple methodologies. But the overall focus of the essays is "postcolonial" in that the literary works are read critically with a mind toward the history and aftermath of US colonialism. The contributors, all experienced scholars in their fields, have their individual emphases and ways of proceeding, but the majority turn to postcolonial modes of understanding as a productive tool to help elucidate the tangles and ironies of cultural encounter.

Shaobo Xie, in "Postcolonialism: Origins, Methodologies, Receptions," gives a detailed overview of the theoretical concerns behind postcolonial thought, which are equally political, literary, and philosophical. Xie's essay explores difficult concepts and employs some stretching of the boundaries of literary conveners as they have conventionally been defined. But the difficulties that Xie unfolds are different from those found in literary theories that exalt difficulty for its own sake. Encounters between cultures are fraught with miscommunication and misunderstanding, and sometimes difficult terminologies must be employed in order to address these difficulties. In discussing critics such as Edward W. Said, Homi K. Bhabha, and Gayatri Chakravorty Spivak, Xie shows how some have found ways to read literary works and the cultures that surround them that address and explain these fundamental difficulties. Xie's distinction between the anticolonial and postcolonial is a cardinal one that explains the original way in which postcolonial criticism defines opposition and resistance.

John Scheckter's essay, "Postcolonialism: Social and Historical Contexts," illuminates the world that called into being the theories explicated by Xie. Scheckter's comprehensive essay explains how racism, colonialism, and imperialism helped constitute today's world and how many pivotal literary texts arose in resistance to these forces or simply in their mesh. Today's globally connoted civilization is not just a phenomenon of the twenty-first century; Scheckter sees its beginnings in a world-girdling novel such as Melville's *Moby-Dick*. Importantly, Scheckter, setting the tone for the entire volume, examines texts from the United States alongside the former British colonies that are more traditionally the focus of postcolonial inquiry. This has the effect of fruitfully disestablishing boundaries and allowing canonical texts such as Fitzgerald's *The Great Gatsby* to come into productive contact with narratives of displacement and cultural assertion in far distant lands. Scheckter pays attention to the way changes in transportation and communication have made this a smaller and more interdependent world, focusing not just on history and politics but on technology and how it has impacted human conduct.

Ferentz Lafargue's comparison of Junot Díaz and Toni Morrison—with an excurses on Paul Beatty—not only compares a Latino-American writer and a writer from the African American tradition, but also addresses the issue of generational identity. Generational rivalry and/ or general difference can be as intense among writers of social resistance as in any other category, and Lafargue shows the very different modes and tones Díaz and Morrison use to address cultural difference as well as the underlying ideals they paradoxically share. A personal essayist as well as an Americanist literary scholar, Lafargue illustrates how both trenchancy of perspective and stylistic craft can help guide the reader in approaching demanding literary works.

Presenting a similar generational contrast is Jonathan Highfield's juxtaposition of Chinua Achebe and Chimamanda Ngozi Adichie, who are both Nigerian writers but are of different generations and are of different genders. Highfield shows how, across these differences, a national tradition of Nigerian fiction has evolved, but he also shows that this very national identity is still contested and that the postcolonial can also involve civil strife within a decolonized nation (such as the horrendous civil war in Biafra, which Highfield rightly positions as a central episode in postcolonial history) as much as it involves the residue of European colonial domination.

We do not think of the United States as having a contested national identity in the way that Nigeria has had. Yet in the eighteenth century, the future of the North American continent was still inchoate, and it was not clear that an independent, English-speaking democracy would eventually dominate it. The writer whose fictions address this era is preeminently James Fenimore Cooper, and Craig White's essay on Cooper shows how the depiction of the frontier and interracial relationships addressed the cultural pluralism of early North America. White compares Cooper to Joseph Conrad—a writer from a colonial background (Russia's subjugation of his native Poland) who devoted his life's work to depicting other colonial situations in Africa and Latin America. White's Cooper–Conrad comparison, obvious once it is seen but original in its conception, is representative of the kind of positive conjunctions that can occur when ideas of cultural encounter unlock too-fixed literary boundaries.

To the south of Cooper's America and over a century after him, Gabriel García Márquez presented another America, one whose incongruities required a different kind of realism, often termed "magic realism." Juan De Castro's essay on García Márquez gives a diligent exegesis of the plot and atmosphere of this writer's most famous novel, *One Hundred Years of Solitude*, while not succumbing to vulgar and patronizing understandings of the meaning of the novel.

As Cooper's and García Márquez's examples show, the novel has been the privileged genre of cultural encounter. Its capacity to represent both individuals and groups, as well as its ability to display different registers of language from high to low, has made this genre overwhelmingly dominant in postcolonial discussions Though this volume features discussions of poetry and drama, fiction receives the greatest amount of attention. In his essay on Daniel Defoe, Gerd Bayer argues that the genesis of the modern novel form and the idea of modern cultural encounter both are jump-started by Defoe's *Robinson Crusoe,* with its primal scene of contact between European and non-European and its intimate connection between colonial expansion and economic profit. Bayer also supplies a sense of Defoe's life and career, providing rich background for the reader to further understand the importance of Defoe's work.

A much later writer who is also a figure of major importance both in discussions of the novel form and in the ramifications of colonialism is E. M. Forster. Nicole duPlessis's essay on Forster's *A Passage to India* captures the novel's dialogue between European and Indian, Hindu and Muslim, male and female, material and spiritual, which underscores the grasp of cultural miscommunication that has made Forster's book prophetic and disturbing nearly a century after it was written. Forster's symbol of the Marabar Caves, as illumined by duPlessis, remains a resonant image of both the aspirations and disappointments of a full understanding of "the other"—and each other.

We tend to think of colonialism as something perpetrated by whites on nonwhites. Jon Curley's study of Irish poetry since William Butler Yeats shows a postcolonial situation in which Ireland remains an island divided between two political sovereignties, while being deeply intertwined with the formation of a modern literary culture. The lyricism and, when he felt it necessary, political forthrightness of Yeats leads to Patrick Kavanagh's solidarity with the poor, Seamus Heaney's mixture of abstraction and embeddedness, and the innovations of younger poets such as Alan Gillis and Leontia Flynn, whose inclusion by Curley gives the essay much added value.

In the volume's other essay devoted to poetry, Maik Nwosu surveys the colossal oeuvre of Derek Walcott, emphasizing his epic *Omeros*. In this narrative poem, Walcott, from the perspective of his birth and maturation on the small Caribbean island of St. Lucia, takes the pulse of the world from the viewpoints of the Homeric epic from which the poem takes its name, a great naval battle of the eighteenth century, and the lives of both whites and blacks in the contemporary Caribbean. Nwosu shows the breadth of Walcott's achievement and his delightful grace notes of attentiveness and evocation. Whereas other Caribbean writers such as V. S. Naipaul—at one point lampooned by Walcott as "V. S. Nightfall"—are pessimistic about the cultural possibilities of the non-European world in the wake of colonialism, Walcott, neither blithe nor unfruitful, discerns hope in the postcolonial tableau.

In many ways, drama is the most concrete literary form because it is enacted physically and in a specified and constricted situation. Walcott, as well as his fellow Nobel Prize winner Nigerian Wole Soyinka, has devoted important portions of his career to drama. In one of the volume's two essays on drama, Frank P. Fury excavates Ntozake Shange's *for colored girls who have considered suicide/when the rainbow is enuf* and shows its delineation of both racial and gender prejudice as well as its experimentation in genre and the exuberance of its language. This essay presents a frequently taught text in ways that at once clarify the basics and reveal new aspects to even the most experienced reader. Fury also discusses Shange's radical originality combined with her grasp of how her work exists in a dramatic tradition going back to the ancient Greeks and Shakespeare. The latter writer is treated by Kirilka Stavreva, whose analysis of *The Tempest* shows how its depiction of a magician exiled on a hidden island became employed as an allegory for colonization and its discontents. Stavreva's essay shows how linchpins such as Shakespeare can continue to yield new, revisionary readings. Yet one of the assets of a postcolonial approach is that it can shed light on recent books, not just longstanding staples of the canon.

Two popular books of the twenty-first century, Monica Ali's *Brick Lane* and Khaled Hosseini's *A Thousand Splendid Suns*, receive whole essays devoted to them here. Dave Gunning's treatment of *Brick Lane* illuminates the existing possibilities and barriers in a Britain beginning to acknowledge its multicultural nature by showing how the lives of Bengali immigrants to Britain carefully straddle the line between excessive separatism and overeager assimilation. Rebecca Stuhr's discussion of *A Thousand Splendid Suns* surveys Hosseini's work against the often-dizzying twists and turns of recent Afghan history, while also paying attention to gender roles as cultural constructs. Both *Brick Lane* and *A Thousand Splendid Suns* are popular books that have been studied in classrooms and in more informal reading groups. But aside from book reviews and brief comments on blogs and Web sites, very little has been written about them. The sustained, academic treatments within this volume are among the first full-fledged analyses of these works and cast a new and more rigorous eye on texts that will continue to remain widely read as they make the shift from being read as current literature to being part of the treasure-trove lovingly tended and explicated by literary academic scholars. Additionally, the popularity of Hosseini and Ali as writers is an illustration of how cultural encounter is not just an abstract academic subject, but it is also an inextricable part of our lived reality.

A danger with respect to the literature of cultural encounter is to try to ignore it as a facet of literary analysis and act as if the world were still the Europe-dominated one of the early twentieth century. Similarly, another pitfall is to imagine that we have already arrived at an era of complete cultural reconciliation in which inclusiveness abounds and tolerance reigns. Though social conditions in the United States have changed drastically since it was written, Richard Wright's *Native Son*, with its sense of the tragic divide between races and the terrible consequences each individual act or choice can have, is an eloquent testimony against the dangers of premature closure and celebration. Robert Butler's essay on *Native Son* leads the reader through Wright's Gothic labyrinth of crime and punishment, moral bewilderment, and existential clarity. Butler also pays attention to the political context in which Wright wrote, to the novel's reception by contemporary criticism, and the role *Native Son* played in Wright's overall career.

Taken together, the essays in this volume present a variegated fabric of cultural encounter in literature, and they reaffirm literature's value in acting as an ambassador between viewpoints and worlds, an ambassador willing above all to deliver both unwelcome and welcome news.

On Cultural Encounters

Nicholas Birns

Beginnings of Cultural Encounters

Cultural encounter can be seen throughout the earliest examples of Western literature. Homer's *Iliad* is the story of the Greeks' siege of Troy, which is a mysterious Asiatic city of uncertain ethnic and linguistic composition that is at once similar to and different from its attackers. The Bible is not only the story of religious revelation and conflict, but it is also the story of the Israelites' encounters with other peoples such as Egyptians, Moabites, Babylonians, Greeks, and Romans. In both these instances, encounter entails confect and understanding, struggle and outreach. The literature of cultural encounter does not provide easy answers to century-long conflicts, but neither does it simply remain within the confines of the perceptions and prejudices of its own culture. It strives to articulate a common ground, often long before such understanding is realized in the external world.

For centuries, the concepts of "self" and "other" have been the prism through which individual groups have viewed their world. Many cultures have language for "us people" or "our people." The Arapaho, a Native American group from present-day Colorado, used *Inuna-Ina*. Similarly, in order to distinguish themselves from foreigners, peoples of Eastern Europe called themselves "Slavic" from the word *Slowo* to refer to those who could understand each other, those whose talk made sense. Conversely, when German-speaking peoples seeped into southern and western Europe in the first millennium AD, the word w*ealhas* was used to refer specifically to foreigners, to others. Forms of the word are scattered throughout Europe from Cornwall and Wales, to Valais in Switzerland, and Wallachia in Romania.

Self and other are also primary categories through which people filter their experience with war, for instance, or with their culture's governance. These prisms are even more intense when viewed through literature, through experience based in the imagination. But imaginative experience has often provided a margin where the "other" might be imagined more generously and the "self" interrogated more rigorously than within such realities as war or governance.

Cultural Encounters: Other and Opposite

When considering the literature of a culture or time period, *other* does not always mean just *opposite*. Often, "other" might refer to a feeling of indebtedness or gratitude to an earlier culture or to an appreciation of the wisdom and learning that has been acquired through the culture's repository of past experience. *Beowulf*, the Anglo-Saxon epic written between the seventh and tenth centuries, was not about Anglo-Saxon England. Rather, it was about the Baltic Sea to which the dimly preserved historical memory of these peoples traced the source of their ethnic traditions. For most of Christianity's history, the Holy Land of Palestine where Jesus lived and taught has been out of Christian hands, and most Christians have come from very different cultural backgrounds than that of Jesus himself. Medieval Christian writing thus became a kind of cultural encounter with a set of doctrines that originated from a very different place. Similarly, the great sixteenth-century Chinese novel *The Journey to the West* chronicles a religious pilgrimage westward from China to India to the source of Buddhist wisdom that had become so important to Chinese culture though not native to it.

So often, writers have desired or elevated the import of what they did not know. John Keats (1795–1821), living in cold, damp England, dreamt of the "sunburnt mirth" of the South of France, whereas the Nicaraguan poet Rubén Dario (1867–1916) grew up in a lush, tropical climate, yet celebrated the *brumas glaciales*, or glacial mists, surrounding northern pine trees. Writers are more prone than other people to desire what they do not have, which parallels the more obvious factors of conquest, warfare, and commercial expansion in prompting the literature of cultural encounter. When Europeans such as the Italian trader, Marco Polo (1254–1324) first saw China, they wrote about it in terms of astonishment and marvel.

Nor does cultural encounter have to be between different ethnic groups. It can be between different social classes in the same society, between different religious or philosophical assumptions that happen to share the same language and milieu, or between groups assigned different roles in a given social framework, such as men and women do. Nonetheless, the paradigmatic model of cultural encounter was the contact between the West and lands in the Americas, Africa, and Asia that in many cases Western explorers colonized during the Renaissance era and after. This evident fact was slow to register within modern literary criticism. While history books, even on the most elementary level, clearly conveyed the magnitude and the often-imperial nature of European expansion, this theme was not often seen in histories of literature or in literary analyses.

The Renaissance

Great works of European literature that very obviously took colonialism as their subject matter—like the sixteenth-century Portuguese poet Luis Vaz de Camões (1524–1580) in his *The Lusiad*s (1572)—were marginalized on the broader world scene. Other works, such as the seventeenth-century Spanish novelist Miguel de Cervantes's (1547–1616) *Don Quixote* (1605–1615), were loved but were not discussed in terms of cultural encounter. When many readers who have heard of Cervantes's story but have not read the full text encounter it in a college class, they are often stunned to find the prominent role given in the early portions of the novel to a tale of captivity among the Moors, mirroring (and overtly incorporating) Cervantes's own life-experience when he was a prisoner in Algiers for five years. Moreover, the fiction of the very origin of Don Quixote's story—Cervantes's playful claim that his source was a manuscript written by an Arab named Cide Hamete Benengeli—bring to mind Spain's geographically proximate but politically troubled relationship with the Arab world. After the fall of Granada, the last Moorish redoubt, not only was Spain wholly part of Christian Europe, but to confirm the connection between national unity and Christian identity, all Jews were expelled as well. As the novelist Salman Rushdie (b. 1947) noted in his novel *The Moor's Last Sigh* (1995), this national consolidation took place the same year Columbus sailed for what turned out to be the Americas. Indeed, the methods and practices used by the Spanish to rule former Arab territories were applied in the administration of the former Aztec and Inca territories in the New World. Europe thus began to probe outward at the very moment it had, at least in its Western reaches, consolidated its identity as Christian. In this way, Christian-Muslim interaction in the Mediterranean was a crucial precursor to oceanic colonialism.

This interaction is seen not only in Cervantes but in Shakespeare's *The Tempest*, which, though long understood to be a depiction of the New World, is, from all geographical indications in the play, set in the Mediterranean. Yet *The Tempest* is also an indication of the relative belatedness of colonial approaches to literature. Taught as a magical tale of knowledge, mastery, renunciation, and exile and return, it is only since the twentieth century that the play has been analyzed in the postcolonial terms in which the student eventually becomes most accustomed to seeing it. Furthermore, the importance of Edmund Spenser's years of colonial landholding in Ireland to the poetic glories of *The Faerie Queene* (1590–1596) and of Sir Thomas Bertram's Antigua slaveholding to Jane Austen's *Mansfield Park* (1814) became routinely analyzed in the late twentieth century. But it took, in the latter case, the critical daring of the late Edward W. Said to unearth a connection that once demonstrated seemed obvious. Why the delay? It is probably too easy to suppose that Europe hoped to suppress the often harsh and disturbing legacy of its colonial deeds. After all, history books may have downplayed the true scale of colonial rule, but they were not silent on the subject. One force might have been nationalism. There was a desire to see works of literature as nationally defined, thereby defining the culture of a nation. One was supposed to understand France, Italy, and

England, for example, by reading their literatures. Acknowledgment that these literatures were rife with encounters with other peoples and traditions and that they were pure or characteristic on a level of national identity would have gotten in the way of the literature's presumed utility in spotlighting a culture. Moreover, until the 1970s, literature was often spoken of in high school and college classrooms as a sanctuary, a respite from politics. Literature was supposed to be the realm of pure art and of the delights of language, imagination, and storytelling. Even while seeing a French or Italian writer as emblematic of those countries, one was not supposed to worry about French or Italian politics too much, other than as background. In other words, it took a willingness among scholars to admit that political readings (and transnational readings for the dimensions of cultural encounter that had been latent in such key writers as Shakespeare, Spenser, and Cervantes) be permitted to rise to the surface.

The Enlightenment

The dimensions of cultural encounter, though, could not always be suppressed. This was particularly true in the eighteenth century when Daniel Defoe's *Robinson Crusoe* (1719) patently took up the subject of colonial appropriation. Aphra Behn's *Oroonoko* (1688), most likely based on the author's own journey to South America, was of one of the first novels in English by a woman writer. Behn (1640–1689) depicts Oroonoko, an African prince enslaved and transported to what is now Surinam, as valorous, eloquent, and noble—an ideal hero. A work of fantasy such as *Gulliver's Travels* (1725) by Jonathan Swift (1667–1745) featured expeditions to faraway lands with strange customs. The book was about difference, even if it did not literally focus on non-European peoples: Every fantastic people encountered was somehow overtly different from the Englishman Gulliver and his culture—smaller than him, taller than him, smarter than him, differently embodied than him.

For all of the era's surface elegance, more divisive issues of race were never far from the stage. As the plays of Shakespeare beamed more popular, his sympathetic depictions of people of African descent, as in the case of Othello, came to be recognized. The late seventeenth-century conservative critic Thomas Rymer (1644?–1713) virulently denounced Othello's race and also mocked the character's creator, Shakespeare. The eighteenth century was also the first period in which non-Europeans began to express themselves in texts written in European languages such as in *The Interesting Narrative* (1789) of Olaudah Equiano (1745?–1797), which tells a story of capture in Africa, slavery in the Atlantic, and eventual freedom in England. Equiano's text exemplifies the eighteenth-century idea of what Srinivas Aravamudan calls "tropicopolitanism," which is a colonial cosmopolitanism extending even to the tropics and that is aware of both Europe and its others and ambiguously traffics between them.

The era's dominant intellectual trend, the philosophy of the Enlightenment, had a paradoxical relation to this spirit. Enlightenment theories of progress and evolution often assumed European civilization had reached a peak of wisdom and that other cultures were wallowing in ignorance. Yet a novel like Voltaire's *Candide* (1759)—with substantial parts of it set in South America—acknowledged a world of difference. In both Voltaire and Swift, the genre of satire—with its inherent practice of contrast and of deflating conventional assumptions—served as a window into the unfamiliar. Enlightenment writers in general spoke appreciatively, if not necessarily knowledgeably, of Chinese and Persian cultures. Enlightenment ideas of universalism meant that there was not a particular "kind" of man, but there was humanity as a whole. These ideals were imperfectly enacted in the Europe of their day. But they were the prerequisites for any hope of cross-communication between peoples of different backgrounds. The replacement of Christian dogma by rational inquiry as the distinguishing mark of European self-awareness meant that those of other religions, whether Muslim or Hindu or Buddhist, were no longer so disparaged. On the other hand, Europeans often felt themselves able to look down on non-Europeans as still superstitious, still enmeshed in religion.

Romanticism

These contradictions might well have brought down any hope of what we might again call an incipient "tropicopolitan" consensus. But something more fundamental emerged to complicate matters: Romanticism.

Romanticism at once gave rise to racial and cultural stereotypes, grounding them in organic national identities and yet also providing the vocabulary of outreach and empathy that would later supply the vocabulary for potential cultural understanding. Jean-Jacques Rousseau's idea of the "noble savage" underlaid the later idealization of the primitive and unfettered vent in the different rhythms of François René de Chateaubriand (1768–1848), Walt Whitman (1819–1892), and D. H. Lawrence (1885–1930). But this idealization enabled a plurality of cultural possibilities even as it helped inscribe the idea of the non-European subject as one hopelessly estranged from critical, conscious knowledge. Thinkers like Johann Gottfried von Herder (1744–1803) paid tribute to distinctive cultural differences. But were they saying all cultures were equally worthy of celebration? Or that one culture was superior to another? This was never fully resolved in Herder's own work, but in his successors' there was often an extolling of some cultures (German, Norse) over others (Latin, Slavic). Another problem here is that the term *culture* as such assumes homogeneity. When we contrast "different cultures," often we assume that, notwithstanding their difference, each culture is alike in being coherent. African and European, French and British cultures might touch each other, but in themselves they were whole, integral. The discipline of anthropology, founded in the later nineteenth century, at once questioned the hierarchies between cultures by pointing out common aspects in all human behavior, but it left the question of whether cultures were in themselves integral when more or less undisturbed. In the later twentieth century, though, this idea began to be more sharply questioned. When one spoke, say, of "the French," did one mean Frenchmen or Frenchwomen? Parisians or provincials? Those who went to church or those who did not? Was a Frenchman a white, heterosexual male?

Or could a gay man be considered characteristically French? Could a lesbian? An Arab migrant? A speaker of a regional dialect? Ralph Ellison (1914–1994) in his novel *Invisible Man* (1952) had his narrator conclude, "Who knows but that on the lower frequencies, I speak for you?" Ellison's narrator was pushing back against the idea that only a white man could be a representative American. Similarly, in her novel *Typical American* (1991), Gish Jen (b. 1955) at once pokes fun at and affirms the way a Chinese-American can be a typical representative of their nation. This sense of diversity within cultures paralleled an increasing skepticism in the humanities and social sciences that we could ever totally grasp any phenomenon, whether in our own culture or that of another. Cultural encounter thus is never unqualified or total. There is always something fragmentary about it, something provisional improvisational—cultural encounter is not necessarily a deep heart's bon; it can be, as the Jewish-American poet Samuel Menashe (1925–2011) put it, "Like a visit / Made on the run." These latter-day amendments in our ideas about cultural encounter all have to do with moving beyond Romantic ideals. Yet Romanticism need not be totally dismissed. Its sense of the importance of place, location, and circumstances as well as its celebration of different standards of beauty, worth, loyalty, and honor helped guide people toward a greater willingness to meaningfully confront and interrogate one another. Indeed, the very idea of cultural encounter would be impossible without Romanticism.

The Nineteenth Century: Limits of Cultural Encounter

In the nineteenth century, novels set in locations where cultural encounter was inevitable canvassed how much could be described and how much yet could not. In *The Last of the Mohicans* (1826) by American novelist James Fenimore Cooper (1789–1851), the reader at first thinks that Cora, a half-African young woman, will end up being married to Uncas, a young Mohican warrior. Both die, however, before the novel's end, and the happy ending of the marriage-plot is restricted to whites. Nonetheless, one cannot dismiss the fact that African Americans and

American Indians are depicted in the novel. Cooper forbids racial mixing on the surface, but he makes clear that given the demographics of the United States, it will one day happen, albeit not in his lifetime. Similarly, Rudyard Kipling (1865–1936), the British writer famous for his stories set in India, was an ardent imperialist who unabashedly believed in the superiority of the white race. Nonetheless, in his fiction he depicted India and other parts of Asia with depth and insight to make clear that to attempt to govern India, his white readership would have to understand Indians as people—their lives, their culture, their hopes.

One can see what Cooper and Kipling were struggling against by examining a writer such as Henry James (1843–1916), an American who spent most of his later life in England. James routinely wrote about cultural encounter, the intermixing of values and background marriages between people of widely different geographical and social origin. But the cultural encounters he described were those between white Americans and white Europeans, and so there was no primordial objection to the intermarriage of his characters. Even here, though, cultural encounter was not a pain-free negotiation. Values were at stake. James presented American innocence and European corruption, American wealth and European prestige, and American optimism and European fatalism in ways that were sometimes schematic but sometimes varied according to individual personality and situation. James showed what was possible in fiction of cultural encounter and that it was possible to operate in areas where overt racial prejudice did not pertain.

Other settler societies had different attitudes toward racial mixing. Brazil, like the United States, had slavery, and indeed Brazil abolished slavery over two decades after the United States did. But mixed marriages were not legally prohibited in Brazil, and many Brazilians were of mixed-race ancestry. This had literary consequences such as in *The Guarani* (1857), a novel by Brazil's first acclaimed writer, José de Alencar (1829–1877), where Ceci, a young white woman, and Pery, a Guarani Indian, end the novel by eloping together into the wilderness. This kind of ending was the one feared by North American (and other

English- and French-speaking) novelists. But in Brazilian literature, it could become a reality. In the next generation, Brazil's most formidable and complex writer, Joaquim Maria Machado de Assis (1839–1908), was himself the product of an interracial marriage.

But even in Brazil, racial hierarchies remained. And the obduracy of racial prejudice was the other major factor, aside from the romantic roots of anthropological speculation as already discussed, in maintaining the strict discursive boundaries that often set the limits for cultural encounter. The legal encouragement of racial segregation in the post–Civil War United States by the Supreme Court's 1896 *Plessy v. Ferguson* ruling encouraged a sense of separate racial identities. Moreover, late nineteenth-century assumptions about men and woman envisioned the existence of separate spheres of what academics later termed "gendered space," where men and women lived related but often separate lives. The rise of certain categories of literature in the late twentieth century, such as literature centered around women, African Americans, and Latinos, was often seen as a form of identity politics, a claim to some sort of essential property in the literature that corresponded to a state of being within the culture. This alone would sound not far from a Romantic thinker like Johann Herder. But the difference is that for many subordinated groups, these identities were imposed as a mark of status, distinction, and hierarchy. In *Contending Forces* (1900), by Pauline Hopkins (1859–1930), a young woman brought up white and privileged in the slaveholding South suddenly finds that she is deemed black and is dispossessed not only of land but identity. Hopkins's use of this racial switch as a plot turn also implies both how basically flimsy and how accidentally consequential arbitrary definitions of race can be.

The Twentieth Century: Questioning Identities
Literature that writes against racism does not do so simply by presuming cultural identities. The solidarity of oppression that seemed to make a group one and separate was imposed by discrimination. But even after discrimination began to end, it did not instantly vanish. Lit-

erature written out of the experience of that identity remained and did not just instantly disperse as a side effect of the erasure of boundaries. That cultural identity politics seemed to so threaten the majority sometimes was probably proof that the need for them had not completely vanished. In other instances, though, the vanishing of fixed boundaries was what truly shook up the situation. Anglo-Canadians were used to French-Canadians being rural, Catholic, and traditionalist. But when those same French-Canadians became more urban, secular, and modern, settled assumptions about national identities were threatened.

Indeed, writers sometimes both affirmed and questioned identities. James Baldwin (1924–1987) uninhibitedly wrote as an African American. Indeed, his essays before and during the civil rights movement often represented African American audience to a newly curious white audience. Baldwin's fiction, however, was very much embedded in African American culture, such as *Go Tell It On the Mountain* (1953), as well as novels stressing a far more fluid, ambiguous set of relations, such as *Another Country* (1962), depicting a Bohemian milieu where artistic and sexual experimentation was as unimportant as racial background. In his most frequently taught book, *Giovanni's Room* (1956), Baldwin dwelt on a relationship between an American and an Italian man in Paris, sounding Henry James–like themes of cultural contact and social hypocrisy and never once mentioning race in the book. Baldwin was homosexual and African American, yet he is thought of as an African American writer far more than a homosexual writer. If, as the critic Leslie Fiedler (1917–2003) has suggested, the key to the American unconscious is a desire for interracial homoerotic relationships, the mainstream's reading of Baldwin might be a defense against its own inner yearnings. But Baldwin's tacit construction of his identity was at once more porous and more resourceful. The signature of Baldwin's achievement was his ability to embrace different aspects of his identity as he needed them. When an interviewer asked Baldwin how he had responded to being poor, African American, and homosexual, he replied not by pitying himself or bewailing his state, but by puckishly saying,

"I thought I'd hit the *jackpot*." For a creative person, cultural encounter, even from a disadvantaged position, can be a recess of tremendous empowerment and affirmation precisely because what one wishes to affirm is so often imperiled.

Baldwin's color was more emphasized than his sexuality because racial prejudice was far more prevalent and because skin color was, in most cases, more obvious than one's sexuality. Often, homosexual writers resorted to various guises and subterfuges to express content that could not be openly aired. This often led to detours, which in turn became revelations. The British novelist Mary Renault (1905–1983) was a lesbian, and in the years after World War II attempted to write novels about homosexual relationships set in contemporary contexts. This strategy failed both commercially and critically, and Renault turned to the topic of ancient Greece, a subject in which she found her life's work. Renault's novels frequently depicted male homo-erotic relationships, which also presented a vision of Greece that stressed its otherness from the modern world. Whereas the conventional tradition had seen figures such as Theseus and Alexander the Great as exemplars for later times, Renault's fiction showed how fundamentally different they were from any model of the modern individual. She thus made the past itself into an object of curiosity and made reading historical fiction a form of cultural encounter. It might have been thought Renault was forced to evade her subject by going to the past as a setting, simply as a matter of recourse. But Renault not only faced the issue but also brought up another very rich layer: that of our encounter with a past that is both crucial to and different from us.

Cultural Encounter in the Postcolonial Era

Writers like Baldwin and Renault were actually rather uncommon in their era, where an emphasis on style and technique often precluded a cross-cultural emphasis. Novels of the African American experience such as Richard Wright's *Native Son* (1940) challenged this consensus. So did work coming from Asia and Africa, which saw many newly independent states being formed between the late 1940s and the early 1960s. These countries entered a global milieu in a condition of formal empowerment, but their citizens still faced practical discrimination. The Nigerian playwright and poet Wole Soyinka (b. 1937) embodied the latter in his famous poem "Telephone Conversation" (1959). Here, a young Nigerian student tries to rent an apartment over the phone from a white woman in London and feels he must apprise her that he is black. This sets up an anxious dialogue as scathingly funny as it is troubling:

> "One moment, madam!" —sensing
> Her receiver rearing on the thunderclap
> About my ears—"Madam," I pleaded, "wouldn't you rather
> See for yourself?"

The literature of cultural encounter is fundamentally about seeing people for themselves. It is not about seeing Nigeria, for example, but seeing Nigerians. The interaction of countries can be studied in the disciplines of history, politics, and sociology. The study of literature involves contact between peoples. Of course, when one is studying peoples enmeshed in the throes of large-scale migration and social change, one must understand the political developments that accompany this change. The fiction that came out of Latin America during its "Boom Generation" of the 1960s and 1970s, epitomized by *One Hundred Years of Solitude* (1967) by Gabriel García Márquez (b. 1927), brought Latin America to world attention and excited readers with its impassioned view of an exotic society rendered in a mode at once vigorous and experimental. But sometimes North American readers assumed they had ingested or consumed Latin America as such and that reading a novel of a nation or region was to know that nation or region. Yet as the literature of Africa indicated, literature was likely to focus on rivalries within a nation or people whose lives were caught and frustrated, not enabled, by national narratives. *Half of a Yellow Sun*

(2006) by Chimamanda Ngozi Adichie (b. 1977) chronicles the suffering of civil war in Nigeria, where national divisions fail to paper over fratricidal rivalries and are more an aspiration than a reality. The point is not that Nigeria, an African nation that gained independence in the recent past, has any more illegitimacy as a nation than a slightly less recently unified state such as Germany or Italy. It is that a national polity defines lives but also, in their concrete materializations, lives often fall between its cracks. Rushdie, whose *Midnight's Children* (1981) was seen as a novel that more or less "presented" India to the West, followed up that capacious national allegory with a shorter book, *Shame* (1983), whose focus was Pakistan. But the book's shape—smaller, more truncated, filled with muted frustration as much as teeming exuberance—in a sense mimed Pakistan much as *Midnight's Children* in much the same way *Midnight's Children* had mimed India. And indeed, Rushdie could claim to be of both countries. Born in India, his Muslim family had moved to Pakistan when he was a teenager. Rushdie was educated at Oxford University in England and became known as a British writer; in his later years he spent much time in the United States. How was a writer to be nationally defined? Successful writers from former European colonies often ended up moving to the former colonial metropolis, in some cases, as V. S. Naipaul (b. 1932) maintained, because the viable publishing markets and critical apparatuses were primarily there. Henry James gave much the same justification a century earlier when he moved from the United States to Britain. Being a writer from a country did not mean one stayed in that country or was stolidly representative of it.

Moreover, the content of literature in the late twentieth century became manifestly transnational. In *De Niro's Game* (2006) by the Lebanese-Canadian novelist Rawi Hage (b. 1964), set amid the Lebanese civil war of the 1970s, two boys grow up to express their image of risk and violence through the metaphor of an American movie. In *The Namesake* (2003) by Jhumpa Lahiri (b. 1967), the protagonist, Gogol Ganguli, gets his name from the nineteenth-century Russian novelist, whose fiction his parents are reading on a railway journey across India when he was born. The character then grows up in America and through the transnational act of reading is raised with both an Indian and a Russian cast to his name.

Sometimes even identities themselves can be exchanged. The frequently taught play *The Golden Age* (1985) by the Australian dramatist Louis Nowra (b. 1950) features a splinter group of white colonists who became separated from the main strand of Australia and in effect develop a separate culture. When, generations later, they are found, the whites that find them treat them as Indigenous Australians: condescendingly and in ways that threaten their continuing viability as a people. If cultural identity is not inherent but acquired or imposed, cultural encounter more than ever proceeds out of how we define one another.

Cultural encounter can integrate or exacerbate, salve or divide. It is not a one-size-fits-all cure for a traumatic past or for contemporary differences. Sometimes cultural encounter is only a record of suffering, as in the account by Janice Mirikitani (b. 1941) of childhood deaths in wartime Japanese American internment camps in "Desert Flowers" (1978):

> Perhaps in easier times
> You would have lived.
> Infants buried at Tule Lake.

Mirikitani's injection to the reader is to remember, to know. She is not fanning the flames of ethnic grievance through recalling past trauma. She is underscoring the way the literature of cultural encounter is not simply a passport to fraternal happiness. Its compass is capacious enough to depict past as well as future, the agony of what has happened as well as the hope that the course of history may change or be rerouted.

In his novel *The Marrow of Tradition* (1901), Charles Chesnutt (1858–1932), an African American writer, tells the story of an African American doctor whose talents go unutilized and unappreciated in the post–Civil War South. When a white baby from a prestigious family is on the verge of death, though, the doctor is finally called. As he ascends the stairs to treat the infant, his white colleague calls out to him, "There's time enough, but none to spare." This sense of urgency has animated the literature of cultural encounter. Contact comes through concrete life-situations, of meetings, confrontations, and dialogues. As Soyinka's speaker in "Telephone Conversation" indicates, the literatures of cultural encounter are literatures that invite readers to see for themselves.

CRITICAL
CONTEXTS

Postcolonialism: Origins, Methodologies, Receptions___

Shaobo Xie

Postcolonialism names an interdisciplinary field of critical inquiry examining the effects of Western colonialism on cultures and societies on both sides of the neocolonial divide. Postcolonialism rethinks the world and its history from the perspective of the colonized. To borrow terms from Robert Young, postcolonialism offers a language of and for the colonized and neocolonized—that is, for all those whose knowledge, histories, interests, concerns, desires, and situations are not allowed to count.[1] In other words, postcolonialism can be taken as a critical genealogy of imperialisms—past and present, covert and overt—with their various strategies of colonization in different social domains and geographical spaces at different historical moments. Like any other globally practiced body of knowledge, postcolonialism involves such a vast network of affiliated and conflicting critical endeavors, it is difficult to determine its discursive and disciplinary boundaries.

Indeed, the boundaries of the field designated by postcolonialism have been expanded to include most disciplines. One reason is that the concepts of colonization and decolonization seem to have enabled a critical methodology for addressing all manner of oppression or dispossession, be it social, political, cultural, and intellectual or whether it concerns class, gender, or race. Additionally, the orthodox Marxist model of class analysis, with its promised utopian vision of the future, seems to have exhausted its force and efficacy. Furthermore, because the colonizing West and the colonized rest are reengaged in a capital-labor relationship in the age of globalization, the cultural logic of late capitalism is essentially "colonizing" the psyche of previously colonized peoples.[2] Another reason for the expanding parameters of postcolonial critique is revealed by the British critic Stuart Hall. According to Hall, the age of capitalist globalization is defined by the sudden emergence of all kinds of margins claiming to rediscover and recover

---

their hidden, repressed, or forbidden histories by speaking about their experiences and representing their lived situations by means of post-modern theories and technologies.[3] In Hall's view, global capitalism constitutes a contradictory process that cancels local differences while encouraging them to flourish.[4] Those social, racial, ethnic, gendered, sexual, and geographical marginalities, emerging from their histori-cally specific situations of colonization, find a new paradigm of episte-mological and cultural decolonization in postcolonial theory.

Although it is widely assumed that Edward W. Said's *Orientalism* (1978) inaugurated what is known as postcolonialism or postcolonial studies and that terms such as *postcolonial* and *postcolonialism* were first used in the mid-1980s and early 1990s, critics like Robert Young assert that postcolonial cultural analysis dates several decades earlier. Young's *Postcolonialism: An Historical Introduction* (2001) defines the historical context of postcolonialism as spanning 150 years and traces the source of postcolonial discursive energy to prior liberation movements, nationalist anticolonialist organizations and activities, and counterdiscourses that interrogated and undermined European colo-nialist ideology and epistemology. The list of original figures respon-sible for the emergence of contemporary postcolonial studies includes such politicians and writers as W. E. B. Du Bois, Kwame Nkrumah, Aimé Césaire, Jawaharlal Nehru, Mohandas K. Gandhi, Mao Zedong, Gamal Abdel Nasser, Ho Chi Minh, Ché Guevara, Fidel Castro, Frantz Fanon, C. L. R. James, and Amilcar Cabral. Events and organizations responsible for the emergence of postcolonial studies include the Non-Aligned Nations association, Pan-Africanism, FLN, the Bandung Con-ference of 1955, and the Organization of Solidarity of the Peoples of Asia, Africa and Latin America of 1966. These mark the beginnings of postcolonial epistemology and cultural analysis as well as the histori-cal sites of social, political, and cultural decolonization. Actually, in Young's view, postcolonialism and tricontinentalism—that is to say, Asia, Africa, and Latin America acting in perceived concert—are sim-ply synonymous.[5] What is particularly interesting and enlightening is that if, as Young insists, Karl Marx, V. I. Lenin, W. E. B. Du Bois, Mao Zedong, Ché Guevara, Aimé Césaire, Antonio Gramsci, Frantz Fanon, Jean-Paul Sartre, Jacques Derrida, Michel Foucault, and Hélène Cixous have all contributed to the political and intellectual context for the formation of postcolonial studies, then not only is postcolonialism the most eclectic in its sources and resources, but it is also arguably the most politically consequent and far-reaching post-marked discourse in the twentieth century. Although it is impossible to determine any singular origin of postcolonialism, one may agree with Young that the material, epistemological, and political condition of possibility for postcolonialism, to a large extent, owes its existence to the tricontinental anticolonialist movements.

However, it is necessary to distinguish between the activities respectively designated by postcolonialism and anticolonialism. Despite their shared opposition to colonialism, it is reductive and even misleading to conflate anticolonialism and postcolonialism. It is acceptable to trace the beginnings of postcolonialism to tricontinental movements, but it is dubious to equate it with anticolonialism for the following reasons. Anticolonialism or tricontinentalism was about the forming of nation-states from previously colonized countries and areas. Its ultimate objectives were to achieve political and economic freedom in their independence from imperial powers. Tricontinental anticolonialism involved the organized political and ideological resistance of individuals, communities, and governments to colonialism through social revolutions and through direct military confrontation between colonized and colonizer. Postcolonialism stands largely different from its predecessor in that it shifts the focus of decolonizing energy from a military and political domain to a cultural domain, from macropolitics to micropolitics, from social revolution to textual revolution. This is not only because in the age of global capitalism, as critics like Arif Dirlik have pointed out, social revolution seems no longer likely to happen, but because a textual or intellectual revolution is urgently needed where anticolonialism has failed in order "to decolonize the mind" and "move the center," to borrow terms from Ngũgĩ wa Thiong'o. As Edward Said notes in *Culture and Imperialism* (1993), former imperial powers may have physically left the lands they had ruled for decades, and in some cases for centuries, but they still dominate them ideologically, culturally, and intellectually. In other words, drawing upon neo-Marxism (Mikhail Bakhtin, Louis Althusser, and Raymond Williams) and poststructuralism (Jacques Lacan, Michel Foucault, and Jacques Derrida) for its conceptual language and analytical frameworks, postcolonialism takes it as its discursive goal to interrogate and deconstruct Eurocentric or West-centered structures of knowledge and feeling located on both sides of the neocolonialist divide. It is arguable that, in this sense, postcolonialism, though more formal and symbolic, is culturally more subversive, theoretically more sophisticated, and perhaps politically more resonant in dealing with colonialism and its effects than anticolonialism has been. It emerges at the historical moment when imperialism and colonialism have been largely displaced from political and military domination to cultural and economic hegemony. Postcolonialism is primarily a mode of cultural critique within the academic world, though its theoretical formulations, concepts, and analytical frameworks can and have passed into various organized decolonization movements outside academia. Indeed, postcolonialism points to a set of critical methodologies aimed at undoing fundamental assumptions underwriting colonialism and imperialism in their variously protean forms.

It is also necessary to distinguish between postcolonialism and poststructuralist theory. According to some critics, postcolonialism, as a progeny of postmodern theory, is only innovative and original in reformulating older problematics of third-worldism in terms of New French Theory.[6] In Aijaz Ahmad's estimate, postcolonial theory is simply an extension of contemporary Western epistemological and intellectual imperialism, a new medium through which the imperial West is recolonizing the rest of the world.[7] Ahmad's criticism is echoed in Stephen Slemon and Helen Tiffin's *After Europe* (1989), which takes postcolonialism with its theoretically sophisticated textual analysis to task for subjugating the colonized and neocolonized subjects to institutionalized Western theory, erasing the actual locus of subversive agency (Slemon and Tiffin xviii). Responses from critics like Gyan Prakash and Robert Young tell a different story of postcolonialism, which they see as "both contestatory and committed toward political ideals of a transnational social injustice," critiquing contemporary hegemonic economic imperialism as well as historical colonialism and imperialism, and seeking to "combat the continuing, often covert, operation of an imperialist system of economic, political and cultural domination" (Young, *Postcolonialism* 58). Postcolonial cultural critique borrows its conceptual language and theoretical frameworks from postmodern critical theory not because it is trendy and highly marketable, as some critics have complained, but because postmodern critical theory such as championed by Derrida, Foucault, and Lacan is itself a deconstruction of Western culture, science, and rationality with their aggressive claims to universal validity. One can argue that postcolonialism and poststructuralism are somewhat halfway fellow travelers. The methodological parallels between them should not be used as an excuse for overlooking their differences. First of all, as Young notes in a different context, the fundamental goal or task of postcolonialism is to "analyse world history and its cultures from a non-European perspective, to explore, articulate and represent subaltern views and their different marginalised knowledges" (Young, "What Is the Postcolonial?" 18). Second, for postcolonial critics to borrow from poststructuralist theories is to recite and resite them in different discursive, historical, and political contexts, which necessarily acts as a catachresis or redeployment of their philosophical formulations and rhetorical strategies against or beyond their original intentions.

To have a more concrete grasp of postcolonialism or postcolonial studies, one needs to meet with its three leading champions: Edward Said, Gayatri Spivak, and Homi K. Bhabha. Said is regarded as a founding figure of postcolonial studies. His monumental *Orientalism* has been praised by postcolonial critics like Spivak herself as "the source book in our discipline" (Moore-Gilbert 35). It is universally assumed, from within and outside the postcolonial field, as a seminal text that is dedicated to indefatigably unmasking overt and covert forms of Orientalism and the complicity between Western culture and Western imperialism. Said has his intellectual apprenticeship in Foucault and Gramsci, who offer him two principal methodological sources. In the earlier phase of his critical career, Said follows Foucault on two accounts: the latter's conception of power and how it operates, and his definition of discourse. According to Foucault, knowledge and power are reciprocally constitutive, for knowledge gives rise to power and is in turn generated and legitimized by power.[8] In Foucault's definition, a discourse is made up of a systematic set of statements, which has its rules of legitimation, and produces the objects of its knowledge and constructs the reality it investigates.[9] Orientalism as defined by Said constitutes a perfect Foucauldian discourse, for it deals with the Orient "by making statements about it, authorizing views of it, by describing it," and, as such, it is "a Western style for dominating, restructuring, and having authority over the Orient" (Said, *Orientalism* 3). Orientalism produces the Orient. What Said inherited and appropriated from Gramsci is the latter's notion of hegemony as well as the perpetual social contest for hegemony and his geographical mode of thinking—that is, "a new geographical consciousness of a decentered or multiply-centered world" (Said, *Reflections* 471)—which Said sees defining Gramsci's whole intellectual career, particularly his seminal essay "The Southern Question." What Said found most inspiring and enlightening is the way Gramsci connected the poor, inferiorized, and vulnerable south Italy to "a north that is dependent on it" (Said, *Culture and Imperialism* 49). Gramsci's geographical analysis of the south-north relationship heralds Said's exploration of the ways Western imperial powers subjugated and depended on colonial peripheries for the maintenance of a privileged life in the metropolitan center.[10] Said's innovative use of the terms *geographical* and *geography* enables him to adopt a useful Marxism against the

Marxist orthodoxy—it takes up all Marxist issues such as class, class struggle, proletariat, hegemony in geographical or spatial terms. That is, Gramsci offers Said all the insights of Marxist analyses unburdened by Hegelian historicism.

Said's Gramscian spatial mode of consciousness performs a double task. On the one hand, it exposes and critiques what he calls imaginative Western imperialist geographies, which conceive the world in terms of self and other, good and evil, barbarian and civilized, justifying colonialism's territorial expansions and economic exploitations overseas. On the other hand, it gives rise to a geographical critical perspective, in which the world is seen as unevenly developed and resistant to colonial modernity. Colonialist imaginative geographies at once cancel genuine difference while also fabricating difference where it does not exist. Geographical imagination, on the contrary, is always at pains to question false difference and unmask the representational violence of the West during its encounter with its geographical and racial Others. Imperialist imaginative geographies divide the world into "us" and "them," designating the familiar spaces as ours and the unfamiliar spaces as theirs and making artificial geographical distinctions. Once those distinctions were established, all the perceived characteristics of the Orient or the indigenous were essentialized in racial terms as "rooted in [their] geography."[11] Imaginative geography transforms times and spaces other or alien to the metropolitan self into hierarchically placed values and meanings. Imaginative geographies of the West serve the purpose of translating "the appetite for more geographical space into a theory about the special relationship between geography on the one hand and civilized or uncivilized peoples on the other."[12] In his geographical or contrapuntal reading of Jane Austen's *Mansfield Park*, for example, Said succinctly maps out the power relations between the metropolitan Mansfield Park and the tropical Antigua whose presence is shadowy but meaningful. The relationship he sees between them is similar to that Gramsci perceives between southern Italy and northern Italy: a metropolitan center depends on a despised, exploited, inferiorized periphery for material and economic sustenance. In *Mansfield Park*, the counterpoint Said discerns or determines is space or spatial relations, or geography, location or relocation. The spatial counterpoint concerns two movements: the movement from Mansfield Park to Antigua and the movement from Portsmouth to Mansfield Park. The spatial relationship between Mansfield Park and Antigua resembles that of country and town, metropolis and colony, center and periphery. The good life in one space, Mansfield Park, is sustained by the other, Antigua. So it is actually a relationship of subjugation and exploitation. All imperial and colonial enterprises aimed at territorial expansion involve a metropolis transforming an outlying territory into a colony, a tributary, an agricultural or manufacturing base, a supplier of resources no longer seen as an independent country with intellectual, cultural, and moral integrity.

Spivak offers a different mode of postcolonial critique. Universally known as a deconstructionist-feminist-Marxist-postcolonial critic, Spivak often speaks to different issues in the same piece of writing, although the gender issue constitutes a recurrent motif in all her writings. As Moore-Gilbert has pointed out, she "consistently seeks to assert the usefulness of classical Marxist analysis for contemporary postcolonial work," for she "finds the orthodox tradition of Marxist political economy more useful than the 'culturalist' strands of Marxism" (Moore-Gilbert 80). In other words, in her view, the economic logic is the organizing dynamic of the world. As a deconstructionist thinker, Spivak always champions the gesture of subverting the dominant discourse from within, and she is well known for what is called strategic essentialism. If and when words are believed to have intrinsic, self-evident, and unchanging meanings, and if and when it is believed that things or social realities have a concrete, objective existence independent of discursive power, then we are dealing with a form of essentialism. In Spivak's as well as many postmodern or postcolonial critics' practices, essentialism is relentlessly unmasked and deconstructed. But the problem is that it is impossible to repudiate essentialism altogether; rather, essentialism is encountered where there is categorical thinking, and there is always a need to use terms such as *nation, third world, subject, subalternity,* and *social economic reality.* That is how and why Spivak advocates the use of strategic essentialism, which is the politically motivated, specifically situated use of the abovementioned concepts either in response to some imperialistic universalism or to "specific policies of exploitation" (Spivak, *Outside in the Teaching Machine* 13). In Spivak's own words, "You pick up the universal that will give you the power to fight against the other side, and what you are throwing away by doing that is your theoretical purity" (Spivak, *The Post-Colonial Critic* 12). Related to her strategy of using essentialism to deconstruct essentialism is her strategy of dismantling the dominant from within. As postcolonial critique undoes colonialism or imperialism by pushing the latter's conceptual language to a crisis, the postcolonial critic's job is to always dismantle the structure one "inhabits *intimately*" (*A Postcolonial Critique of Reason* 191; emphasis added). One of the most effective tactics Spivak uses is *catachresis,* which "involves wrenching particular images, ideas or rhetorical strategies out of their place within a particular narrative and using them to open up new areas of meaning" (Moore-Gilbert 84). To apply *catachresis* to colonial discourse is to prove the limits of its control, to turn its language against itself. This is how she rigorously and productively negotiates with Western texts, values, and theories. Catachresis in Spivak's hands serves not only to unsettle colonial discourse, but it also serves to recuperatively revise or rewrite contemporary Western theories including Derridean deconstruction and Lacanian psychoanalysis for postcolonial analysis.[13]

In her analysis of literature, Spivak always alerts one's attention to the sites and moments where the portrayals of the non-Western subaltern or her relationship with the metropolitan West betray what is called axiomatics of imperialism, according to which the natives, or non-Western others, are conceived as degraded, monstrous, uncivilized, and corrupt and need to be morally and spiritually reformed in order to meet the metropolitan canon of humanity. Such axiomatics of imperialism and the soul-making or subject-constituting project derived thereby are best illustrated in Charlotte Brontë's *Jane Eyre*, particularly through the characterization of Bertha Mason and St. John Rivers: The former is monstrous and an imbecile who is violent, dangerous, and needs to be restrained and reformed, whereas the latter is in India as a Christian warrior dedicated to "bettering their race," "carrying knowledge into the realms of ignorance," "substituting peace for war—freedom for bondage—religion for superstition—the hope of heaven for the fear of hell" (Spivak, *Postcolonial Critique* 124–25). One of the most persistent motifs spanning Spivak's entire critical career is her concern with the subaltern. In her definition, the subaltern are not those who belong to the oppressed working class or a certain discriminated-against minority, but they are those who enjoy the benefits of cultural imperialism or hegemonic discourse. The subaltern are those individuals or populations of the world who constitute the excluded who are outside of Eurocentric modernity, whose feelings, desires, and thoughts are not accommodated in the conceptual language of that modernity.[14] This is why and how the subaltern cannot speak. As Judith Butler succinctly notes in a different context, when Spivak famously asserts that the subaltern cannot speak, she "does not mean by this claim that the subaltern does not express her desires, form political alliances, or make culturally and politically significant effects, but that within the dominant conceptualization of agency, her agency remains illegible" (Butler, "Restaging the Universal" 36). In order to ensure that the subaltern agency is not erased in the conceptual language of the West, Spivak advises and encourages her metropolitan colleagues, those who attempt to understand or represent the subaltern, to humbly open up and listen to the subaltern "with care and patience," in the normality of the other" (Spivak, "Translation as Culture" 22).

Bhabha foregrounds different issues than explored by Said and Spivak, and this can be seen from the list of his key concepts such as ambivalence, mimicry, in-betweenness or third space, and cultural translation. As Moore-Gilbert has pointed out, Bhabha "seeks to emphasize the mutualities and negotiations across the colonial divide.

For Bhabha, the relationship between colonizer and colonized is more complex and nuanced—and politically fraught—than Fanon and Said imply" (Moore-Gilbert 116). Methodologically, Bhabha is as eclectic as Spivak and Said, and his intellectual and theoretical beginnings can be traced back to Derrida, Lacan, Benjamin, Bakhtin, Fanon, and Kristeva. In Bhabha's view, what happens at the point of contact between the colonizer and the colonized is the emergence of a third space of cultural production, the ambivalent, indeterminate space of signification. Just as Derrida adds a third term, the temporal dimension, to the Saussurean sign, so Bhabha constructs a third space, an interstitial locus of meaning, between the indigenous and the European, the colonizer and the colonized. This newly emergent cultural space proves subversive to both the indigenous and the Western, allowing neither of them cultural and discursive continuity. Bhabha's ambivalent colonial subject, which recalls the Lacanian split subject, not only threatens to defeat the Western Enlightenment historicist representation of the non-Western, but it undermines the unity of the Western nation itself. As Bhabha writes, "The problem is not simply the 'selfhood' of the nation as opposed to the otherness of other nations. We are confronted with the nation split within itself, articulating the heterogeneity of its population" (Bhabha 148). Because of postcolonial migrations, or what is called voyages-in, which have characterized the past several decades, the whole world has become restructured by a global cultural liminality or hybridity. There are no longer homogeneous cultural spaces and times. As Bhabha notes in the last chapter of *The Location of Culture*, the old national boundaries have collapsed, and the center has disappeared. Culture has become a translational and transnational process of production of meaning. It is in these translational and transnational interstices that newness enters the world. Living in the interstices of culture and history, he maintains, the subject of cultural difference assumes the status of what Walter Benjamin describes as the element of resistance in the process of translation (Bhabha 224).

Any productive discussion of Bhabha has to rehearse his discursively and politically consequent notion of performative translation. To get a good idea of what he means by cross-cultural translation, examine the following passage: "The sign of translation continually tells, or 'tolls' the different times and spaces between cultural authority and its performative practices. The 'time' of translation consists in that *movement* of meaning, the principle and practice of a communication that, in the words of de Man 'puts the original in motion to decanonise it, giving it the movement of fragmentation, a wandering of errance, a kind of permanent exile'" (Bhabha 326). Cultural or cross-cultural communication always involves performative or transformative translation. Cultural translation as such discloses and conceals, cancels and preserves the agonistic temporalities between cultural authority and its performative citation or interpretation. Performative translation deconstructs the authority of the original, and hence deconstructs the ceaseless process of democratic dissemination of meaning or power. This is how the Master's power is defused by the Slave's skilled hands, or how the colonizer's Master Signifier is uncontrollably at the disposal of the colonized. The core concept of the foreignness of languages encountered in Benjamin's seminal essay on translation lends well to Bhabha's innovative theory of mimicry or hybridity. As the foreignness of languages is irresolvable or irreducible, no mimicry can "faithfully" carry meaning or value or intention across cultural boundaries, and an act of mimicry can be either a moment of insufficiency or excessiveness. Either way, mimicry as such tends to undermine or subvert the colonizer's authority. That is also why hybridity as a *third space*—a space of cultural translation—alters, expands, and hybridizes self and Other at the same time, for at the other end of the translation process neither remains the same that has been known and both become displaced, enriched, and revised. It is in this sense that Butler contends that Bhabha's notion of mimicry or hybridity exposes the limits of the dominant discourse.[15]

Like any other newly emergent critical discourse, postcolonialism has been evolving in the midst of objections from different sides.

Russell Jacoby, for example, in his 1995 *Lingua Franca* article chastises postcolonial theorists for intruding upon fields of history, economy, sociology, and anthropology with no training or no educated knowledge about these fields, just tinkering around "with reference to Gramsci and hegemony" (Moore-Gilbert 14). John MacKenzie in his 1995 book, *Orientalism: History, Theory, and the Arts*, shows a similar distrust and dismissal of postcolonial critics, particularly the author of *Orientalism*, who he complains only "deals in truisms that had long been common currency among historians" (Moore-Gilbert 14). The late Cambridge professor of social anthropology Ernest Gellner, in his review of *Culture and Imperialism*, simply dismisses this book and Said's *Orientalism* as "quite entertaining but intellectually insignificant" (Moore-Gilbert 14). In Gellner's estimate, Said "was straying into academic fields not proper to the literary critic and claiming competence on issues which were, in fact, beyond his jurisdiction" (Moore-Gilbert 14). Another objection to postcolonialism is the argument raised in Michael Hardt and Antonio Negri's *Empire* that postcolonialist theory and criticism are "entirely insufficient for theorizing contemporary global power" (Hardt, Negri 146), and that they coincide with and reinforce global capitalism's strategies of rule, for both postcolonialism and global capitalism celebrate and deploy difference in the form of hybridity, circulation, mobility, diversity, and mixture (Hardt, Negri 138, 152). From a different perspective, but in an equally harsh tone, Slavoj Žižek takes postcolonial theorists to task for canceling the existing politico-economic struggle of the world. "The problem of postcolonialism is undoubtedly crucial," he writes in *Revolution at the Gates*; "however, postcolonial studies tend to translate it into the multiculturalist problematic of the colonized minorities' 'right to narrate' their victimizing experience, of the power mechanisms which repress 'otherness,' so that, at the end of the day, we learn that the root of postcolonial exploitation is our intolerance towards the Other, and, furthermore, that this intolerance itself is rooted in our intolerance towards the 'Stranger in Ourselves,' in our inability to confront what we have repressed in and of ourselves—the politico-economic struggle is thus imperceptibly transformed into a pseudo-psychoanalytic drama of the subject unable to confront its inner traumas" (Žižek 171).

Criticisms and objections also arise from within the field of postcolonial studies. Kwame Anthony Appiah, for instance, critically describes postcolonial critics as "a *comprador* intelligentsia: a relatively small, Western-style, Western-trained group of writers and thinkers who mediate the trade in cultural commodities of world capitalism at the periphery," making a living through selling images of an invented non-West in metropolitan centers (Appiah 348). Similar scathing remarks come from Aijaz Ahmad, in whose opinion postcolonial theorists make a career of trading in intellectual commodities between metropolitan center and periphery. He argues that the postcolonialists reproduce in the academic domain "the contemporary international division of labour authorized by global capitalism," using third-world cultural producers as informants and selling refined academic products made of such informational raw material back to the third world (Moore-Gilbert 18). In Ahmad's view, postcolonial critique, dedicated to explicating literary texts, increasingly divorces itself from organized political struggles outside the academy. According to Stephen Slemon and Helen Tiffin's *After Europe*, postcolonial theorists like Spivak and Bhabha evade the real politics of the postcolonial predicament, in that they are merely obsessed with theoretical issues, which, arising from the Anglo-American cultural and intellectual climate, are not necessarily concerns of third-world intellectuals (Slemon, Tiffin xviii). Critics like Arif Dirlik, Ella Shohat, and Ann McClintock fault the term *postcolonial* for glossing over contemporary global power relations. McClintock objects to the term for its premature celebration of the pastness of colonialism (McClintock 88). In Dirlik's estimate, postcolonialism is a progeny of postmodernism, and postcolonial critics' most original contributions consist in their rephrasing of old problems in new language, but they have deliberately avoided examining the relationship between postcolonialism and global capitalism (Dirlik 352). In Shohat's estimate, the term *postcolonial* fails to address the issue of contemporary power relations; it lacks a political content that can account for U.S imperialism in the 1980s and 1990s (Shohat 105). She explicitly expresses her preference for *Third World* over *postcolonial*, for the former term contains a common project of allied resistances to neocolonialisms, "usefully evoking structural commonalities of struggles among diverse peoples" (Shohat 111). Critics like Chandra Talpade Mohanty and Benita Parry have charged postcolonialism with its potential homogenizing tendency to cancel the geographical and historical specificity of colonial experience in different parts of the world. The postcolonial discourse imposes universal conceptual frameworks on "different degrees, forms and histories of colonization" and on "many different degrees, forms and histories of postcoloniality" (Moore-Gilbert 12).

While some of the above-cited criticisms are insightful, some obviously seem to have proved misdirected or irrelevant. What David Harvey admiringly writes of Said's *Orientalism* in a different context can be taken as a contestatory response to the opinions entertained by Jacoby, Kellner, and MacKenzie. In Harvey's estimate, it is Said who "so brilliantly demonstrates in his study of Orientalism, the identity of variegated peoples can be collapsed, shaped, and manipulated through the connotations and associations imposed as outsiders name places and peoples"; it is Said who draws "attention to the power of naming as a power over others as well as over things" (Harvey 265). Indeed, Said's *Orientalism*, in spite of its shortcomings and boomeranging implications, has not only initiated contemporary postcolonial studies, but along with *Culture and Imperialism* has inspired the desire and agency of decolonization in almost all disciplines of academic inquiry. It is a questionable assumption that postcolonial theory and criticism are entirely inadequate for understanding contemporary global power and that they coincide with and reproduce global capitalism's strategies of rule in celebrating difference, hybridity, circulation, mobility, diversity, and mixture. For postcolonialism's vindication of difference is to assert the equality of being on behalf of the previous and present colonized, while global capitalism deploys the strategy of differentiation only to recolonize the underdeveloped of the world. Only by legitimating and celebrating ethnic and racial difference can the dominated and marginalized peoples achieve recognition as equal and justify their right to equality despite their insufficient technological and infrastructural modernization. According to Prakash, postcolonial critique obviously owes its critical methodologies to poststructuralists' deconstructive readings of Western thought, but it is because these readings provide "a powerful critique of the rule of modernity that the colonies experienced in a peculiar form" (Prakash 10). Or, as Young persuasively notes, although structuralism and poststructuralism developed in Europe, both were "fundamentally anti-Western in strategy" (Young *Postcolonialism* 68). It is necessary to distinguish between Western modernity and its critique from within and between New French Theory and its postcolonial catachretized uses. Many of the concepts deployed in postcolonial studies such as "diaspora" and "subaltern" have indeed been taken from European intellectual sources, but they are never used unrevised or unreinvented in postcolonial studies. One major lesson we learn from the gloomy global present is that the world is far from being decolonized. As Butler writes in *Precarious Life*, millions of people, whose existence as the racial or cultural Other is understood as "neither alive nor dead but interminably spectral" are being excluded from the domain of "the human as it has been naturalized in its 'Western' mold by the contemporary workings of humanism" (Butler 32–3). These people are brutally subjected to the "violence of derealization" every day. It is to be hoped that as long as racially and culturally different people(s) are being subjected to derealization or dehumanization, and as long as imperialism in its various forms is taking place in our everyday world, postcolonialism as a strategy of cultural decolonization and a theory of cross-cultural communication will always act in its present continuous tense.

Notes

1. See also Young, "What Is the Postcolonial?" 14.
2. See also Jameson 47; Wenders 98.
3. See also Hall 183.
4. See also Hall 182.
5. See also Young, "What Is the Postcolonial?" 15.
6. See also Dirlik 352.
7. For this point, see Moore-Gilbert 18.
8. See also Childs and Williams 98.
9. See also Moore-Gilbert 27, 36.
10. For this point, see Said, *Culture and Imperialism* 58–9, 96.
11. See also Said, *Orientalism* 216.
12. See also Said, *Orientalism* 108, 217, 251.
13. For this point, see Moore-Gilbert 84.
14. For more discussion on the subaltern, see de Kock 46–7.
15. See also Butler, "Restaging the Universal" 37.

Works Cited

Appiah, Kwame Anthony. "Is the Post- in Postmodernism the Post- in Postcolonial?" *Critical Inquiry* 17.2 (1991): 336–57.

Bhabha, Homi K. *The Location of Culture*. London: Routledge, 1994.

Brontë, Charlotte. *Jane Eyre*. Oxford: Oxford UP, 1975.

Butler, Judith. *Precarious Life: The Powers of Mourning and Violence*. London: Verso, 2006.

_____. "Restaging the Universal." *Contingency, Hegemony, Universality: Contemporary Dialogues on the Left*. Judith Butler, Ernesto Laclau, and Slavoj Žižek. London: Verso, 2000. 11–43.

Childs, Peter and R. J. Patrick Williams. *An Introduction to Post-Colonial Theory*. New York: Prentice, 1997.

Dirlik, Arif. "The Postcolonial Aura: Third World Criticism in the Age of Global Capitalism." *Critical Inquiry* 20.2 (1994): 328–56.

Hall, Stuart. "The Local and the Global: Civilization and Ethnicity." *Dangerous Liaisons: Gender, Nation, and Postcolonial Perspectives*. Ed. Anne McClintock, Aamir Mufti, and Ella Shohat. Minneapolis: U of Minnesota P, 1997. 173–87.

Hardt, Michael, and Antonio Negri. *Empire*. Cambridge, MA: Harvard UP, 2000.

Harvey, David. *Justice, Nature, and the Geography of Difference*. Cambridge, MA: Blackwell, 1996.

Jameson, Fredric. *The Ideology of Theory: The Syntax of History*. Minneapolis: U of Minnesota P, 1988.

de Kock, Leon. "Interview With Gayatri Chakravorty Spivak: New Nation Writers Conference in South Africa." *ARIEL* 23.3 (1992): 29–47.

McClintock, Ann. "The Angel of Progress: Pitfalls of the Term 'Postcolonialism.'" *Social Text* 31/32 (1992): 84–98.

Moore-Gilbert, Bart J. *Postcolonial Theory: Contexts, Practices, Politics.* London: Verso, 1997.

Prakash, Gyan. "Postcolonial Criticism and Indian Historiography." *Social Text* 31/32 (1992): 8–19.

Said, Edward W. *Culture and Imperialism.* New York: Knopf, 1993.

_____. *Orientalism.* New York: Pantheon, 1978.

_____. *Reflections on Exile and Other Essays.* Cambridge, MA: Harvard UP, 2002.

Shohat, Ella. "Notes on the 'Postcolonial.'" *Social Text* 31/32 (1992): 99–113.

Slemon, Stephen, and Helen Tiffin, eds. *After Europe*: *Critical Theory and Post-Colonial Writing.* Sydney: Dangaroo Press, 1989.

Spivak, Chakravorty Gayatri. *Outside in the Teaching Machine.* New York: Routledge, 1993.

_____. *The Post-Colonial Critic: Interviews, Strategies, Dialogues.* Ed. Sarah Harasym. New York: Routledge, 1990.

_____. *A Critique of Postcolonial Reason: Toward a History of the Vanishing Present.* Cambridge, MA: Harvard UP, 1999.

_____. "Translation as Culture." *Parallax* 6.1 (2000): 13–24.

Wenders, Wim. *The Logic of Images: Essays and Conversations.* Trans. Michael Hofmann. London: Faber and Faber, 1991.

Young, Robert. *Postcolonialism: An Historical Introduction.* Oxford: Blackwell, 2001.

_____. "What Is the Postcolonial?" *ARIEL* 40.1 (Jan. 2009): 13–25.

Žižek, Slavoj. *Revolution at the Gates: Žižek on Lenin, The 1917 Writings.* London: Verso, 2002.

Postcolonialism: Social and Historical Contexts_____

John Scheckter

During the second half of the twentieth century, the world grew much larger. The usual claim is that the world has grown smaller, but that really describes speed, not distance or quantity: In a single night, we can cross oceans that once took weeks to sail; for a century, information has come to us almost instantaneously through the speed of radio, television, and now the Internet so that we scarcely know what it means to wait for news; our fresh food arrives from hemispheres away, defying the seasons. These are all signs of growth, not shrinkage. What we call "the world" in an ethical sense, meaning all of our relationships to the world—to the variety of information available and to the ways we try to understand it—is exponentially larger than the world any previous age was required or privileged to accommodate. In 1851, for example, when Herman Melville wanted to stress the cosmic insignificance of human events in *Moby-Dick*, he sandwiched his protagonist's action "as a sort of brief interlude and solo between more extensive performances. I take it that this part of the bill must have run something like this:

"Grand Contested Election for the Presidency of the United States.
"WHALING VOYAGE BY ONE ISHMAEL.
"BLOODY BATTLE IN AFFGHANISTAN." (Melville 16)

Everything points to unimportance. Few printed texts are more ephemeral than programs announcing "performances," and Melville's irony quiets the clamor of the "more extensive" events. The United States was an important economy, but not yet a political power, and Melville could count on his readers to feel that Afghanistan was too far away to matter. Things have changed, of course, as the world has grown larger: The American political scene is closely watched around the world, and everyone knows where Afghanistan is. We can assume that the role, purpose, and value of Ishmael have changed as well, as the growing awareness of the larger world, and increasing recognition of its variety, have generated the most powerful influences shaping literary and cultural expression of all types, in all places.

Melville's nineteenth-century irony, to which we will return, works by referring to several modes of generalization that originated hundreds of years before him and have lasted in some forms to the present time; we need to examine these patterns in order to understand the great movements of decolonization and liberation and the reconsiderations of race, class, and gender that have most deeply influenced society and culture in the past sixty years. Such thinking includes processes of universalizing social assumptions, totalizing perceptions of experience, and normalizing evaluation and judgment. These form what is called a "social construction," the set of underlying rules that influence a society's understanding, and in this case, the social construction depends most deeply upon a belief in hierarchy. In Europe, the European-settled Americas and Australasia, and every place Europe colonized or influenced, rankings and evaluative differences stem from the introduction of Aristotle in the Middle Ages. In the early 1300s, for instance, Dante's *Divine Comedy* describes a journey through clearly organized and ranked categories of punishment and reward. In the Renaissance, hierarchy was codified in The Great Chain of Being, conceived as a chain literally hanging (in Latin, "dependent") from the Heaven of Christianity. Every type of existence is described as occupying a link in the chain, in order—angels, humans, and then the three great kingdoms: animal, vegetable, and mineral. Further, the figure of the chain does not permit side-by-side equality or analogy. Among humans, for instance, any observed difference, whether of gender, race, religion, or social standing must be ranked in vertical hierarchy— superior or inferior to other items in its category. As a religious formulation, indicating relative closeness to or distance from God, the model acquires great force by claiming to originate in divine will. Challenging a particular placement, much less declaring "independence," can be condemned as blasphemy. The habits of mind thus instilled, involving close observation with the goal of discovering difference, grow even stronger when, in the seventeenth century, scientific method begins to evolve as the dominant European epistemology, or path of understanding, supplanting the "ancient authority" of Greek and Latin and the "revealed knowledge" of religion. The urge to categorize—and always, thereby, to rank—is vastly reinforced as Europe in the same period expands its reach by contacting, trading with, and often colonizing other areas of the world. Such observations often reveal their motives. In the eighteenth century, for example, Thomas Jefferson wrote a "scientific" justification of racial division and white domination. By the middle of the nineteenth century, many of Darwin's followers applied his theory of biological evolution to justify an "inevitable" separation of society into rich and poor along the same lines as the older argument that God favors some people and not others. Karl Marx, likewise, portrayed the roles and interests of different economic classes as the matter of ceaseless, unresolvable conflict. Because categorization and hierarchical order can be described as universal principles, applicable to all situations, these habits of thinking become self-reinforcing; any impulse to revise the process of evaluation, then, requires terrific effort, and while the system is frequently challenged, systematic counter-proposals will hardly be seen to gain ground before the twentieth century.

Assumptions of continual or even endless conflict, whether explained in terms of Darwinian "survival of the fittest" or Marxist "class struggle," tend to create hardened binary categorizations, totalizing the encounter of others as conflict between "all of us" and "all of them," friends or enemies, forces of good or evil, wholly victorious or entirely unredeemed. The implacable nature of such a mindset is demonstrated in Frederick Jackson Turner's famous 1893 characterization of the American frontier as "the meeting point between savagery and civilization." Native America, in all of its historical and cultural aspects, and all of the individuals within its many varied societies, can be subsumed within a single, aggressive, negative judgment. All European-American actions, on the other side of that hard line, are enrolled in the destiny of truth, progress, and deserved reward. At the time Turner formulated his hypothesis, America was in the midst of triumphal public celebrations of the four-hundredth anniversary of Columbus's "discovery"; the 1890 massacre of some three hundred Sioux at Wounded Knee, marking the end of Native American independence in the northern United States, was included in the price of that triumph. Further, having spun Manifest Destiny across the continent, America would shortly initiate overseas colonization by going to war against Spain in 1898.

Acquiring the Philippines, Guam, Puerto Rico, and part of Cuba, the United States followed the imperial examples of Britain and France— or, more accurately, joined the recently formed Germany and Italy in a late scramble for power and prestige. That is, for nations or individuals on the "right" side of social generalizations, categorical hierarchies produce directed opportunities for mobility. According to the model, the desire to improve will always lead to progress and improvement through emulation of the categories above. This universalizing of social direction reinforces the established order—the rich must be better if so many people want wealth—while distracting attention from other models of social organization that might be more just, rewarding, or peaceful. In the United States, independence from hereditary distinctions of class and origin emphasized the contrast with Europe but not without anxious questioning about what should replace those known values. America lacked a long history and developed cultural traditions, at least as these were represented by Europe; the resulting crisis influences such disparate novels as James Fenimore Cooper's *The Pioneers* (1823), Henry James's *The American* (1877), and Ernest Hemingway's *The Sun Also Rises* (1926), all of which consider whether political democracy must necessarily be accompanied by social opportunism and cultural mediocrity. Condemnation of imperialism is easier in the twenty-first century, but we should also understand that as European and American empires expand, their intrusion into the cultural patterns of those they encounter is not entirely a cynical matter of developing markets and extracting resources, but is often accompanied by social and religious missionizing based upon the most liberal, benevolent principles of a previous age. Deep assumptions of human inequality that were based upon patterns of characterization and hierarchy were everywhere in the social construction so that emulation and assimilation were seen as the clear pathways to full citizenship. The much-criticized Indian Schools in the United States, described first-hand by Charles Eastman and like the Australian policies of removing Aboriginal children from their parents, which was portrayed in Phillip Noyce's film, *Rabbit-Proof Fence* (2002), proceeded from thoroughly racist assumptions, to be sure, but at the same time represented the more benign end of the spectrum of possibilities that also included the subject peoples' continued loss, displacement, and annihilation.

Even in the metropolitan centers of imperial power, methods of categorical thinking, with the tendency to subsume other models of evaluation, produce habits of normalizing on the basis that certain behaviors or usages are the most logically, legally, or morally appropriate. Responses to normalization are always part of the discussion of race, class, gender, and belief because references to norms, as we have seen, insist that all others emulate them or else be regarded as inferior, perverse, or even dangerous. Such totalizing practices extend high and low. In the eighteenth and nineteenth centuries, dictionary makers and language experts sought to regularize spelling and grammar in part to facilitate communication and commerce but more broadly out of a sense that language *should* be regulated. In France in the 1800s, this effort lent quasi-legal power to academies of language and art in the form of committees charged with ruling upon acceptable styles of literature and painting. At the same time, English and American law formulated "the reasonable man," a general characterization of logical evaluation in matters of evidence and motive. As access to education increased throughout the nineteenth century, particularly with the public school movement in the United States, curriculum development focused upon producing good citizens, emphasizing not only usable skills but socialization into existing structures. Systems of handwriting, for example, instilled clarity and conformity in miniature along with practice for larger realms of responsibility. As with the Chain of Being, each element in this unified schooling was said to represent the nature of the whole: small aspects reflected larger patterns so that a child's poor handwriting might be considered a warning of intellectual deficiency, social deviation, or incipient criminality.

Processes of acculturation aim at internalizing patterns of conformity, which permit them to function quietly and powerfully. Frequent claims of simplicity or common sense—"things that everyone knows"—reinforce these behaviors, making them very difficult to challenge and sometimes rendering alternatives literally "unspeakable." In this manner, Virginia Woolf quite generously describes "the common reader" whose sensibility will generate a book of literary essays in 1925: "above all, he is guided by an instinct to create for himself, out of whatever odds and ends he can come by, some kind of whole—a portrait of a man, a sketch of an age, a theory of the art of writing" (Woolf 1). The common reader, then, is both an ordinary individual, admirably doing the best he can and the ideal citizen of a polite society who is increasing his knowledge in order to form a more comprehensive view of his world. In the same year as *The Common Reader*, however, this appeal to accepted attitudes in two other works now seems far less ennobling. In the short story "The Battler," Hemingway describes a character speaking "in a low, smooth, polite nigger voice" (Hemingway 138). He does not use the term as Mark Twain did in *The Adventures of Huckleberry Finn* (1884) to condemn the hideous ease of racist assumption; rather, Hemingway makes that very assumption and assumes as well that his narrator's vocabulary is everyone's and that the common reader will see no offense. Similarly, in *The Great Gatsby*, F. Scott Fitzgerald offers Meyer Wolfsheim, "a small, flat-nosed Jew" (Fitzgerald 69), as the only ugly character in a novel of beautiful people and the only speaker of orthographically substandard English. Here, Wolfsheim tells the first-person narrator, a Yale graduate, about Jay Gatsby:

> "He's an Oggsford man."
> "Oh!"
> "He went to Oggsford College in England. You know Oggsford College?"
> "I've heard of it."
> "It's one of the most famous colleges in the world." (Fitzgerald 72)

Like Hemingway, Fitzgerald—who resented his own treatment as a Catholic at Princeton—here assumes an easy acceptance of deep discrimination. Like Woolf with her equally deep humanism, they are people of their time who are living within their social constructions; to be sure, they do little more than perform common tropes of discrimination, but their comfort with such generalizations makes it easier for extremists to practice sharper cruelties and more difficult for their victims to protest and demand change. The smaller world, where fewer points of view need to be considered, does not become the larger world without some growing pains. Even Woolf, with her careful attention to the public and internal lives of women in *Mrs. Dalloway* (1925) and *To the Lighthouse* (1927), uses the first-person masculine pronoun in *The Common Reader*, acquiescing to the accepted grammar of her time. The idea behind the usage—often, again, a benevolent notion—was that "he" proceeded from "mankind," or "man" as a species. It was meant to be inclusive, but this positive interpretation nonetheless encloses vast reservoirs of assumed inequality and institutional silencing. Here, as elsewhere, accepted generalization and normalizing tend to forestall critical observation and intervention. The underlying tension between Woolf's discourse as a feminist writer and the public language available to her in 1925 represents the difficulties encountered by all of those who promote more direct enfranchisement in both political and artistic senses.

The habits of thought that limited recognition and expression in 1925 seemed more obvious as the twentieth century progressed and as the world became larger with increased speed and consequence. It has been said that one could begin adding zeroes, or even orders of magnitude, to almost any quantification of human experience. The fastest a human could move in 1800 was on horseback at fifty miles an hour or so over short distances; by 1900, steam locomotives commonly approached one hundred miles per hour and traveled for several hours at that speed. The first English ships that were sent to Australia in order to establish a penal colony took eight months to get there in 1787 and 1788. Even considering time spent in layovers, in 2011, it takes about twenty-four hours to travel from London to Sydney, a city of over four million people. Likewise, connections and interdependencies increased and have been assisted by new technologies. Undersea cables and radio transmissions, succeeded by satellites and the Internet, allowed the delivery of information at speeds previously unimaginable. Refrigerated cargo ships that allow New Zealand lamb to be served at European dinner tables and Latin American fruit to be served atop North American breakfast cereal also link regions and hemispheres in economic mutuality. The technology of war added more zeroes. World War I was fought in Europe, the Middle East, and Africa, but World War II was global in that it stretched from Montevideo, Uruguay, to Vladivostok in the Soviet Far East. The 47,000 casualties of the Battle of Waterloo in 1815 became the half-million casualties at the First Battle of the Marne in 1914. The 300 Sioux killed at Wounded Knee in 1890 became the 22,000 Poles murdered by the Russians at Katyn in 1940. Then there was the Holocaust.

Horrifying or hopeful, these patterns of growth and development are not new, of course. As Kwame Anthony Appiah notes, people since biblical times have moved around and encountered others unlike themselves through conquest or trade, for diplomacy or religion, in hope or on the run (Appiah xiv). In the 1700s, Jefferson and his colleagues inscribed the possibilities of such mobility with the freedom and dignity of mankind, offering the new United States as a place of unprecedented human opportunity. Beethoven pressed the same point in setting a poem by Friedrich Schiller in the last movement of his Ninth Symphony: "all men will be brothers." Melville in *Moby-Dick* presented Queequeg and the other exotic crew members of the *Pequod* as "an Anacharsis Clootz deputation from all the isles of the sea" (Melville 108), referencing a diverse band of petitioners during the French Revolution and representing the global possibilities of liberty, equality, and fraternity. We know the failures of these visions because they have been before us constantly; but while obvious brutality continues around us, the increased magnitude of human interaction has brought some very positive results. Importantly, three factors have coincided to generate the demands for ethical recognition that are the most powerful influences on cultural expression in the past sixty years: the logical extension of nineteenth-century European liberalism, the progress of information technologies, and the growing acceptance of uncertainty, once a principle of scientific method, within fields of social science, humanities, and art and, indeed, in many aspects of everyday life.

As the speed, frequency, and sheer quantity of global interchange increase throughout the twentieth century, the presumable isolation of Melville's "Affghanistan" begins to break down. More specifically, the assumption that a place is so subordinated through colonization or remoteness that no one outside needs to pay attention to it, that such a place has no voice of its own worth hearing, comes under increasing challenge both externally (as people claim a place on the world stage) and internally (as people express their particular characteristics and circumstances). In many ways, these assertions are based upon extending liberal concepts familiar to the powerful countries that ruled much of the nineteenth-century world: ideas of enfranchisement, access to education, social mobility, and economic opportunity. While efforts at extension can take a long time to succeed or achieve viable representation even in societies that like to see themselves as progressive, and while enlarging franchise is never unopposed, it is clear that ideas spread in a kind of viral pattern in many directions, and once released are very difficult to contain. Appiah points out, for example, that the major figures of South Asian independence in 1947—Gandhi, Nehru, and Jinnah—moved familiarly within the British establishment and used their training in common law to forge arguments against colonialism (Appiah 79). Likewise, the Charter of the United Nations, asserting in 1945 "the principle of the sovereign equality of all its Members" (Article 2.1), was strongly guided by the powerful imperial and quasi-imperial nations, which thus acknowledged the immense task of redrawing the political world in the decades to come. With greater irony but no less seriousness, the great Ghanian leader Kwame Nkrumah, "who went to college in Pennsylvania and lived in London" (Appiah 79), took Winston Churchill's speeches during World War II as a basis for expanding the discussion: "All the fair brave words spoken about freedom that had been broadcast to the four corners of the earth took seed and grew where they had not been intended" (Toye 262).

At the same time, after World War II there were fewer ways to speak nicely of the human hierarchies that for centuries had dictated approaches to race, class, and sexuality (gender and orientation alike). This is not to say that the West had simply painted itself into an ideological corner. Rather, the postwar period brought a vast rethinking of social configurations in all areas, much of which took place within post-Holocaust recognitions that political action would affect entire civilian populations and that the development of atomic weapons presented the possibility of annihilation on an even greater scale. It is difficult now to conceive that the legal term *crimes against humanity* did not exist until 1945; until then, nations were considered free within their territory to deal as they wished with "unwanted" indigenous populations (e.g., the Sioux Indians within the United States) or ethnic groups (e.g., the Armenians in Turkey). Once the underlying concepts change, such actions can be redefined as matters of global moral imperative, justifying international condemnation and intervention. Wartime conquests by Germany in Europe and by Japan in Asia and the Pacific islands similarly undermined traditional claims on the part of the remaining imperial powers that their intentions were benign and their rule brought the benefits of civilization to their subjects. Further, as the Cold War settled in and throughout the late 1940s and early 1950s, the Western allies found strength in continued references to freedom by asserting the contrast between the openness of their societies and the captive nations of the Soviet bloc (just as the Communist countries pointed to the equality of their citizens in contrast to the cruel inequalities of capitalism); the Berlin Wall was an effective symbol of repression, but it also pushed the Western societies to validate the openness they claimed to represent. These changes in political outlook (and even more evident in moral awareness) combined with the economic crises among the victors of World War II where rebuilding domestic economies and meeting social demands at home meant directing resources and energy away from imperial rule toward overseas commonwealths and cooperative exchange. In 1942, it was useful for Churchill to proclaim famously, "I have not become the King's First Minister in order to preside over the liquidation of the British Empire" (Toye 230), but by the end of the decade the direction was clear.

The great human migrations of the postwar period—West Indians to Britain, for example, or southern Europeans to Australia—continued to use ships as did evacuations, invasions, and tourism. The development of large passenger aircraft, however, changed all aspects of travel: the length and cost of the journey, the numbers of people moved, the possibility of visiting or returning to the country of origin. The introduction of jet airliners in the 1950s, and especially the 747 in 1970, promoted experience of a larger world through migration, vacationing, and study abroad and through short-term conferences for business, diplomacy, and scholarly exchange. Orchestras could go on tour, art museums could loan exhibits, and sports teams could participate in distant contests. Meanwhile, the exchange of information grew at a similar pace. When World War II ended, word arrived by newspaper and radio. Into the 1990s, students and professors worked in libraries using card catalogues; they typed their papers and submitted them by mail or in person; if they were smart, they made carbon-paper copies of their manuscripts. The computer, and particularly the Internet, have changed every aspect of information gathering, presentation, and storage, but even at such a pace, the skills required for disciplined work, careful planning, and clear expression have not lost their importance.

It is often feared that technological development will kill previous skill sets and formats. While this has happened in some specific cases, such as with the Morse Code, the usual pattern is that mechanisms change faster than methods. The replacement of mechanical adding machines and slide rules with electronic calculators did not change the functions or value of mathematics. Television did not finish off movie-making in the twentieth century any more than photography ruined painting in the nineteenth century. Rather, the new forms produced an evolutionary pressure on the older ones: Filmmakers and artists had to determine what they could do that the new competitors could not. The rise of digital photography put an end to acetate film (and to the chemical pollution from developing it), but photography as an aesthetic practice certainly did not die, and the social aspects of casual photography have vastly improved with Internet exchanges. Online news sources will hugely impact the appearance of paper media such as newspapers and magazines, and many will disappear, but the activities of editors and reporters will not cease to exist; as news sources proliferate, there will in fact be a greater need for careful observation and clear writing. Books that quickly grow outdated, such as travel guides and scientific reports, will be supplanted by electronic forms, but, again, the skills required to produce them will remain in demand. Literary books will last, not only for the pleasures of physically handling them, but also because of their easy access, their archival qualities, and, not insignificantly, the security of their contents.

The spread of liberal ideas and the progress of technology laid foundations for the third and most monumental development between the end of World War II and the present: the general acceptance of uncertainty as an organizing principle. This uncertainty is more than just ordinary confusion or the intellectual perplexity that leads, for instance, to agnosticism. Rather, it is a scientific position beginning with two axioms. The first axiom, which was written into scientific method from the beginning, is the recognition that absolute knowledge—what the seventeenth century called the Mind of God—is unobtainable for humans; the second axiom, which is from the nineteenth century, is that increased data results in decreased order. Truthful understanding is certainly possible, but so many factors must be taken into account across space and time that assumptions of certainty come under substantial challenge. Beginning in physics with Albert Einstein and Max Planck, new theories at the beginning of the twentieth century offered a new episteme, or way of looking at the world, that pulled away from the claim of universal applicability the idea that conditions were constant under all circumstances and at all times. Slightly later, Werner Heisenberg offered an Uncertainty Principle, asserting that the position of the observer and the structure of the experiment affect the outcomes of the observation. As these ideas spread from the hard sciences to the social sciences and the humanities, they produced a revolution that enabled potentially unlimited bases of observation and parameters of evaluation: At last, there is a disciplined, nuanced methodology capable of challenging the dreadful injustices of categorical and hierarchical judgment. In ethical terms, observations based upon relativity and uncertainty, rather than a priori assumptions of constant value, help us encounter flowing, increasing information—our widening world—with greater flexibility and faster adaptation. Recognizing, with Appiah and others, that social constructions are human developments and that all of them are limited in some way does not imply an abandonment of difficult moral decisions; instead, this knowledge demands more from us and insists that we interrogate our methods of observation even as we judge what we observe. With Jefferson's assertion, for example, that "all men are created equal," the older categorical thinking assumes that the meanings of such terms as equality, freedom, manhood, and even creation are fixed, limited, and knowable to all. Taken within a modern field of uncertainty, however, Jefferson's claim, losing none of its grandeur, becomes an ideal to be worked toward, a process rather than a prefigured conclusion, shared among many peoples whose senses of justice, freedom, and dignity may differ nonetheless. We cannot dismiss these differences as illogical or morally wrong: they form the very basis of a new approach to human understanding. Frederick Jackson Turner's envisioned contest of civilization versus savagery, the brutal binarism that leads directly from Wounded Knee to Auschwitz, gives way to Mary Louise Pratt's formulation of the "contact zone," a dynamic meeting place of interchange where cultural beliefs, languages, and habits interchange unpredictably and sometimes sloppily in ways that always challenge the methods of judgment brought from every side.

In cultural areas, and especially in literature, acceptance of indeterminate evaluations came well after the great waves of decolonization and indigenous liberation that transformed the political world roughly between 1945 and 1975. (Pratt's essay on the contact zone appeared in 1991.) During much of the postwar period, writers from newly independent nations or from newly recognized sub-populations labored in a critical climate of publishing, marketing, and academic discussion that hardly possessed the means of appreciating them. Cultural recognition was greatly advanced by the self-interrogating practices of postmodernism beginning in the mid-1970s, although these initially lacked the useful dimension of political commitment they would later acquire. In particular, however, a growing body of material, works of undeniable quality produced by "nontraditional" artists, encouraged both a general de-centering of cultural assumptions and the specific development of postcolonial theory that were devoted precisely to appreciating such authors as Chinua Achebe (Nigeria), Gabriel García Márquez (Colombia), and Leslie Marmon Silko (Native American: Laguna Pueblo). Thus, in 1978, Edward W. Said's pioneering critical work *Orientalism* demonstrated the errors and agendas underlying many Western assumptions about the Middle East; Said's discourse and his commitment widely influenced examinations of cultures everywhere—including, importantly, the metropolitan institutions that had dominated discussion heretofore. In 1989, Bill Ashcroft, Bareth Griffiths, and Helen Tiffin wrote *The Empire Writes Back: Theory and Practice in Post-Colonial Literatures*. It was revised in 2002, and remains a vital summation of postcolonial literary issues and a model of accessible, clear, and supple applications of theory. Hyphenating the term *postcolonial*, the authors emphasize that their scope takes in not only the "postcolonial" era following a nation's independence, but also the entire enterprise of imperialism from its beginnings in the Age of Exploration (and perhaps before) to the full historical sum of its effect upon cultures—home and colony alike. As with Said's work, this expansive range is extremely important because one of the easiest ways to contain or dismiss challenges to established methods is to claim that the new articulations appeal only to a fringe group or apply merely to a limited range of work. By showing, on the contrary, that postcolonial examination produces useful insights with regard to mainstream writing as well—Shakespeare's *The Tempest* (1623) or Dickens's *Great Expectations* (1861), for example—the new methods demonstrate their value not only to the socio-political margins but also within long traditions of cultural study as a field.

With its concern for the cultural expressions of previously excluded or suppressed people, postcolonialism offers a beneficial level of ethical commitment to postmodernism; the resulting interchange produces supple and rapid ways of handling the massive varieties of information in a widening world. The result is a view of literature that is more inclusive, more fair, and capable of greater self-critique and thus able to advance its own development. An example of this growth is the movement beyond the early-phase urge to dismiss the traditional canon of literary study as the work of "dead white men"; while this posture was historically necessary after centuries of domination, such categorical dismissals of entire types and affiliations were quickly recognized as reproducing the very fallacies they oppose and have thus abated almost entirely. Among larger academic fields, the old boundaries of subject disciplines or "majors," formulated in the nineteenth and early twentieth centuries (the same time as Turner's hypothesis), came to be seen as excluding a vast amount of information at the same time as they promoted "the best" or "most worthy" topics of study. By redefining a specialty in literature or film or physics not as a defense of contested borders but as a means of entry into a globalized, encompassing contact zone, the participant in twenty-first century culture can approach the fullness of character that has long been the goal of liberal thought. Melville's "one Ishmael" who begins *Moby-Dick* by stating his own insignificance can matter a great deal in the larger world we now envision.

Works Cited

Appiah, Kwame Anthony. *Cosmopolitanism: Ethics in a World of Strangers*. New York: W. W. Norton, 2006.

Ashcroft, Bill, Helen Tiffin, and Gareth Griffiths. *The Empire Writes Back: Theory and Practice in Post-Colonial Literatures*. 2nd ed. London: Routledge, 2002.

"Charter of the United Nations." *un.org.* United Nations, n.d. Web. 30 Dec. 2011.

Eastman, Charles A. (Ohiyesa). *From the Deep Woods to Civilization: Chapters in the Autobiography of an Indian*. 1916. Lincoln: U Nebraska P, 1977.

Fitzgerald, F. Scott. *The Great Gatsby*. 1925. New York: Scribner, 1953.

Hemingway, Ernest. "The Battler." 1926. *The Short Stories of Ernest Hemingway*. New York: Scribner, 1966. 127–38.

Jefferson, Thomas. *Notes on the State of Virginia*. 1787. *Thomas Jefferson: Writings*. Ed. Merrill D. Peterson. New York: Library of America, 1984.

Melville, Herman. *Moby-Dick; or, The Whale*. 1851. Ed. Harrison Hayford and Hershel Parker. New York: Norton, 1967.

Pratt, Mary Louise. "Arts of the Contact Zone." Profession (New York: MLA) 1991: 33–40.

Said, Edward W. Orientalism. New York: Pantheon, 1979.

Toye, Richard. *Churchill's Empire: The World That Made Him and the World He Made*. New York: Henry Holt, 2010.

Turner, Frederick Jackson. "The Significance of the Frontier in American History (1893)." *Internet Archive*. 30 Sept. 2009. Web. 27 Dec. 2011.

Woolf, Virginia. *The Common Reader. First Series*. 1925. New York: Harcourt, 1953.

A Thousand Splendid Suns:
Sanctuary and Resistance

Rebecca Stuhr

In his novel *A Thousand Splendid Suns*, author Khaled Hosseini provides a vivid portrait of a country shattered by a series of ideological leaders and wars imposed on it by foreign and internal forces. The narrative, which spans several decades, is driven by the stories of two women, Laila and Mariam, who, despite starkly different beginnings, find themselves intimately connected and dependent upon one another. Hosseini's women, much like the country of Afghanistan itself, appear to be propelled by the whims of outside forces, familial and societal, with little chance of influencing their own lives and futures Yet Laila and Mariam are neither passive nor helpless as they make choices and accept consequences to affect desired ends, both hopeful and tragic. In interviews and talks, Hosseini claims to write simple love stories, but his portrayal of Laila and Mariam and their dreams, trials, and challenges presents a complex view of women in Afghanistan that goes beyond oppression and the stereotype of the veil.

If was set in an Afghanistan at peace, it would perhaps have been a novel of contrasts: an urban life with educational and professional opportunities for Laila in Kabul, and a rural life of strict mores and stark deprivation for Mariam growing up outside the city of Herat. Because it is a novel of Afghanistan at war and in upheaval, however, it is a story of shared experiences. The women's lives come together and intertwine with a shared desire for their family's survival. The differences in their upbringing and circumstances become inconsequential as personal survival becomes less important than caring for each other and their children. The story of their lives runs parallel to the story of Afghanistan as the novel stretches over four decades.

Resistance and Sanctuary: Afghanistan

Through his characters, Hosseini introduces the reader to an Afghanistan that existed before the war and beyond the media's twenty-first-century coverage of the country. He paints a picture for his readers of a land of culture and abundance. As the novel opens, Jalil, Mariam's father, tells her as she sits on his lap that Herat, Mariam's birthplace, "had once been the cradle of Persian culture, the home of writers, painters, and Sufis" (Hosseini 4). He evokes the glory of the city through its ancient architecture and history. He impresses Mariam as he describes its current lushness, "the green wheat fields of Herat, the orchards, the vines pregnant with plump grapes, the city's crowded, vaulted bazaars" (Hosseini 4). Jalil attests to an Afghanistan with its own tradition of literature and a history of autonomous rule that precedes the era of the Great Game and the wars yet to come. Laila's father continues these idyllic history lessons as he relates the story of Afghanistan as a country of poetry and architecture, but from the perspective of Kabul. Finally, as the novel draws to a close, Laila returns to Herat to visit Mariam's birthplace. At this sad and reflective moment, despite the evidence that Soviet soldiers made use of Mariam's house, her *kolba,* Laila experiences only the peace and quiet beauty of the spot. As the tragedy of this novel plays out within the devastation of wars, civil chaos, mindless cruelty, and rampant injustice, Hosseini never abandons the thread of the narrative of Afghanistan's rich heritage and its capacity for beauty.

In the background of the main narrative, Afghanistan is buffeted from power to power. It becomes clear that no one can successfully rule or dominate the country. Its people, willing to sacrifice everything to fight for their political and religious autonomy, as well as the country's geography, eventually defeat each invading power. As Babi travels with Laila and Tariq to Bamiyan to see the famous (and now destroyed) Buddhas, Babi points out *Shahr-e-Zohak*, the Red City. The Red City was built as a fortress to defend its surrounding valley. Babi explains that it withstood the invasion of Genghis Khan's grandson but was then destroyed by Genghis Khan himself. The taxi cab driver comments on this story, saying,

> And that, my young friends, is the story of our country, one invader after another. . . . Macedonians. Sassanians. Arabs. Mongols. Now the Soviets. But we're like those walls up there. Battered, and nothing pretty to look at, but still standing. (Hosseini 132)

Babi concludes that the "only enemy an Afghan cannot defeat is himself." During the lifetimes of Tariq and Laila, the Soviet invasion will be followed by the warring rebels seeking to gain control of Kabul, the Taliban takeover, the American bombing campaign to take Kabul from the Taliban, and the ensuing partisan conflict that follows the American intervention. Just as Laila and Mariam experience abuse from Rasheed in their home and from random men as they venture out on the streets of Kabul, the country has been abused and traumatized by outside forces. When freedom seems to be within its grasp, as with the signing of the peace treaty with the Soviet Union, events and circumstances lead to continued conflict and violence. Even the Taliban forces bring with them many foreigners. When Rasheed and Mariam go to the hotel to use a telephone to call Mariam's father, Mariam hears "bits of Pashto and Farsi," the two major languages of Afghanistan, "but Urdu and Arabic too." As Rasheed notices this, he tells Mariam, "Meet our *real* masters . . . Pakistani and Arab Islamists. The Taliban are puppets. *These* are the big players and Afghanistan is their playground" (Hosseini 274).

The history of Afghanistan's wars and conflicts is morally complex. Despite the horrifying nature of the Soviet invasion of Afghanistan, it also brings constructive elements in its train. Although Laila's father loses his teaching job to the Soviets, he can see positive aspects of their control as well, especially in Soviet policy toward women. The Soviet-backed government raised the status of women by providing them with educational and professional opportunities. At the same time, this interference with entrenched tribal practices (Rasheed's sense of *nang* and *namoos*: honor and reputation) leads to the fierce resistance against the regime. "It is a good time to be a woman in Afghanistan," Babi tells Laila, but he also points out that the freedoms women have now are "also one of the reasons [Afghans in the tribal areas] took up arms in the first place" (Hosseini 121). This complexity is further highlighted later when, after the Taliban have taken control and begun their decimation of Afghan culture and the eradication of what remains of the rights of women to work, be educated, or to move freely outside the home, Laila declares that the Taliban are savages. Rasheed laughs at Laila's declaration, "Compared to what? The Soviets killed a million people. Do you know how many people the Mujahideen killed in Kabul alone these last four years? Fifty Thousand. *Fifty thousand!*" (Hosseini 251).

Despite its fluctuating fortunes, Kabul serves as a kind of sanctuary for Laila and her family. During the Soviet occupation, war raged beyond the boundaries of Kabul. Tariq's lost leg and the death of Laila's brothers serve to symbolize the devastation that is taking place in the areas beyond the city; the prevalence of land mines, tanks, and raging battles can be seen when Babi takes Laila and Tariq beyond the city's borders. Life in Kabul is not without difficulties for Laila, but she goes to school, has friends, the warmth of a home, a father's love, plus her special friendship with Tariq and the affection of Tariq's parents. This sanctuary is violated completely as the battle of the warring Mujahideen take over the streets of Kabul. The Mujahideen, having sacrificed everything for the sake of Afghanistan's independence, come out of the mountains and into Kabul having spent all of their adult years fighting. Just as the celebratory party Laila's mother hosts in honor of the fall of Najibullah turns into a scuffle of differing opinions originating out of ethnic loyalties, so does the brief period of harmony among the different rebel parties end in war. Hosseini writes, "The Mujahideen, armed to the teeth but now lacking a common enemy, had found the enemy in each other" (155).

Later, as the Taliban establish themselves as the rulers of Kabul, they root out what remains of the Kabul so beloved by Babi: the elements that contributed to Kabul as sanctuary. The Taliban smash the remnants of the Kabul museum and do away with any aspects of Afghan culture that predate or conflict with Islam.

The university was shut down and its students sent home. Paintings were ripped from walls, shredded with blades. Television screens were kicked in. Books, except the Koran, were burned in heaps, the stores that sold them closed down. The poems of Khalili, Pajwak, Ansari, Haji Dehqan, Ashraqi, Beytaab, Hafez, Jami, Nizami, Rumi, Khayyam, Beydel, and more went up in smoke. (Hosseini 250)

Many years later, after leaving Kabul, Laila returns to the new post-2001 Kabul. But even as Laila, once again pregnant, finds purpose and healing in her work with the children at Zalman's orphanage, outside forces are once again threatening to destroy the promise of sanctuary.

Resistance and Sanctuary: Mariam and Laila

A Thousand Splendid Suns is divided into four parts. Part One tells the story of Mariam and Part Two tells that of Laila. Part Three centers on the shared lives of Mariam and Laila living under the same roof, and Part Four serves as an epilogue relating Laila's life with Tariq and her children in the aftermath of Rasheed's and Mariam's deaths. Mariam's story begins in 1964 when she is five years old. Ten years later, at the age of fifteen, she is walking away from her one-room home or kolba on the outskirts of the village of Gul Daman into the big city of Herat to find her father. Laila's story begins in 1987 when she is nine years old. She is born the same spring as the Communist takeover of Kabul in 1978. Mariam is nineteen at that time. Their stories come together in 1992, as Laila turns fourteen and the Mujahideen battle for control of Kabul. Laila is separated from her family and married to Rasheed at almost the same time that this happens to Mariam. Their circumstances are different, but the results are virtually identical. Eventually, Laila will provide sanctuary for Mariam through the love that she and her children share with her—giving her a family, a sense of belonging, and a purpose. Mariam provides Laila and the children with the prospect of sanctuary through her decisive actions at the climax of the novel. Not only does she save Laila from death, but she also provides the chance and the inspiration for Laila to realize her full potential.

The novel begins with Mariam as a child living in near solitude with her mother, Nana, and anxiously awaiting the arrival of her father. It is a harsh, uncompromising existence. Her mother's stern manner is in contrast to her father's cheerfulness, gifts, and affection. Mariam impatiently anticipates her father's visits and does not recognize the stable if spare life she has with her mother and their few but trustworthy friends. Mariam also enjoys a fair amount of independence with her mother. Her mother will not let her attend school, but she has regular visits from the village Mullah who teaches her to read and write and to recite the Koran. Nana's bitterness stems from her experience with rejection time after time throughout her life. After suffering an epileptic fit, she is rejected by her fiancé, and when she becomes pregnant with Jalil's child, she is rejected both by him and then by her own father. She has little ability to reassure Mariam or to raise her with a sense of security and family having experienced little or none of these comforts herself.

When Nana believes that Mariam has left her to live with Jalil, her love for Mariam and her fear of one more rejection induce her to commit suicide. Her feelings for Mariam are deep, but she has not been able to express any such feeling to Mariam. The remote kolba beyond the borders of Gul Damen could have been a refuge for Mariam, but it is, in her mind, a place to escape. And yet Nana has cared for Mariam, providing her with the skills she needs to know to support and care for herself. In Hosseini's description of Nana's teaching of Mariam, it appears that they indeed do have sufficient resources to live on and, however emotionally inadequate, Jalil makes sure they have their physical needs met.

Mariam and Nana milked the goats, fed the hens, and collected eggs. They made bread together. Nana showed her how to knead dough, how to kindle the tandoor and slap the flattened dough onto its inner walls. Nana taught her to sew too, and to cook rice and all the different toppings: shalqam stew with turnip, spinach sabzi, cauliflower with ginger. (Hosseini 15)

In addition to Nana, there is Mullah Faizullah who teaches Mariam and the family friend Bibi jo who is a regular visitor to the kolba. In contrast with what Mariam experiences later under Rasheed, the Mujahideen who take control of Kabul, and finally the Taliban, this little plot of land is an Eden from which Mariam is expelled. In fact, later in the novel, when Laila returns to visit Mariam's birthplace, Laila sees a peaceful, idyllic setting and imagines Mariam as a happy child playing on the dirt floor of the kolba.

The city of Herat, her father, his nine children, his wives, and his cinema are temptations for Mariam. They form a mirage that lures her out of her home, away from her mother, away from the people and things that belong to her. She doesn't realize this until much later in her life. "She gave herself over to the new life that awaited her in this city, a life with a father, with sisters and brothers, a life in which she would love and be loved back, without reservation or agenda, without shame" (Hosseini 29). The idealization of this much-dreamed-of life disintegrates as Mariam approaches closer to what she believes to be its realization. After Mariam sees her father's face disappear behind a window curtain and she sleeps all night on his doorstep, the dream is gone. As Mariam leaves her father's house, she loses everything, including her mother and her childhood. She is expelled from her childhood home and Herat altogether, and she is forced into a marriage with an unknown man from Kabul.

In Kabul, Mariam seeks for ways to feel part of a unit, however it might be formed. In the early days of her marriage she quickly responds to the attention and praise Rasheed gives her. "It surprised her, this thrill she felt over his small compliment" (Hosseini 63). She is taken aback when he makes clear the extent of his will and his possessive nature, "Where I come from, one wrong look, one improper word, and blood is spilled. Where I come from, a woman's face is her husband's business only. I want you to remember that" (Hosseini 63). But later, she finds that Rasheed's insistence that while out in public she wear a *burqa*, a garment that covers her from head to foot with just a small mesh opening to see through, is, though at first shocking, a source of comfort. The burqa provides "a refuge from the scrutinizing eyes of strangers. She no longer worried that people knew, with a single glance, all the shameful secrets of her past" (Hosseini 66). Similarly, when Rasheed holds a celebration in recognition of Mariam's first pregnancy, Mariam does all the preparation and then is confined to her room until it is time for her to clean up. But, just as the burqa gives her a sense of sanctuary from prying eyes, Mariam convinces herself that Rasheed's protective nature is flattering, "Rasheed saw sanctity in what they had together. Her honor, her *namoos*, was something worth guarding to him. She felt prized by his protectiveness. Treasured and significant" (Hosseini 74).

She continues to look for signs of a bond between Rasheed and herself. She comes across his gun and tells herself that he has it for "their safety. Her safety" (Hosseini 74). Years later, ironically it is her awareness of this same gun and her now diametrically changed conviction that Rasheed will use it against her and Laila that motivates her to kill him. But early on, when Mariam finds a picture of Rasheed's son and first wife, Mariam feels a "kinship with her husband . . . she [tells] herself that they would make good companions after all" (Hosseini 77). As time passes and Mariam is unsuccessful in bearing children, she finds that Rasheed's affection turns to indifference and then animosity. There is no refuge, no sanctuary in her life with Rasheed because of

> his scorn, his ridicule, his insults, his walking past her like she was nothing but a house cat. . . . Mariam saw clearly how much a woman could tolerate when she was afraid. . . . She lived in fear of his . . . volatile temperament, his . . . punches, slaps, [and] kicks. (Hosseini 89)

Despite Mariam's anger and humiliation as she realizes that Rasheed will take Laila as a second wife, this second marriage turns out to be Mariam's salvation. When Aziza, Laila's first child is born, she becomes no less than a miracle in Mariam's life. Everything changes for her. Aziza becomes attached to Mariam, responding to her as though she is a second mother.

> Mariam had never before been wanted like this. Love had never been declared to her so guilelessly, so unreservedly. . . . She marveled at how, after all these years . . . she had found in this little creature the first true connection in her life of false, failed connections. (Hosseini 226)

At the novel's climax, when Mariam makes a calculated decision to kill Rasheed as he is in the act of murdering Laila, she makes sure that he sees her so that he can acknowledge her action. At this crucial juncture, Mariam, who has done all she can to appease and accommodate Rasheed, who has lived in fear throughout her marriage, is able to resist not only his brutal force but her own revulsion of violent action to save Laila. *"He's going to kill her. . . . He really means to.* And Mariam could not . . . allow that to happen. He'd taken so much from her. . . . She would not watch him take Laila too" (Hosseini 310). In these remaining seconds, she remains clearheaded enough to assure her results. "Mariam raised the shovel high. . . . She turned it so the sharp edge was vertical, and, as she did, it occurred to her that this was the first time that *she* was deciding the course of her own life" (Hosseini 311).

In the aftermath of her decisive action, Mariam comforts Laila by sharing with Laila her vision of a future sanctuary that very much resembles the simplicity and isolation of her childhood home, "a remote village where the road was narrow and unpaved but lined with all manner of plants and shrubs" (Hosseini 315). In this place, children play, there is abundance and tranquility. "They would make new lives for themselves—peaceful, solitary lives—and there the weight of all that they'd endured would lift from them . . ." (Hosseini 315). Thoughts of her loved ones are in her mind as Mariam goes to her death. She is aware of what she will miss: her companionship with Laila and seeing Aziza grow, marry, and have children of her own. "She would have liked that very much, to be old and play with Aziza's children" (Hosseini 329). Despite this, she is at peace with her actions and is cognizant that although she came into the world unwanted, she leaves it "as a woman who had loved and been loved back. . . . This was a legitimate end to a life of illegitimate beginnings" (Hosseini 329).

In contrast to Mariam's marriage, where the semblance of choice is part of the wedding ceremony, there is no evidence of choice in Mariam's execution, yet she is forced into marriage and she makes her own decision to take the actions that she knows and accepts will lead to her death. When she is married in her father's living room, the mullah asks Mariam three times if she accepts the marriage. She acquiesces only after her father urges her. In contrast, from the moment Mariam makes her decision to kill Rasheed, she fully accepts the consequence of each step that leads to her execution, even as Laila begs her to change her mind. In response to Laila's pleading, Mariam is assured and succinct, "Think like a mother Laila jo. Think like a mother. I am" (Hosseini 319).

Mariam's death, significantly, does not end the book. Rather than focusing on her action as sacrifice and martyrdom, the narrative continues and by doing so emphasizes the practicality of Mariam's act. It is one of many actions taken in the novel, including Laila's own failed attempt to effect their escape from Rasheed. Laila and the children must go on despite the loss of their mother, aunt, and friend. Their future gives meaning to Mariam's sacrifice, making it more than a glorious gesture. Mariam's action is heroic, but, as the narrative suggests, she is doing what mothers have always done and continue to do for the sake of their families and children. She has chosen death so that Laila and the children, together with Tariq, can find a sanctuary where they will thrive in peace and security.

Laila follows Mariam's instructions, and she and Tariq, with her two children, go to Murree in Pakistan, a small tourist town where Tariq lived and worked previous to finding Laila. Murree was Tariq's sanctuary, and he describes it as "worlds removed from the wretchedness he'd known but one that made even the notion of hardship and sorrow somehow obscene, unimaginable" (Hosseini 302). Murree does offer all of them the sanctuary imagined by Mariam with its natural setting; its isolation from the troubles of war, violence, and abuse; and in the loving nature of the community.

Ultimately, Laila chooses to leave this safe haven to return to Kabul. This is just one of many choices Laila makes throughout the novel as she strategizes for her survival. Although Laila's mother has neglected her as she mourns the absence and then the deaths of her two sons who fought in the battle against the Soviet Union, Laila has found a refuge in her father, who dotes on her. He is a teacher who has been removed from his post by the Soviets. Now, working in a bread factory, Babi teaches Laila about poetry and Afghan history while giving her parental love that her mother cannot. Babi and Laila are a supportive team. She protects him from the anger of her mother almost as much as he protects her from her mother's indifference. Her father's expectations for her to be educated and to pursue a profession set Laila aside from her friends who plan to marry and raise children. "Babi had made it clear to Laila from a young age that the most important thing in his life, after her safety, was her schooling" (Hosseini 103). Laila accepts her father's expectations for her and is proud of them.

When she loses her mother and father during the Mujahideen shelling of Kabul following the fall of Najibullah and the failed attempt at a shared government, Laila, who miraculously survives the blast, is left to her own wits and resources to survive. Initially it appears that Rasheed has acted generously and selflessly when he pulls Laila from the rubble. On the surface, it seems as though Rasheed is offering Laila refuge, and in a way he is, but strictly according to his terms. He has plans for Laila. Rasheed points out to Mariam when she protests his desire to marry Laila that Laila has little choice in the matter. It is sanctuary with him or exile into an even more unforgiving world with

> no food, no water, not a rupiah in her pockets, bullets and rockets flying everywhere. How many days do you suppose she'll last before she's abducted, raped, or tossed into some roadside ditch with her throat slit? Or all three? (Hosseini 192).

Laila, although demonstrating signs of childishness as Mariam nurses her to health, devises her own agenda as she realizes that she is pregnant with Tariq's child. For her, time is of the essence, and she quickly agrees to Rasheed's offer of marriage. Laila believes that she has hidden the truth from Rasheed, but he realizes before too long that this child, who has already disappointed him by being a girl, is not his. Despite this knowledge, he does not expel Laila, but he can use this knowledge to threaten her and her child and it justifies his violent anger against her. Laila, having been raised with a strong sense of self by her father, is not as willing to submit to her circumstances as is Mariam. When she does, it is because she has something to gain by doing so.

Although her first attempt to deceive Rasheed about Aziza's real father fails, Laila, undeterred, schemes once again to deceive him and, through deception, escape him and his superficial refuge. She gradually steals money from Rasheed, saving it to escape to Peshawar. As she and Mariam bond after the birth of Aziza, she includes Mariam in her escape plans. This attempt also fails, not because Rasheed discovers the plot, but because the women are too dependent on strangers to make their plan succeed. They place their trust in a man who takes their money and turns them in to the police. The policeman returns them to Rasheed whose reception of Mariam, Laila, and Aziza serves to demonstrate that Rasheed is capable of murder. He locks Laila and Aziza in a hot, airless room, where they nearly die of heat and dehydration. Mariam is locked in a shed.

Laila partially redeems herself with Rasheed when she gives birth to a son. Rasheed then places all of his focus on this small child and excludes the women from his attentions as much as possible. This fragile situation begins to crumble as drought and disaster exhaust the city's and the family's resources. Aziza is sent to an orphanage, which is a weak refuge for the starving children of Kabul. After one of Mariam and Laila's trips to visit Aziza, they return to find Tariq waiting outside their house. It is this fateful and nearly fatal event that brings about the pivotal moment in the novel leading to Mariam's decisive action against Rasheed and Laila's ultimate escape from him and into a true sanctuary.

This sanctuary could be a simple happy ending to a tragic story. Because of Mariam's sacrifice, Laila is back with her childhood sweetheart and both of her children are alive and thriving. But the narrative of Afghanistan is not so neatly brought to a conclusion, nor does Hosseini choose to end his novel with such an unambiguous and unlikely ending. In this final portion of the narrative, Laila's character evolves out of the remains of her childhood and into a mature woman who is able to make her own sacrifices, this time on behalf of Afghanistan and Kabul. After the events of September 11, 2001, and the subsequent American invasion, Laila begins to hear about positive changes in Kabul, the rebuilding of roads and schools and improvements for women, and she wants to be a part of it. She retains the ambition instilled in her by her father. She recalls his words and wants to fulfill them: *"You can be anything you want, Laila, he says. I know this about you. And I also know that when this war is over, Afghanistan is going to need you"* (Hosseini 343).

She wonders if living her life as a maid in a "foreign land" would be what Mariam wanted for her. "Maybe it wouldn't matter to Mariam what Laila did as long as she and the children were safe and happy. But it matters to Laila. Suddenly, it matters very much" (Hosseini 343). And so Laila chooses to abandon what peace her family has found and returns to Kabul to realize her full potential. When Laila and her family return to Kabul, they are also choosing to exile themselves from the sanctuary of Murree, much as Mariam did when she left her kolba and mother, but they are more aware of their choices than Mariam was of hers. They consciously choose to live within an insecure world in hopes of bettering it rather than opting for the security and peace of Murree. Just as Mariam did in accepting her fate, they choose to sacrifice their comfort and safety to help others.

The family returns to Kabul by way of Herat. While there, Laila visits Gul Daman and her kolba outside the village. But now, in Laila's eyes, the abandoned remains of Mariam's and her mother's small hut are set in a peaceful and bucolic corner of Afghanistan. At first glance, it seems to be far from the years of Soviet conflict, Mujahideen shelling, and their torturous life with Rasheed. Perhaps, had Mariam stayed there, her life would have been different; it might have been a safe haven with Mullah Faizullah and his family to look after her. And yet, along with the flowers, birds, grasshoppers, and other verdant aspects of the spot, Laila sees graffiti and debris; she sees evidence of the past presence of Soviet soldiers. But Laila's mind is filled with Mariam's stories and imagines her playing on the kolba floor as a small child. She recognizes that this child will grow into a woman who has no expectations for herself or from others. Despite this apparent meekness, she knows in fact Mariam had "something deep in her core, that neither Rasheed nor the Taliban [would] be able to break. Something as hard and unyielding as a block of limestone" (Hosseini 355).

The narrative of Mariam and Laila merges with the narrative of the rebuilding of Afghanistan and of Kabul in particular. As Tariq and Laila set to work at Aziza's old orphanage, Laila feels Mariam's spirit everywhere and senses it as a force behind Kabul's reconstruction.

Laila sees . . . that Mariam is never far. She is here, in these walls they've repainted, in the trees they've planted, in the blankets that keep the children warm, in these pillows and books and pencils. She is in the children's laughter. (Hosseini 366)

Mariam's sacrifice is infused into Laila's purpose and the reconstruction of Kabul. As Laila comes to realize, "every Afghan story is marked by death and loss and unimaginable grief. And yet she sees that people find a way to survive, to go on" (Hosseini 350), as such, Mariam's death is not so unusual and her sacrifice is not so remarkable. It is part of the continuing narrative of Afghanistan. Yet, Laila's knowledge that Mariam not only chose this fate but chose it for Laila's well-being gives Laila a sense of purpose and allows her to grow beyond the tragedies she has experienced and to choose to devote her life to others and to something as seemingly impossible as the reconstruction of Kabul and Afghanistan.

Works Cited

Abu-Lughod, Lila. "Do Muslim Women Really Need Saving? Anthropological Reflections on Cultural Relativism and Its Others." *American Anthropologist* 104.3 (2002): 783–90.

Ayotte, Kevin J., and Mary E. Husain. "Securing Afghan Women: Neocolonialism, Epistemic Violence, and the Rhetoric of the Veil." *NWSA Journal* 17.3 (2005): 112–33.

Bezhan, Faridullah. "A Woman of Afghanistan: A Warning Portrait, Afghanistan's First Novel." *Critique: Critical Middle Eastern Studies* 15.2 (2006): 171–86.

———. "Women's Causes in Spozhmai Zaryab's Narrative Works." *Comparative Studies of South Asia, Africa and the Middle East* 28.2 (2008): 260–72.

Broxup, Marie. "Afghanistan According to Soviet Sources, 1980–1985." *Central Asian Survey* 7.2/3 (1988): 197–204.

Donnell, Alison. "Dressing with a Difference." *Interventions: Journal of Postcolonial Studies* 1.4 (1999): 489–99.

Edgar, Adrienne. "Bolshevism, Patriarchy, and the Nation: The Soviet 'Emancipation' of Muslim Women in Pan-Islamic Perspective." *Slavic Review* 65.2 (2006): 252–72.

Goodson, Larry. "The Fragmentation of Culture in Afghanistan." *Alif: Journal of Comparative Poetics* 18 (1998): 269–89.

Green, Nile. "Tribe, Diaspora, and Sainthood in Afghan History." *The Journal of Asian Studies* 67.1 (2008): 171–211.

Grima, Benedicte. *The Performance of Emotion Among Paxtun Women.* New York: Oxford UP, 2004.

Hanifi, M. Jamil. "Editing the Past: Colonial Production of Hegemony Through the 'Loya Jerga' in Afghanistan." *Iranian Studies* 37.2 (2004): 295–322.

Hosseini, Khaled. *A Thousand Splendid Suns.* NY: Riverhead Books, 2007.

Khan, Shahnaz. "Between Here and There: Feminist Solidarity and Afghan Women." *Genders* 33. Genders Journal/Ann Kibbey, 2001. Web. 31 July 2011.

Matzke, M. "On the Position of Women in Afghan Society of the Seventeenth Century (Khushal Khan Khatak's Dastarnama)." Marián Gálik, ed. *Proceedings of the Fourth International Conference on the Theoretical Problems of Asian and African Literatures*. Bratislava: Literary Institute of the Slovak Academy of Sciences, 1983. 262–67.

McGonegal, Julie. "Postcolonial Metacritique: Jameson, Allegory and the Always-Already-Read Third World Text." *Interventions* 7.2 (2005): 251–65.

McLarney, Ellen. "The Burqa in Vogue: Fashioning Afghanistan." *Journal of Middle East Women's Studies* 5.1 (2009): 1–24.

Naghibi, Nimi. "Bad Feminist or Bad-Hijabi?" *Interventions: Journal of Postcolonial Studies* 1.4 (1999): 555–71.

Nichols, Robert. "Afghan Historiography: Classical Study, Conventional Narrative, National Polemic." *History Compass* 3.1 (2005): 1–16.

Shahrani, Nazif M. "War, Factionalism, and the State in Afghanistan." *American Anthropologist* 104.3 (2002): 715–22.

Singh, Amardeep. "Republics of the Imagination." *The Minnesota Review: A Journal of Committed Writing* 68 (2007): 147–57.

Snyder, Jack. "Empire: A Blunt Tool for Democratization." *Daedalus* 134.2 (2005): 58–71.

Stabile, Carol A. "Unveiling Imperialism: Media, Gender, and the War on Afghanistan." *Media, Culture & Society* 27.5 (2005): 765–82.

Whitlock, Gillian L. "The Skin of the Burqa: Recent Life Narratives from Afghanistan." *Biography: An Interdisciplinary Quarterly* 28.1 (2005): 54–76.

Identity and Popular Culture in Toni Morrison's *The Bluest Eye* and Junot Díaz's *The Brief Wondrous Life of Oscar Wao*_____

Ferentz Lafargue

If there was no Toni Morrison, there could not be a Junot Díaz. To some this may seem like a controversial statement. After all aren't Díaz and Morrison writing out of two distinct literary traditions, African American and Latino, respectively, and Morrison's midwestern sensibilities would have very little, if any, relation to the northeastern Quisqueya landscape that pollinates much of Díaz's work. However, both writers share an affinity for rattling the echo chamber of American identity by displaying that the African American or Latino presence is a vital aspect of cultural encounters that have long defined the United States in particular and the Americas as a whole. Through this shared affinity, Morrison and Díaz are carrying out an extended dialogue with American literary masters spanning from their forerunners Sherwood Anderson and Ralph Ellison, to contemporaries such as Paul Beatty and Alice Walker. Moreover, the cultural encounters presented in *The Bluest Eye* and *The Brief Wondrous Life of Oscar Wao* range from meditations on Shirley Temple to Dungeons and Dragons, and work to reveal how these African American and Latino characters (echoing the synchronistic acts of their enslaved ancestors) reconfigures these pop-cultural icons to suit their own imaginations. To that end, this essay will explore Díaz and Morrison's attempts at revealing the reverberations of popular culture in ethnic American communities in *The Brief Wondrous Life of Oscar Wao* and *The Bluest Eye,* respectively, as well as the pertinent links between the works of these two writers and their predecessors in American literature.

Junot Díaz's 2007 novel *The Brief Wondrous Life of Oscar Wao* is a recanting of the life of Oscar de León and his family. Although residing in Patterson, New Jersey, Oscar's family is originally from the Dominican Republic, the island that serves as the secondary setting in the novel. The story is told from the perspective of Yunior, a fledgling writer, a former college roommate of Oscar's, and his sister Lola's longtime boyfriend.

Díaz's Oscar Wao bears a close resemblance to a number of other prominent literary figures. American literary history is rife with precocious young men, chief among them include Mark Twain's Huckleberry Finn, the main character from the novel of the same name; J. D. Salinger's Holden Caulfield from *The Catcher in the Rye*; John Kennedy Toole's Ignatius J. Reilly from *A Confederacy of Dunces*; as well as a more recent character, Paul Beatty's Gunnar Kaufman, the main character in *The White Boy Shuffle*. Of these four figures, Oscar is most reminiscent of Toole's Reilly and Beatty's Kaufman.

Like Ignatius Reilly, Oscar is an incredibly smart, hypersensitive social outcast who finds refuge in a world of his own design. Whereas Oscar finds solace in the imaginary worlds of comic books, science fiction books and films, and role-playing games, Ignatius has found asylum in Greek mythology and the writings of sixth-century philosopher Boethius.

Similarly, there are also notable overlaps between Oscar and Gunnar Kaufman. Like Gunnar, Oscar is a late twentieth-century young man dwelling in an American suburb and seeking to traverse an intricate race, class, and gender matrix:

> My inability to walk the walk or talk the talk led to a series of almost daily drubbings. In a world where body and spoken language were currency, I was broke as hell. Corporeally mute. (Beatty 52)

Beatty uses Gunnar to challenge and satirize conventional notions of African American male identity, not unlike how Díaz unleashes Oscar as the penultimate antithesis of the Dominican male:

> [Oscar] had none of the Higher Powers of your typical Dominican male, couldn't have pulled a girl if his life depended on it. Couldn't play sports

for shit, or dominoes, was beyond uncoordinated, threw a ball like a girl. Had no knack for music or business or dance, no hustle, no rap, no G. And most damning of all: no looks. (20–21)

Both Gunnar and Oscar are "corporeally mute" characters devoid of the cultural currency capable of enriching their young adult lives. Beatty and Díaz emphasize their characters' depleted cultural currency within their respective communities in order to generate renderings of African American and Dominican males that run against the grain of stereotypical perceptions. In fact Beatty and Díaz employ Gunnar and Oscar to probe and illuminate how these perceptions extend beyond the realm of stereotype and into the netherworld of cultural ethnic mores. They are both heretical figures in these communities because of their inability to erect the physical and verbal comportment commonly associated with young African American and Dominican men. To that end, both of these novels are about young men who are in their own right novel characters.

Yet, both of these characters are endowed with profound historical sensibilities. As is suggested early in both *The White Boy Shuffle* and *The Wondrous Life of Oscar Wao,* Gunnar and Oscar's plights are not accidental but are inherited destabilizing traits passed down from their similarly accursed forefathers:

Unlike the typical bluesy earthly folksy denim-overalls noble-in-the-face-of-cracker-racism aw shucks Pulitzer-Prize-winning protagonist mojo magic black man, I am not the seventh son of a seventh of a seventh son. I wish I were, but fate shorted me by six brothers and three uncles. (Beatty 5)

And:

They say it came first from Africa, carried in the screams of the enslaved; that it was the death bane of the Tainos, uttered just as one world perished and another began; that it was a demon drawn into Creation through the nightmare door that was cracked open in the Antilles. *Fukú americanus*, or more colloquially, fukú—generally a curse or a doom of some kind; specifically the Curse and the Doom of the New World. (Díaz 1)

The two passages are excerpted from the opening monologues of *The White Boy Shuffle* and *The Brief Wondrous Life of Oscar Wao*, respectively. In the first example, Beatty tips his hand at the object of his satire. Beatty's novel satirizes African American first-person narratives, a genre that runs the gamut from nineteenth-century slave narratives to Richard Wright's 1945 autobiography *Black Boy,* and Ralph Ellison's landmark 1952 novel *Invisible Man.* The "seventh son" quip is an allusion to W. E. B. Du Bois's famous declaration in the *The Souls of Black Folk:*

After the Egyptian and Indian, the Greek and Roman, the Teuton and Mongolian, the Negro is a sort of seventh son, born with a veil, and gifted with second-sight in this American world,—a world which yields him no true self-consciousness, but only lets him see himself through the revelation of the other world. (615)

In the *The Souls of Black Folk*, Du Bois brandishes his own peculiar approach to the first-person narrative as he couples it with social commentary and socio-historical analysis of African American life after the Civil War. As evidenced in *The Souls of Black Folk,* "the bluesy earthly folksy denim-overalls noble-in-the-face-of-cracker-racism aw shucks Pulitzer-Prize-winning protagonist mojo magic black man" is to be acknowledged and celebrated as the purveyor of the spirituals, the quintessential African American contribution to American culture. This figure is also in dire need of restoration and elevation if he is to keep pace with the onslaught of modernity. In satirizing this literary tradition, Beatty is not only resuscitating Wright and Du Bois, among others, for further scrutiny, he is also conjuring the work of Ishmael Reed, who himself trebles the tropes of African American narrative forms in his own work. Beatty borrows his free-form narrative approach from both his mentor, acclaimed poet Allen Ginsberg, and also from Reed, who utilizes the technique in his fiction.

Díaz owes a great deal to a famous poet as well—in his case, Nobel laureate Derek Walcott from whose 1978 poem "The Schooner 'Flight'" Díaz extracts the epigraph for *The Brief Wondrous Life of Oscar Wao*. This allusion to Walcott's epic poem immediately establishes the wide arching historical sweep that Díaz is intent on sustaining throughout his novel—what the editors of *BOMB* magazine have cited as the novel's epic qualities:

> *The Brief Wondrous Life of Oscar Wao* is epic, not only in its historical rendering of heartbreaking violence, of a cross-generational, exiled family, but in its language: a courageous patois from the streets of New Jersey, via the Spanish-speaking Caribbean, flying right up and into the face— and the canon—of great literature. (Danticat)

As in much of Walcott's work, the channel through which Díaz's epic is streamed is the history of the New World. Díaz places particular emphasis on the island of Hispaniola, which is shared by Haiti and the Dominican Republic. And as noted in the passage above, Díaz's novel is imbued with a number of the motifs commonly associated with epics, exile, family relations, and heartbreaking violence—in other words, tragedy. The same motifs permeate any number of Walcott texts ranging from *Omeros* to the aforementioned "The Schooner 'Flight.'" Where these two authors differ, however, is that while Walcott often transposes classical Greek literature onto narratives of the Caribbean in order to show the region's heroic and mythological attributes, Díaz delves into another canon in order to accomplish the same feat, that of the role-playing game Dungeons and Dragons.[1]

D&D's significance to *The Brief and Wondrous Life of Oscar Wao* extends far beyond the fact that it's Oscar's favorite pastime. The board game is a vital anchor in the construction of this narrative, particularly the aforementioned epic characteristics. Unlike other war-inspired board games, D&D is not predicated on military strategy. Instead, D&D is based on storytelling. In other words, it's a story-telling game as much as it is a war game. Each player is assigned a character for which an imaginary story is developed and the game is refereed by a Dungeon Master who is essentially the chief storyteller.

In its own way a game of D&D is akin to a Homeric epic in that they are both filled with stories of contests and conquests and are told over the course of many days. Thus, if one is reading *The Brief and Wondrous Life of Oscar Wao* as a D&D game, then Yunior is the Dungeon Master and Oscar is his character. Extending this logic a bit further, Yunior is a latter-day Homer and Oscar is his Odysseus.

Although neither Homer nor the *The Odyssey* is ever cited in *The Brief Wondrous Life of Oscar Wao,* traces of Homer are present throughout the novel. Díaz uses an episodic structure to relay the story. Hubris propels Yunior's demise. And in lieu of saturating this text with Greek gods and goddesses, Díaz fills *The Brief Wondrous Life of Oscar Wao* with a bevy of superhero and comic-book allusions that help outline certain characteristics of Oscar's personality. Similarly, these superheroes and comic-book characters also function as figures to which Oscar is beholden and shape his destiny in a manner comparable to how Greek gods and goddesses served as overseers to the fortunes of Homer's mortals.

In addition to Derek Walcott, the list of literary and pop-cultural allusions in *The Brief Wondrous Life of Oscar Wao* also includes references to authors Samuel Delany and Stephen King, and we are told that Oscar aspires to be "the next Gary Gygax" (co-creator of Dungeons & Dragons). Furthermore, Oscar read Tom Swift, "gorg[ed] himself on a steady stream of Lovecraft, Wells, Burroughs, Howard, Alexander, Herbert, Asimov, Bova, and Heinlein" (Díaz 21). We learn that the title of the book is derived from a derogatory reference to Oscar Wilde (when Oscar is dressed up for Halloween as Doctor Who, the title character from the British television series that ran from 1963–1989) (Díaz

180). Oscar is well versed in the travails of the televisions series *Star Trek*, is capable of writing "in Elvish, speak Chakobsa, could differentiate between a Slan, a Dorsai, and a Lensman in acute detail, [and] knew more about the Marvel Universe than Stan Lee" (Díaz 21). Also present in the canon being constructed in this novel by Díaz are allusions to comic book characters such as Doc Savage, The Watchers, and The Avengers.

This litany of pop-cultural and literary allusions arguably has another purpose in *The Brief Wondrous Life of Oscar Wao*. It frames a reader's understanding of Oscar's unwavering dedication to the characters he creates during his Dungeons and Dragons games, which in turn serve as an allegory for the type of conviction that Yunior aspires to have in his own life. One must remember that not only is Oscar the hero of this story, but he's Yunior's hero. Save for an admission to sharing Oscar's affinity for the Japanese anime series *Akira*, it is never fully explained how Yunior manages to be so insightful about the countless other superheroes and Dungeons and Dungeons characters that populate this novel. In light of this omission, one can infer that while Yunior may have been drawn to Oscar as a way to get closer to his sister Lola, another reason that their friendship endures is because Oscar's unconventional Domicanness alleviates the pressure on Yunior to act like a stereotypical Dominican man. Oscar's presence relieves Yunior from being a two-dimensional character simply interested in weightlifting and womanizing, and it offers him an opportunity to hone his talents as a writer.

Whereas *The Brief Wondrous Life of Oscar Wao* is saturated with literary ephemera related to comic books, science fiction novels and movies, and the role-playing game Dungeons and Dragons, the cultural artifacts present in Toni Morrison's . are arguably far more familiar. One reason for this is that Morrison's text has fewer recurring symbols, and the most prominent of these symbols are early twentieth-century movie stars such as Shirley Temple, Greta Garbo, and Ginger Rogers. In addition to being the living embodiment of a white doll that the novel's narrator Claudia receives as a Christmas gift one year, Temple, Garbo, and Rogers represent an image of beauty that the young black girls in *The Bluest Eye* are expected to embrace even though it's impossible for them to replicate.

A casual reader might deduce that since *The Bluest Eye* was published in 1970 and offers a chilling indictment of the effect that the proliferation of white images has on black children, that it is a novel born out of the Black Arts Movement. However, unlike contemporaries such as Toni Cade Bambara or Gayl Jones, Morrison never emerged as one of the movement's proponents. One reason for this is that during the 1970s, the Black Arts Movement was supplanted by the black feminist movement as the most critical voice in African American literature.

In addition to the publication of Morrison's first novel in 1970, the 1970s was also marked by the emergence of writers such as June Jordan, Audre Lorde, and Alice Walker, all three of whom would make indelible contributions to African American literature not only as creative writers, but also as instructors at prominent universities and as literary and social critics. Walker is a particularly important figure in this period because of her work to revive interest in Zora Neale Hurston, whose *Their Eyes Were Watching God* (1937) was virtually out of print prior to Walker's landmark essay "In Search of Zora," published in *Ms. Magazine* in 1975. Walker's essay was her contribution to a crusade in which young scholars such as Nellie McKay, Barbara Smith, and Sherley Anne Williams were also working tirelessly to restore Hurston to her rightful place in the American literary canon. In revitalizing Hurston's career and interest in other then-overlooked African American women writers such as Nella Larsen and Jessie Redmon Fauset, these scholars and creative writers permanently amended the historical narrative of African American literature, which up to that point was essentially comprised of Frederick Douglass, W. E. B. Du Bois, Richard Wright, Ralph Ellison, and Amiri Baraka.

Morrison eventually went on to become not only the most celebrated writer of the 1970s Black feminist era, but also the most celebrated African American writer in US history. In addition to winning a Pulitzer Prize for fiction and being a finalist for an American Book Award for her 1987 novel *Beloved,* Morrison was also the first African American woman to receive a Nobel Prize in Literature, the highest international honor a writer can receive.

The Bluest Eye was the genesis of Morrison's path to literary greatness. The novel is told from the perspective of Claudia MacTeer, who along with her sister Frieda and Pecola Breedlove, the foster child taken in by their mother, represent the three little girls at the heart of this narrative. In addition to Claudia, there is also an omniscient narrator who occasionally oversees storytelling duties. The novel is set in a small Ohio town, presumably Lorain, where Morrison herself was born and raised. As various characters cycle in and out of the text, one cannot help but be reminded of Sherwood Anderson's *Winesburg, Ohio* (1919), and Toshio Mori's *Yokohama, California* (1949), a text inspired by Anderson's 1919 classic. Both Anderson and Mori give readers a snapshot of small-town life in their respective works. Each novel is episodic and is invariably a collection of short stories in which the town is simultaneously the main character and the thread connecting the disparate tales. It is undoubtedly Anderson's *Winesburg, Ohio* that looms most heavily over Morrison's *The Bluest Eye*. Along with using small Ohio towns as a setting, both Anderson and Morrison deftly illustrate a tragic nature that has become synonymous with, or rather has been ingrained into, these towns. Despair, isolation, self-loathing, and shame are just some of the overlapping themes explored in both of these texts, all of which combine to shed light on communities hamstrung by their tragic flaws, or as Morrison asserts in the novel's foreword:

> The death of self-esteem can occur quickly, easily in children, before their ego has "legs," so to speak. Couple the vulnerability of youth with indifferent parents, dismissive adults, and a world, which, in its language, laws, and images, re-enforces despair, and journey to destruction is sealed. (x)

For example, in *The Bluest Eye*, it's not simply a matter of these characters hating themselves, but more so they are unable to actualize and articulate their self-worth. The clearest examples of this can be found via Claudia's narration of her encounter with images of Shirley Temple as well as her own struggle to defeat and destroy the white doll she's been given as a Christmas present. While Shirley Temple and the white doll are related, it is very much worth noting the distinct socio-cultural and socio-political histories that Morrison is mining by including them in the novel. Moreover, tensions surrounding preferential treatment allotted white movie stars and how white dolls impact a black girls' understanding of beauty still figure heavily in African American discourses on popular culture.

In 2005, then New York City high school student Kiri Davis made a short documentary called "A Girl Like Me" that explored race and representation, or "colorism" (preferential treatment and appreciation of light-skinned blacks over darker blacks within the black community), from the perspective of her peers. Reflecting on the perceived standards of beauty within black communities, one of the young women introduced in the film declares, "You're prettier if you're light-skinned." Davis's film addresses the proliferation of skin bleaching creams and how "colorism" even has the potential to factor into marriage decisions, "I've heard people say I would never marry a dark-skinned man because I wouldn't want that in my gene pool."

Arguably the most powerful statement made in Davis's documentary emerges during her re-creation of Kenneth and Mamie Clark's famous doll-experiments of the late 1930s and early 1940s. During this period, the Clarks, a husband-and-wife team of black psychologists, conducted a study where they presented young black children with a pair of dolls, one black and the other white, to explore their perceptions of race. The overwhelming majority of the students in the study preferred the white dolls. The Clarks went on to serve as expert witnesses in the landmark *Brown v. Board* of Education case that overturned segregation in public schools in the United States.

Sixty years after the Clarkses conducted their study, and thirty-five years after the publication of *The Bluest Eye*, Davis recreated the same experiment. Fifteen out of the twenty-one black children interviewed preferred the white doll over the black doll. Below is an excerpt of one of the more moving exchanges between Davis and one of the study's subjects:

Davis: Can you show me the doll that looks bad?
Black Girl: (Selects black doll)
Davis: Why does that look bad?
Black Girl: Because it's black.
Davis: Why do you think that is a nice doll?
Black Girl: Because she's white.
Davis: Can you give me the doll that looks like you?
Black Girl: (Leans to grab white doll, before correcting herself and handing over the black doll)

The young girl featured in this exchange is roughly the same age as Claudia, Frieda, and Pecola in *The Bluest Eye*. She's about the same age as Morrison and her childhood friend, whose admission of her desire for "blue eyes" was the genesis of this novel:

We had just started elementary school. She said she wanted blue eyes. I looked around to picture her with them and was violently repelled by what I imagined she would look like if she had her wish. (x)

Similar to *The Bluest Eye* and the Clarkses' experiment, Davis's *A Girl Like Me* depicts how codified racial language, laws, and images "re-enforce despair." However, Morrison is careful to show that in spite of their vulnerability, young black girls are not minimally broken by the power embedded in and associated with these white dolls. Rather, it is the apathy adults exhibit toward what a child might really want, appreciate, or find beautiful that unnerves Claudia:

From the clucking sounds of adults I knew that the doll represented what they thought was my fondest wish. . . . I had no interest in babies or the concept of motherhood. I was interested only in humans my own age and size, and could not generate any enthusiasm at the prospect of being a mother. (20)

Claudia's distaste for the doll is unassailable. That said, the additional layer of nuance that Morrison ascribes to this relationship in these two scenes is incredibly profound. In addition to being a re-creation of a white image of beauty that she could never attain, this doll is also repulsive to Claudia because by giving it to her, Claudia's parents are incorrectly presupposing that she has an interest in childrearing. Moreover, as one learns later in the novel when Pecola decides to keep her child, were this doll an actual child, Claudia would have been ostracized from her community if she decided to take on the responsibilities of motherhood.

The sensible nature of Claudia's ambitions is further amplified when she declares:

Had any adult with the power to fulfill my desires taken me seriously and asked me what I wanted, they would have known that I did not want to have anything to own, or to possess any object. I wanted rather to feel something on Christmas day. The real question would have been, "Dear Claudia, what experience would you like on Christmas?" (22–23)

Claudia's desire "to feel something on Christmas day" eloquently encapsulates what all the other characters are searching for in this novel. They are not all seeking to feel something on Christmas, per se. Rather, theirs is a broader aspiration that applies especially to the adults whose lives have become flaccid. In fact, the tragic incident at the center of this novel, Pecola's rape by her father, Cholly,[2] is incited by Cholly's desire to feel something. Morrison exposes Cholly's rape of Pecola as an example of an extreme to which a person might succumb in an attempt to resuscitate an inert existence.

Claudia's desire is also noteworthy in light of Cholly's tragic act because the experience that she says she would have asked for were someone to ever inquire would be "to sit on the low stool in Big Mama's kitchen with my lap full of lilacs and listen to Big Papa play his violin for me alone." In stark contrast to the traumatic encounter that punctuates Cholly and Pecola's relationship, Claudia articulates a vision of a tender moment with her own father. The fetid stench of Pecola's rape that hovers over this novel and the lives of these characters is for a moment replaced with an idyllic image of a young girl sheltered in lilacs enjoying the warm, soothing presence of her parents.

As mentioned earlier, the white doll is not a singular object/trope in *The Bluest Eye.* It resides in the same zip code of racial representation and allegory as movie stars Greta Garbo, Ginger Rogers, and Shirley Temple, who are alluded to multiple times throughout this novel. Garbo and Rogers are invoked as a term of endearment for Claudia and Frieda by Henry Washington, an older black gentleman who rents a room from the girls' mother. This term of endearment does not undergo much scrutiny in the novel. Still, it is worth noting that Washington's penchant for alluding to these young girls by the names of two of Hollywood's earliest starlets, and sex symbols, is lecherous. Moreover, these allusions to Garbo and Rogers are examples of how white women are the lynchpins and preeminent icons of the language of beauty spoken by characters in *The Bluest Eye.*

Chief among these aforementioned white starlets is Shirley Temple, whose silhouette is a constant presence in the MacTeer home via a cup bearing Shirley's face. Not surprisingly, unlike Frieda and Pecola who are diehard Temple fans, Claudia is not a Temple admirer:

> I hated Shirley. Not because she was cute, but because she danced with Bojangles, who was *my* friend, *my* uncle, *my* daddy, and who ought to have been soft-shoeing it and chuckling with me. Instead he was enjoying, sharing, giving a lovely dance thing with one of those little white girls whose socks never slid down under their heels. So I said, "I like Jane Withers." (19)

This passage is instructive for a number of reasons. Again Claudia is found pining for an "experience." In this fantasy, Claudia has replaced her real father with Bill "Bojangles" Robinson, the famed African American actor and dancer of the early part of the twentieth century. Instead of a shared experience in Mama's kitchen with Big Papa, Claudia is alongside Robinson as they glide across the dance floor. Remaining true to the register of films released between 1934 and 1935 and cited in *The Bluest Eye*, the film that Claudia is most likely alluding to in the passage is *The Little Colonel* (1935), which in addition to marking Robinson and Temple's first appearance together on screen[3] is also the film that featured their famed staircase dance scene and a cameo appearance by Jane Withers.

Ironically, by alluding to Withers in attempting to show that her dislike of Temple is not solely based on the fact that Temple is "cute" or white, Claudia unmasks how deep her distaste for Temple actually runs. In addition to being another one of the most popular child stars of the 1930s and early 1940s (although she never came close to matching Temple's stature as a brand), Withers was Temple's antagonist in the 1934 film *Bright Eyes*. *Bright Eyes* is the film that catapulted Temple from fledgling child star to one of the most profitable brands of the era. Along with her movie roles, Temple was able to generate revenue by licensing her image for a variety of consumer goods such as the cup referenced in *The Bluest Eye*.

Bright Eyes is one of the two other important films from the 1930s alluded to in *The Bluest Eye*. Also featured in this directory is *Imitation of Life* (1934), which was based on the best-selling Fannie Hurst novel of the same name. Both films feature young orphaned girls who triumph over their circumstances. The references to these films are undoubtedly deployed by Morrison to further re-enforce Pecola's tragic existence. Not only is Pecola the young black girl who desires to have blue eyes and is a Shirley Temple fan, but as her schoolmate Maureen Peal unveils to the reader, Pecola is also named after Peola, the light-skinned black girl in *Imitation of Life* who abandons her black family members when she decides to pass for white.

Unlike Temple in *Bright Eyes* or Sebie Hendricks (the child actress who plays a young Peola in the 1934 version of *Imitation of Life*), there is no victory for Pecola Breedlove. She does not find caring relatives to take her in like Temple does in *Bright Eyes,* nor is she capable of passing for white like her namesake in *Imitation of Life.* Thus, in *The Bluest Eye,* Pecola emerges as a character living a dystopian version of the lives led on film by Temple and Hendricks.

Tragically, as Claudia asserts at the end of this novel, it is Pecola's putrid existence that enables others in the town to see the beauty or take pride in their own:

> [We] felt wholesome after we cleaned ourselves on her. We were so beautiful when we stood astride her ugliness. Her simplicity decorated us, her guilt sanctified us, her pain made us glow with health. . . . Her inarticulateness made us believe we were eloquent. (205)

Here Claudia punctuates Pecola's ascent to becoming the inverse of the cinematic starlets found in this novel. It is not because she's not white or light-skinned or does not have bright eyes like Garbo, Hendricks, Rogers, Temple, or even her classmate Maureen Peal that makes her the antithesis of these women. Ironically Pecola is their opposite because she performs the same function as these women in her Ohio town; Pecola is the fantasy on which the "egos" of her neighbors are based. Inverse to how Garbo, Rogers, Temple, and Maureen Peal represent examples of beauty the heights of which these characters could never hope to attain, Pecola symbolizes a level of ugliness the depths of which, in their minds at least, they could never descend.

Garbo, Rogers, and Temple are part of Morrison's contribution to the index of pop-cultural references that also includes the litany of figures cited by Díaz in *The Brief Wondrous Life of Oscar Wao.* Díaz and Morrison deploy these pop-cultural references to situate their protagonists

Oscar de Leon and Pecola Breedlove, and to an extent Yunior and Claudia, in a socio-cultural maze where concepts such as hero and beauty are simultaneously omnipresent and elusive. Emblematic of their respective communities' futility, Oscar and Pecola fall prey partly because of their innate vulnerability and also because of their Promethean-like acquisitions of the items that they coveted most. In Oscar's case, it was his fling with the Captain's mistress Ybon during his final visits to the Dominican Republic, and for Pecola, it was her attainment of the infamous blue eyes. Tragically, the ironic twist of both novels is that it is Oscar and Pecola's pursuit of these classical ideas—the hero and beauty—that leads to the unraveling of these modern characters.

Notes

1. Dungeons and Dragons (D&D) first premiered in 1974, and by the end of the decade and through the next twenty-five years, it was the most popular role-playing game. D&D's popularity is especially impressive given the degree to which video games proliferated the market beginning in the 1980s. One reason for D&D's ability to retain its market share despite the emergence of best-selling video game consoles such as Nintendo and PlayStation is that the game has been successfully adapted to various video game consoles since its inception. Dungeons and Dragons also found a second life on television and in film. The television adaptation had a successful three-year run in the United States during the mid-1980s and was then shown in syndication two decades later. International versions of the television show, however, continued producing new content through the early 1990s, and in 2000 and 2005, profitable screen adaptations were produced. There have also been extensive books published related to the game and a magazine that was revived online in 2007 that further reinforces the notion that D&D is a culture unto itself.

2. Morrison's depiction of Cholly's rape of Pecola is eerily similar to Jim Trueblood's defilement of his own daughter in Ralph Ellison's *Invisible Man*. And like Trueblood, Cholly's act leads to his eviction from his black community.

3. *The Little Colonel* was the first of four films in which Robinson and Temple collaborated.

Works Cited

Anderson, Sherwood. *Winesburg, Ohio*. New York: Modern Library, 1995.

Beatty, Paul. *The White Boy Shuffle*. New York: Holt, 1997.

Bright Eyes. Dir. David Butler. Perf. Shirley Temple, Jane Withers. Fox Film Corporation. 1934. DVD.

Díaz, Junot. *The Brief Wondrous Life of Oscar Wao*. New York: Riverhead, 2007.

_____. Interview with Edwidge Danticat. *BOMB Magazine* 101 (2007): 88–95.

Du Bois, W. E. B. "The Souls of Black Folk." *Norton Anthology of African American Literature*. Ed. Henry Louis Gates Jr. and Nellie McKay. New York: Norton, 1997.

Ellison, Ralph. *Invisible Man*. New York: Vintage, 1995.

Girl Like Me, A. Dir. Kira Davis. Reel Works Teen Filmmaking. 2005. Film.

Hurston, Zora Neale. *Their Eyes Were Watching God*. New York: Harper, 1990.

Imitation of Life. Dir. John Stahl. Perf. Claudette Colbert, Warren William, Sebie Hendricks, and Jane Withers. Universal Pictures. 1934. Film.

The Little Colonel. Dir. David Butler. Perf. Shirley Temple, Lionel Barrymore, Bill Robinson. Fox Film Corporation. 1935. DVD.

Mori, Toshio. *Yokohama, California*. Seattle: U of Washington P, 1985.

Morrison, Toni. *The Bluest Eye*. New York: Vintage, 2007.

Toole, John Kennedy. *A Confederacy of Dunces*. Baton Rouge: Louisiana State UP, 1980.

Wright, Richard. *Black Boy*. New York: Harper, 2008.

CRITICAL READINGS

Island Noises: Sound Imprints of the Cultural Encounters in Shakespeare's *The Tempest*

Kirilka Stavreva

Shakespeare's last single-authored play, *The Tempest*, takes place on a sparsely populated island in the Mediterranean Sea, albeit one on a route between the Neapolitan kingdom and North Africa that has been traversed for centuries. Alonso's Neapolitan courtiers are returning home from the wedding of the king's daughter Claribel in Tunis—the North African country bordering on Algiers, which is the birthplace of Caliban's mother, "the foul witch Sycorax" (1.2.257).[1] Isolated as the island may be, its history is enmeshed in myths of empire building as notably developed in Virgil's *Aeneid* and of the Christianization of the Mediterranean as historicized in the Acts of the Apostles.[2] The stories about the island's turbulent present, in turn, dramatize the turmoil of Italian political life in the Renaissance era, and they evoke the geopolitical clash of Christian and Muslim civilizations on a sea road frequented by buccaneers and privateers whose allegiances and religions shifted with the change of the winds of profit.[3] Echoes of the English colonization of Ireland and of the experiences of first contact in the "New World" are also audible. The island, in other words, is inscribed within a history of power contests among and within multiple sets of ethnic and cultural groups and polities.

Nonetheless, it appears to be a place that calms the senses. Caliban, son of the one of the earlier colonizers of the island and subject to its current one, describes the land as "full of noises, / Sounds, and sweet airs that give delight and hurt not" (3.2.133–34). His description agrees with Gonzalo's observation about the "sweet music" he hears not long after the shipwreck (3.3.19). However, an analysis of the islanders' speech, including their songs, reveals that both "the most ignorant monster" and the wise old councilor are mistaken about the quality of what they hear. The musical "airs" carried in the wind feature contending voices; they can be bitter, misleading, or downright dangerous. In turn, the islanders' Creole-inflected language can pack a considerable rhetorical punch, whether subtly or directly. So can their silence. There is nothing accidental about these enticing, yet injurious, sounds and languages. They are the vehicles and expressions of encounters between worlds—a term that may appear benign enough, but one that, as Roland Greene reminds us, was tied in the Renaissance to the Latin root *computare*, and thus carried both economic and narrative overtones. *Count* is related to both "account" and "recount." Given the economic underpinnings of "encounters," Greene contends, they "have a palpable investment in alterity . . . ; at its most basic level an encounter happens between a subject and an other who are, and go, against one another—'in contra'" (139). In this contentious process, the participants in an encounter formulate identities that, once the initial "wonder" of the experience has worn off, incorporate recognition of the other in the notion of the self.

The play is triggered into centrifugal action by a horrific sea-storm as the Neapolitan party returns from Claribel's wedding in Tunis. The storm is memorably dramatized in the opening scene where the original stage directions indicate the dominance of "tempestuous noise" over intelligible speech. In most performances, language is indeed obliterated by noise in a scene that allows for little characterization (no names are given in the dialogue). There is no room for the steady beat of poetry here, as social hierarchies collapse in the riot of the elements. It may well be the case that the scene dramatizes a first-time encounter between crew and courtiers, who would have had no cause to cross paths during a less eventful voyage. Alonso's inquiry after the ship's master and his inept encouragement of the mariners, "Play the men" (1.1.10), signals the king's social unease about interacting with any mariner beneath the rank of captain. The Boatswain, in turn, seems unable or unwilling to recognize the king, and addresses the lords collectively in his curt response, "Keep your cabins: you do assist the storm!" (1.1.14). If Gonzalo manages to maintain some civility in his satiric references to the imagined fate of the Boatswain ("Methinks he hath no drowning mark upon him; his complexion is perfect gallows. Stand fast, good Fate, to his hanging" (1.1.29–31), this is not the case with Sebastian and Antonio. Their curses—"a pox o' your throat, you bawling, blasphemous, incharitable dog!" (1.1.37–38), "Hang, cur, hang, you whoreson insolent noise-maker!" (1.1.40–41)—are not the speech decorum one would expect of aristocrats. As the members of the two social groups go at each other, the class distinction between courtiers and crew thus collapses—a point swiftly grasped by the Boatswain who challenges the lords to work (1.1.39).

The diminishment of the lords' status as vocalized in the storm scene is a logical outcome of the larger political context of Alonso's journey. The dynastic marriage of the Princess of Naples to the King of Tunis implies the political preeminence of the African state in the ideological and military conflict between the Islamic and Christian civilizations unfolding in the Mediterranean during the sixteenth and the seventeenth centuries. Questions of the practicality of such a union aside—marrying the King of Tunis would have necessitated Claribel's conversion to Islam, which no Italian king would have consented to—Alonso himself acknowledges once he regains his senses on the island that he regrets the decision (2.1.103–07). It is apparent that Alonso's ship—traditionally, as Robin Kirkpatrick points out, "an emblem both of commercial enterprise and of imperial ambitions"— is headed home with no exotic goods, nor is it charting new routes of trade and imperial conquest. In the cultural encounter that makes possible the events on Prospero's island, Claribel is lost "to an African" (2.1.121). To the mind of her Neapolitan family, the possibility that she might be able to construe a hybrid identity is negated as resolutely as the prospects for cultural and economic exchange between Italy and Africa.[4]

Gonzalo, always one to seek the silver lining in stormy clouds, casts a vision of Claribel as Dido, Queen of Carthage, reassuring the courtiers that "This Tunis . . . was Carthage" (2.1.80). In the old councilor's mythologizing account, Claribel does not get lost "to an African," but rather, is inscribed into a European history of empire building. Even a casual reflection, however, would reveal that Gonzalo's story is hardly optimistic. As commentators on Virgil's *Aeneid* throughout the Middle Ages and beyond noted repeatedly, the Tyrean princess Dido (a refugee from the dynastic plots in her homeland) indeed founded a kingdom in Carthage. She accomplished this by swindling the local inhabitants into selling her a much more substantial plot of land than what they believed could be covered by a bull's hide—the price that she modestly offered. Once this request was granted her, Dido cut the bull's hide into narrow strips with which she encircled a considerable amount of land, including a hill.[5] But as the original audiences of *The Tempest* would have known too well from reading their *Aeneid*, it was not long before Dido's colonization enterprise was sacrificed to Aeneas's empire building, and the abandoned love-struck queen committed suicide. So much for the prospects of the marriage of the Neapolitan princess to the Tunisian king.

The spiteful commentary by Antonio and Sebastian upon Gonzalo's attempt to render Claribel's future in classical literary terms reveals how awkwardly tuned is the speech of the courtiers themselves. "His word is more than the miraculous harp," teases Antonio, comparing Gonzalo's soothing story-telling to the Greek myth of Amphion raising the walls of Thebes as he played his magical harp and had the stones follow him and gently glide into place (2.1.83). There is an ideological and perhaps generational divide between Gonzalo and young Adrian, on the one hand, with their wide-eyed admiration of the "temperance" of the island and the Golden Age utopia of its future governance, and, on the other hand, Antonio's and Sebastian's political cynicism. As Gonzalo waxes poetic about his vision of a plantation on the island without commerce, writing, daily labor, taxation, land inheritance, or government (yet one that he would rule as king), Antonio and Sebastian undercut the delicately balanced syntax of his poetic lines by parodic commentary in casual prose (2.1.139–65). In the long term, neither ideology is politically viable. Gonzalo's regressive fantasy blurs the distinction between a state of nature and the workings of civilization;

Antonio and Sebastian appear invested in exacerbating the divisions among the survivors of the shipwreck. As Andrew Hadfield discusses, such pipe-dreaming, factionalism, and inconstancy, which by the end of the scene have culminated into a treasonous plot to kill King Alonso, was precisely what the Kingdom of Naples was notorious for in the Renaissance (215–25). Even before the Italian courtiers encounter the island's people, the prospect of colonial expansion has brought out among them a dissonance of ideologies and visions of history.

Sharply differentiated from the Neapolitan squabbles and the hair-raising sounds of the tempest is the 3 of the island. It is most closely associated with Ariel, whose name puns on the element of air and on Renaissance musical "airs," or songs. We first *see* Ariel perform music as he leads Ferdinand onstage after the shipwreck. The stage direction has him "playing and singing," likely accompanying himself on the lute. This music is described by Ferdinand as divine, soothing, and enticing:

> . . . sure it waits upon
> Some god o' th'island. Sitting on a bank,
> Weeping again the King my father's wrack,
> This music crept by me upon the waters,
> Allaying both their fury and my passion
> With its sweet air. Thence I have followed it,
> Or it hath drawn me rather . . . (1.2.387–92)

No musical record survives of the song in question, "Come unto these yellow sands." Ferdinand perceives it as having a "sweet" power, but his impression may well be accounted for by his relief to be alive and the enchantment with the unfamiliar landscape. A more wary listener would note the song's disconcerting combination of instrumental music, human song, and animal sounds. Certainly anyone familiar with accounts of sirens' songs from classical epics would be on the alert. Analyzing the layout of the song in the First Folio of 1623, the only source of *The Tempest*, David Lindley points out how confused it appears in terms of both verse form and the indication of what constitutes the "burthen," or refrain. It is unclear who performs it (Ariel or the spirits), which of the performers are visible to the audience, what instruments may have been used (3). Clearly, the multiple voices of the song presented a challenge to Ralph Crane, the scribe who prepared the play for publication. Modern editors have tried to straighten the meter and rhyming scheme and usually relegate the animal sounds to the invisible spirits. But the Folio printing of the song may well suggest a deliberate confusion of sounds. Ariel's voice could contend with those of the spirits or mimic them; the spirits' voices may at times enhance Ariel's music or could, at times, overwhelm it. It is conceivable that Ariel's instrumental music, likely performed on the lute (the harmonious string instrument associated with the god of music, Apollo) would have been at odds with the Dionysian pipes of the spirits. Such discordant orchestration fits in with the disparate music genres referenced in the text. If music is the language of the islanders, the song certainly offers quite the mixture of stately court-dancing music ("Curtsied when you have, and kissed" [1.2.376]), the angel choir of "sweet sprites," and the natural sounds of the barnyard (according to the arrangement of the Arden 3 edition, "SPIRITS: Hark, hark! Bows-wow / The watch-dogs bark, bow-wow. / ARIEL: Hark hark, I hear / The strain of strutting chanticleer / Cry cock a diddle dow" [1.2.380–87]).

The medley of voices, instruments, and genres in the song can be accounted for by the long history of settlers and conquerors on the island. The jarring song functions, in effect, as an acoustic map of the waves of voyagers that have washed upon this land, each group drawing its own profit and each one intent on spinning its own account of cultural encounter and dominance. Another memorable instance of jarring music is the rebellious song performed by Stephano, Trinculo, and likely Caliban as the three join forces to murder Prospero and destroy his cultural heritage (burn his books). As implied by Caliban's request to Stephano, "Will you troll the catch/ You taught me but whilere?," the song has its origins in the drunken butler's tavern world (3.2.115–16). However, Caliban's recognition that "That's not the tune" (3.2.122) may suggest that Stephano and Trinculo are singing out of tune, signaling thus the preposterousness of their attempted "conquest." It is also possible that their performance does not match Caliban's understanding of what a song of freedom should sound like. The latter interpretation points to discordant notions of conquest by the conspirators. The stage direction following this line, "Ariel plays the tune on tabor and pipe," opens up another reason for Caliban's observation, namely that he finds the instrumental accompaniment at odds with the vocal performance. Lindley conjectures that "if Ariel takes up the same tune, it becomes a powerful dramatic image of the way Prospero co-opts and transforms this rebellious music" (*Shakespeare and Music* 222). One should be cautious, however, in equating Ariel's music unequivocally with Prospero's bidding. In this scene, Ariel may be keeping an eye on the rebels as Prospero ordered, but that does not necessarily diminish the appeal of their song of freedom for the airy spirit. Of course, the ideas of what this freedom may be remain disparate among the characters in the scene, as do their musical languages.

By the time we see Ariel perform his music, playgoers have also realized that he is the composer and performer of the cacophony of the tempest. Although by no means a malevolent spirit, Ariel's account to Prospero of the terror he struck into the lords and mariners when he executed the tempest was delivered with considerable glee: "I flamed amazement" (1.2.198). Similarly spiteful is the choice of the song addressed directly to Ferdinand shortly after Ariel leads him on stage. The surviving musical setting by Robert Johnson for this song, "Full fathom five," has been characterized by Howell Chickering as possessing "a sense both of continuity and continuing transformation." Jacquelyn Fox-Good similarly notes that "the song's music does not refer to or summarise 'sea change' but rather enacts it" (qtd. in Lindley, *Shakespeare and Music* 225). Heeding to the lyrics, we learn that the "change" in question is the fossilization of the allegedly drowned body of Ferdinand's father, Alonso: "Full fathom five thy father lies, / Of his bones are coral made; / Those are pearls that were his eyes" (1.2.395–97). If the music indeed enacts the change of the body, Ariel's musical art here is at once viscerally morbid and psychologically cruel.

Perhaps the reason for such proficiency in "inflaming" others with pain—and for the spirited accompaniment of the "freedom" song sung by the conspirators discussed earlier—is that Ariel has had a long, ruthless training in expressing pain vocally. In a story that appears to have been drummed into his ears on numerous occasions, we learn from Prospero that the "delicate" spirit had spent twelve years confined "into a cloven pine" (1.2.277) upon refusing Sycorax's behest. "Thy groans," taunts Prospero, "Did make wolves howl, and penetrate the breasts / of ever-angry bears" (1.2.287–89). Howling is the soundmark of islanders pressed into service or punished for disobedience by powerful colonizers. Prospero, having recalled Ariel's howling in the pine tree, threatens to "peg" him into the "knotty entrails" of an oak until the spirit has "*howled* away twelve winters" (1.2.295–96, emphasis added). At this, Ariel promptly acquiesces to serve his master as required. Still, he does not refrain from subtle parody —as when he makes an entrance "like a water nymph," just as Prospero has called the "tortoise" Caliban (1.3.316), or when he raises, but does not press upon the forgetful Prospero, the question about the timeliness of his entertainment for Ferdinand and Miranda given the advanced stage of Caliban's, Stephano's, and Trinculo's plot against the duke (4.1.41).

If the acoustic signature of Ariel and the other island "spirits" is the lute and the pipe, while Caliban, Stephano, and Trinculo are recognized by their voices, the scene dramatizing the encounter of Prospero with Caliban is characterized by a menacing and intensifying rhythm. Heeding to this rhythm we realize what Prospero means when he says that he has a "beating mind" (4.1.163). Rarely in this play do we encounter as relentless an iambic pentameter as when Prospero threatens to unleash his malevolent magic upon Caliban:

For this, be sure, tonight thou shalt have cramps,
Side-stitches that shall pen thy breath up; urchins
Shall, for that vast of night that they may work,
All exercise on thee; thou shalt be pinched
As thick as honeycomb, each pinch more stinging
Than bees that made 'em. (1.2.325–28)

This measured threat (rudely interrupted in the last line by Caliban's call for his dinner) is shot back in response to the quickly intensifying "beating" of Caliban's mind. The latter is delivered venomously as soon as he makes his first entry on stage:

As wicked dew as e'er my mother brushed
With raven's feather from unwholesome fen
Drop on you both! A southwest blow on ye
And blister you all o'er! (1.2.321–24)

The play offers divergent possibilities for the genealogy of the vicious "beats" in the speech of the colonizer and his subject. On the one hand, as Miranda claims in a passage that in production is frequently given to Prospero, Caliban has never had a language other than that of his colonizers:

I pitied thee,
Took pains to make the speak, taught thee each hour
One thing or other. When thou didst not (savage)
Know thine own meaning, but wouldst gabble like
A thing most brutish, I endowed thy purposes
With words that made them known. (1.2.352–57)

As a "savage" lacking a language, Caliban would have been akin, in the eyes of the audience members from Shakespeare's era, to colonial subjects such as the Irish or the Amerindians of North and South

America. As Paul Brown clarifies in his analysis on the involvement of *The Tempest* in the multivalent British colonialist projects of the era, "the savage other needed to be civilized, conquered, dispossessed." Doing it without coercive power (as Prospero did early in his sojourn on the island, and as Miranda did during the language lessons) was the highest measure of royal power. At its most optimistic, the colonial subject was a white page to be patiently inscribed by the colonizer. However, as Brown points out, far more prevalent was a concept of the colonial "other" as "bestial or only marginally human, and, as such, totally irreformable" (275–78). Caliban's opening salvo, in this context, would be a savage corruption of Prospero's and Miranda's "civilizing" efforts. His guttural response to the mention of the attempted rape of Miranda—"O ho, O ho! Would't had been done! Thou didst prevent me; I had peopled else / This isle with Calibans" (1.2.349–50)—would be an apt linguistic demonstration of his inherent depravity.

While this analysis of Caliban's speech in the context of English Renaissance colonialism may explain its phonetic and rhetorical thrust, it does little to account for the rhythm and imagery of Prospero's verbal assaults against his subjects. As several critics have noted, Prospero's learned Neo-Platonic magic bears disturbing parallels to the "mischiefs manifold, and sorceries terrible" of the witch Sycorax, the island's previous ruler.[6] Theater productions have been more hesitant in bringing out Prospero's indebtedness to Sycorax. A notable exception, however, was Paul Jesson's rendition of Prospero in the 1995 Royal Shakespeare Company (RSC) production of the play. The actor attempted to convey his conviction that the duke's magic had been inherited from Sycorax by donning a cloak decorated with island memorabilia and consulting (for a few performances) with a tattered human skull, presumably that of the witch (Lindley, *Shakespeare at Stratford* 62–63).

On the Jacobean stage, Sycorax's magic—and Prospero's—could not have had anything to do with African ritual. Rather, they likely evoked descriptions in popular Elizabethan docu-fiction of low-born witches' capacity to suggest vividly the physical and mental suffering of their opponents through the acoustic contour of their speech, body language, and word choice. As I have argued elsewhere, the "cramps," "side-stitches," and "stinging" pinches with which Prospero frightens Caliban, and later, Stephano and Trinculo, are the stuff of popular English witchcraft. So is his use of small animals such as apes, hedgehogs, and adders for suggesting and/or causing pain—tools of the magic trade that are no different from Sycorax's toads, beetles, and bats, or from the familiar spirits of English countryside hags (Stavreva 221–22). Contextualized in this way, Prospero's "bad tongue" associates him with malevolent witchcraft and seriously undermines his moral status. Furthermore, the beats of Caliban's cursing turn out not to be imprints of his "savage" nature, but rather, they have been learned from his master. In other words, when Caliban lashes out against Miranda, "You taught me language, and my profit on't / Is I know how to curse" (1.2.362–63), he may be entirely literal about his language lessons. This statement is also a blunt recognition of how significant the colonizer's "bad tongue" is for the articulation of his subject's identity.

In the play's last scene, Prospero famously renounces "this rough magic" (5.1.50)—his means of conquering the nature and "spirits" of the island—and calls for "heavenly music" instead (5.1.53). At this point, he seems to care little about the social harmony among the island's inhabitants; rather, Prospero is focused on harmonizing the political discord among the marooned Italians. Not long afterwards, Gonzalo delivers a thanksgiving hymn of reconciliation and affirmation of common European identity among the previously fractious courtiers:

> Was Milan thrust from Milan that his issue
> Should become kings of Naples? O, rejoice
> Beyond a common joy, and set it down
> With gold on lasting pillars: in one voyage
> Did Claribel her husband find at Tunis,
> And Ferdinand her brother found a wife
> Where he himself was lost; Prospero his dukedom

In a poor isle; and all of us ourselves
When no man was his own. (5.1.205–13)

The hymn condenses the multivalent accounts of cultural encounters into a bare-bones dynastic chronicle, fit for inscription on palace pillars. It completely disassociates the European sense of self from the unsettling experience of first contact, from the power contestations among colonizers and colonized, from the trade considerations of intercultural encounters. In Gonzalo's proclamation, issues of colonialism and empire are expunged from the play's narrative. Ironically, this gloss of the outcome of the play matches closely the call to keep politics out of the study of literature, issued by proponents of a conservative cultural agenda during the culture wars of the 1990s.[7]

The dramatic action of *The Tempest*, however, concludes much more messily with the racial and social mix on stage reintroducing forcefully the political issue of cultural encounters. As Ariel drives in the rebels, Antonio and Sebastian immediately start evaluating their market value:

SEBASTIAN   Ha, ha! What things are these, my Lord Antonio?
Will money buy 'em?
ANTONIO   Very like. One of them
Is a plain fish, and no doubt marketable. (5.1.264–66)

Accounting for Caliban, Prospero assigns him—twice—to the realm of the diabolical ("His mother was a witch" [5.1.269]; "this demi-devil" [5.1.272]), but eventually claims responsibility and even affinity with him: "this thing of darkness I / Acknowledge mine" (5.1.275–76). He then sends Caliban and his companions to "trim" his cell and promises the courtiers the story of his life, focusing on the events on the island and a safe voyage back to Naples.

At this critical moment, the nature of leave-taking and stage exits should map parallels and differences in the identity of the characters as they have developed through the dramatic action. Frustratingly, however, the playtext features a single explicit stage direction for all of the characters crowded on stage at the end of the last scene before Prospero's epilogue: Alonso, Antonio, Sebastian, Gonzalo, Adrian, Francisco, Ferdinand, Miranda, Ariel, the Master, Boatswain, Caliban, Stephano, Trinculo: "Exeunt omnes" (exit all). Most directors have felt that an en masse exit would not do justice to characters as important as Caliban and Ariel (to say nothing about the traffic jam that would result on stage), and have invented "business" to underscore the end-point of character and relationships development.

One way to do this is to follow Shakespeare's implied stage direction for Caliban's exit after he promises (earnestly? hypocritically? ironically?) to "be wise hereafter, / And seek for grace" (5.1.294–95). At this point, Prospero commands him, "Go to, away" (5.1.297), and Alonso orders Stephano and Trinculo "Hence" (5.1.298), presumably showing them off the stage after Caliban. Directors' decisions regarding the nature of Caliban's exit and the power balance of his relationship with Prospero vary widely. Some final visions of the character have cast him as Prospero's finally reformed servant, whether kneeling at Miranda's feet (in Herbert Beerbohm Tree's 1904 production for His Majesty's Theatre) or kicking Stephano and Trinculo into the cell (Ben Iden Payne's 1941 production for the Royal Shakespeare Company). Contrastingly, in Giorgio Strehler's famous 1978 revival of the play for Teatro Lirico in Milan, Caliban's exit demonstrated his severing ties with the Europeans as he dropped a stick and sword at Prospero's feet and jumped with his arms raised high into the trap, out of which he had crawled in. If the trap door to Caliban's cave remained open in Strehler's production in the Stratford run of Sam Mendes's 1993 RSC production, Prospero's line, "As you look / To have my pardon" was cut. Caliban was, in Lindley's description, "clapped howling into the theatrical skip," although the severity of the ending was modified when the production transferred to London (*Shakespeare at Stratford* 146). In Jonathan Miller's landmark 1970 RSC anticolonial production, Caliban was last seen on stage shaking his fist at the departing ship. Postcolonial renditions focusing on reconciliation have had Prospero give Stephano's crown to Caliban and Miranda curtsy to him (Bill Alexander's 1994 production for the Birmingham Rep); Caliban reach up to touch Prospero as he sought forgiveness (Adrian Noble's 1997 RSC production); or Prospero (played by Vanessa Redgrave in the Shakespeare's Globe 2000 production) give Caliban her hat, perhaps as a deed of ownership. In Janet Honeyman's 2009 collaborative production of Cape Town's Baxter Theatre Center and the RSC, Caliban reentered to face Prospero as he delivered his Epilogue so that its final couplet ("As you from crimes would pardon'd be, / Let your indulgence set me free" [5.119–20]) became an act of penance. The final tableau of the production, as Anston Bosman relates in his analysis of the production, had Caliban standing tall on top the rocky steps on the stage, yet frozen in a bewildered stare after Prospero's exit, "as if to ask, *What now?*" (115). A 2002 production directed by Edward Isser at the College of Holy Cross in Worcester, Massachusetts, attempted to transcend the anticolonial/postcolonial discourse by having Prospero admonish the cowering Caliban to stand up straight and invite him to board the ship, leaving the island to the singing and dancing indigenous "spirits." Deliberately optimistic as such a reconciliatory ending may be, it eschews the question of the market value of the Carib/cannibal/Caliban in the Italian states.[8]

If most stagings of Caliban's exit have Prospero determine the final terms of the relationship, Ariel typically takes his leave on his own terms at Prospero's final words before the Epilogue: My Ariel, chick, / That is thy charge. Then to the elements / Be free, and fare thou well (5.1.31618). True, as Lindley reminds us, "In 1957 it had been possible for Gielgud simply to bless a kneeling Ariel, thus seeming 'to validate a master-servant relationship.'" However, he goes on to describe how in 1982 on the RSC Stratford stage, "Jacobi began his instruction 'My Ariel,' only to realize he was not there, pause, and deliver the endearment 'chick?' as a question, before pacing the stage and delivering his instruction to the empty air" (*Shakespeare at Stratford* 109). As Ralph Berry suggests, when Ariel departs so abruptly and without a word of gratitude, Prospero is left with a diminished status, "desolated by this desertion" (139). His plaintive "Please you draw near" (5.1318), so uncharacteristic of one who had given fire "to the dread rattling thunder" (5.1.44), may be directed to Ariel, or else, desperately, to the off-stage audience. As a weak response to what Philip McGuire has termed Ariel's "open silence," the half-line marks the nadir of Prospero's power on the island (44). In Mendes's 1993 production, this nadir was punctuated poignantly when Simon Russell Beale's Ariel paused on being given his freedom and then spat in Prospero's face before walking slowly offstage. The spit, which got a mix of strong responses from reviewers, was replaced by a stare in later shows, one described by Beale as "a mixture of hatred, anger, confusion, and love" (Lindley, *Shakespeare at Stratford* 109–10).

The Tempest offers no projection of how the cultural encounters on the island would affect the characters' lives after the departure of the Neapolitan ship from the island. But it makes it clear that once the initial "wonder" or the stupefaction of first contact has worn off, travelers and "islanders" alike begin to conceive of themselves, of their speech, silence, actions, and transactions as inflected by the speech, silence, and actions of cultural others. Prospero despairs about the possibility for his cultural readaptation to Milan, where, he says, "Every third thought shall be my grave" (5.1.311). But Miranda, Caliban, and Ariel—though arguably not Gonzalo, Alonso, Antonio, or Sebastian—have gained an acute awareness of cross-cultural expressions and manipulations of power. And so has a careful play-reader or play-goer.

Notes

1. Unless indicated otherwise, all quotes are taken from Shakespeare, William. *The Tempest: A Norton Critical Edition.*

2. See, among others: Hamilton, "Defiguring Virgil in *The Tempest*," and *Virgil and* The Tempest, 12–21; Hulme 109; Barbara A. Mowat, "'Knowing I loved my books': Reading *The Tempest* Intertextually," in Hulme and Sherman, The Tempest *and Its Travels*, 27–36. Additional classical contexts relevant to *The Tempest* include the *Odyssey*, Ovid's *Metamorphoses*, and Apollonius's *Argonautica*.

3. Most famous among the English privateers in the Mediterranean was Captain John Ward, whose Tunis-based pirate fleet raided Christian and Ottoman ships throughout the Mediterranean. This flamboyant individual is featured in a 1612 play, Robert Dadborne's *A Christian turn'd Turk, or the Tragicall Lives and Deaths of the two Famous Pyrates, Ward and Danisker*. See Hess, 127–28; Nabil Matar, *Islam in Britain 1558–1685* (Cambridge: Cambridge UP, 1998), 1–72, 120–90; Daniel J. Vitkus, "Turning Turk in *Othello*: The Conversion and Damnation of the Moor," *Shakespeare Quarterly* 48.2 (1997): 145–76.

4. Unlike Alonso and Prospero, England's Elizabeth I derived considerable profit and political advantage from her alliance with the Ottoman Empire, which resulted in establishing English commercial outposts in Northern Africa and the Eastern Mediterranean and a robust trade in clothing and military equipment. See Hess 124–29.

5. For a discussion of Dido as a figure for English imperial nationalism, see Ferguson, especially Chapter 4, "An Empire of Her Own," 179–224. In modern mathematics, the circumscription of Carthage is known as the "isoperimetric problem" of enclosing a maximum area within a fixed boundary (the "Dido problem" in calculus of variations).

6. The extended debate on the blackness or whiteness of Prospero's magic has been summarized in Corfield. See also Orgel.

7. To get a sense of the heated debate over the focus on politics and ideology in the study of canonical authors such as Shakespeare, see the exchange between George Will ("Literary Politics") and Stephen Greenblatt ("The Best Way to Kill Our Literary Inheritance Is to Turn It into a Decorous Celebration of the New World Order") in Graff 110–15.

8. For the theater renditions of Caliban's exit, see Horowitz 192; Isser 117–18, 124–26.

Works Cited

Berry, Ralph. *Shakespeare in Performance: Castings and Metamorphoses.* New York: St. Martin's, 1993.

Bosman, Anston. "Cape of Storms: The Baxter Theatre Centre–RSC Tempest, 2009." *Shakespeare Quarterly* 61.1 (2010): 108–17.

Brown, Paul. "'This Thing of Darkness I Acknowledge Mine': The Tempest and the Discourse of Colonialism." The Tempest. *A Case Study in Critical Controversy.* Eds. Gerald Graff and James Phelan. Boston: Bedford, 2009. 268–92.

Corfield, Cosmo. "Why Does Prospero Abjure his 'Rough Magic'?." *Shakespeare Quarterly* 36.1 (1985): 32–33.

Ferguson, Margaret W. *Dido's Daughters: Literacy, Gender, and Empire in Early Modern England and France.* Chicago: U of Chicago P, 2003.

Graff, Gerald, and James Phelan, eds. The Tempest. *A Case Study in Critical Controversy.* Boston: Bedford, 2009.

Greenblatt, Stephen. "The Best Way to Kill Our Literary Inheritance Is to Turn It into a Decorous Celebration of the New World Order." The Tempest. *A Case Study in Critical Controversy.* Eds. Gerald Graff and James Phelan. Boston: Bedford, 2009. 113–15.

Greene, Roland. "Island Logic." The Tempest *and Its Travels.* Eds. Peter Hulme and William H. Sherman. London: Reaktion, 2000. 138–45.

Hadfield, Andrew. *Shakespeare and Renaissance Politics.* London: Thomson Learning, 2004.

Hamilton, Donna B. "Defiguring Virgil in The Tempest," *Style* 23.3 (1989): 352–73.
_____. *Virgil and* The Tempest: *The Politics of Imitation.* Columbus: Ohio State UP, 1990.

Hess, Andrew H. "The Mediterranean and Shakespeare's Geopolitical Imagination." The Tempest *and Its Travels.* Eds. Peter Hulme and William H. Sherman. London: Reaktion, 2000. 121–30.

Horowitz, Arthur. *Prospero's "True Preservers": Peter Brook, Yukio Ninagawa, and Giorgio Strehler—Twentieth-Century Directors Approach Shakespeare's* The Tempest. Cranbury, NJ: AUP, 2004.

Hulme, Peter. *Colonial Encounters: Europe and the Native Caribbean, 1492–1797.* London: Methuen, 1986.

Hulme, Peter, and William H. Sherman, eds. The Tempest *and Its Travels.* London: Reaktion, 2000.

Isser, Edward. "Permissive, Implied, and Missing Stage Directions: 'Exeunt Omnes' and *The Tempest.*" *Staging Shakespeare: Essays in Honor of Alan C. Dessen.* Eds. Lena Cowen Orlin and Miranda Johnson-Haddad. Cranbury, NJ: AUP, 2007. 124–29.

Kirkpatrick, Robin. "The Italy of The Tempest." The Tempest *and Its Travels.* Eds. Peter Hulme and William H. Sherman. London: Reaktion, 2000. 78–96.

Lindley, David. *Shakespeare and Music.* London: Thomson Learning, 2006.
_____. *Shakespeare at Stratford:* The Tempest. London: Thomson Learning, 2003.

Matar, Nabil. *Islam in Britain 1558–1685.* Cambridge: Cambridge UP, 1998.

McGuire, Philip C. *Speechless Dialect: Shakespeare's Open Silences*. Berkeley: U of California P, 1985.

Mowat, Barbara A. "'Knowing I loved my books': Reading The Tempest Intertextually." The Tempest *and Its Travels*. Eds. Peter Hulme and William H. Sherman. London: Reaktion, 2000. 27–36.

Orgel, Stephen. "Prospero's Wife." *Rewriting the Renaissance: The Discourses of Sexual Difference in Early Modern Europe*. Eds. Margaret W. Ferguson, Maureen Quilligan, and Nancy J. Vickers. Chicago: U of Chicago P, 1986. 50–64.

Shakespeare, William. The Tempest: *A Norton Critical Edition*. Eds. Peter Hulme and William H. Sherman. New York: Norton, 2004.

_____. *The Tempest*. Eds. Virginia Mason Vaughan and Alden T. Vaughan. London: Arden Shakespeare, 2011.

Stavreva, Kirilka. "'There's Magic in Thy Majesty': Queenship and Witch-Speak in Jacobean Shakespeare." *High and Mighty Queens of Early Modern England: Realities and Representations*. Eds. Carole Levin, Debra Barrett-Graves, and Jo Eldridge Carney. New York: Palgrave, 2003. 151–68.

Vitkus, Daniel J. "Turning Turk in Othello: The Conversion and Damnation of the Moor." *Shakespeare Quarterly* 48.2 (1997): 145–76.

Will, George. "Literary Politics." The Tempest. *A Case Study in Critical Controversy*. Eds. Gerald Graff and James Phelan. Boston: Bedford, 2009. 110–13.

Crusoe's Empire

Gerd Bayer

The history of the English novel has been retold from the point of view of various scholarly traditions, but the place awarded to Daniel Defoe's publication, *The Life and Strange Surprizing Adventures of Robinson Crusoe* (1719), is frequently one of prominence. In his influential study *The Rise of the Novel* (1957), Ian Watt famously awarded Defoe's novel a central role in the development within narrative fiction away from the frequently supernatural events of medieval and early modern romances that ushered in the kind of formal realism that would become the hallmark of the novel: the genre that increasingly came to dominate literary taste from the eighteenth century onwards. In his study, Watt presents a sequential development that led from the rise of the middle class to the rise of a new reading public and, ultimately, to the rise of the novel. Defoe's work fits this ticket quite nicely in that its protagonist, Robinson Crusoe, comes from a relatively modest social background and manages, through perseverance and a belief in his own fate, to survive a number of ordeals, the most memorable of which, to his readers at least, is his being stranded on a remote island off the coast of South America.

Defoe was inspired by various publications that told of genuine cases of ship-wrecked castaways, most famously Alexander Selkirk, and he also benefited from the general interest in travel writing. Some of these popular travelogues were clearly based on actual journeys—for instance the writings of Richard Hakluyt (1552–1616)—while others were blatantly fictional, as in the fourteenth-century work associated with John Mandeville. Defoe cleverly positioned his own work in between fact and fiction by passing his fiction off as the actual biography of his invented character, Crusoe. In the preface to his book, Defoe claims that he is merely the editor of what he calls "a just History of Fact" (3). His readers were thus invited to believe that they in fact read a truthful relation of a man's survival. The overall realism of his work allowed readers to identify with the protagonist and suspend their disbelief. Many readers must have taken *Robinson Crusoe* at face value (see Mayer), having become used to the reading of news as a consequence of the newly established format of print journalism around the beginning of the eighteenth century (see Davis).

Defoe presents Crusoe's survival as both a physical and a psychological process: Crusoe learns how to build himself a home and provide for his own food, but he also must come to terms with his own fate. The process of maturation that this involves might be recognized by modern readers as psychological: to Defoe's contemporaries any struggle of an individual with his social and natural environment played out more as a religious experience than as a psychological process. If one remembers all the religious turmoil that marked the English seventeenth century—including a civil war, the execution of a supposedly God-anointed king, the changing fates of Puritan and other dissenting groups, as well as the recurring conflicts between Catholicism and Protestant groups—Crusoe's search for atonement and redemption, figured in his return from a desert island to his English homeland, clearly takes on religious dimensions. In the wake of Sigmund Freud's early twentieth-century research, modern readers will nevertheless be tempted (and permitted) to see psychological developments in Crusoe's biography: The fact that this book allows for such diverse readings and interpretations testifies to its literary merit and explains, at least in part, its continued success through the centuries.

What is easy to overlook, though, for modern readers is the extent to which allegorical and symbolic references to biblical events and Christian practice shape Defoe's work. *Robinson Crusoe* therefore benefits if read in conjunction with other literary works popular at the time—for instance, John Bunyan's *The Pilgrim's Progress* (1678) or even John Milton's epic *Paradise Lost* (1667). Such comparisons also help to understand how significantly Defoe contributed to the history of the novel in his transformation of abstract religious and ethical discussions and the sources of evil into a tale of human survival and individual growth. Whereas Bunyan's pilgrim manages to overcome all kinds of religious hurdles and obstacles to save his soul, Defoe's Crusoe battles a reality that his readers would have recognized from their own personal lives, even if they had never set foot on a ship, let alone the New World. Crusoe's practical and hands-on approach to problem-solving has made him a role model for private enterprise and the entrepreneurial spirit. He literally builds his own world, adapts his environment to his own needs, and eventually is rewarded with riches and glory. This raft-to-riches story of perseverance resonated widely with Defoe's contemporary audience, which started to realize that anybody can potentially be champion of his or her own life.

Defoe himself, while not belonging to the aristocracy, grew up under rather privileged circumstances. The son of a wealthy Presbyterian tallow chandler (a candle maker) who had become a full citizen of London, young Daniel was sent to a prestigious nonconformist academy. There, he benefited from its modern curriculum with its emphasis on English (rather than on Greek) and the natural sciences. He later became a merchant in London, married a rich woman, and added the "De" to his last name to appear nobler. His religious background and support of the Glorious Revolution brought him in conflict with the Catholic King James II, and business trouble took him to debtor's jail. He soon became a writer of pamphlets (pro-trade and frequently critical of the monarchy), a journalist (active for both Tory and Whig causes), and eventually a successful author of literary works. Even though he died in poverty, his final business scheme having faltered, his work is filled with the notions that trade and enterprise are potentially to the benefit of everybody.

It is little surprising, then, that the inherent optimism of Defoe's tale continues to inspire readers, even including the modern-day inhabitants of the very Caribbean islands that Crusoe presents quite negatively in his tale as uncivilized and barbarian backwaters. The Caribbean poet and Nobel Prize laureate Derek Walcott, whose work frequently relates canonical European works of literature to the political and cultural realities of the postcolonial sphere, has famously pointed out that Defoe's Crusoe is anything but a character that can be described as single-minded or flat. In fact, Walcott evokes a different kind of figure: "It is not the Crusoe you recognize. I have compared him to Proteus, that mythological figure who changes shapes according to what we need him to be" (35). He goes on to compare Crusoe to the biblical Adam, to Christopher Columbus, and to various heroes known from tales of adventures. In short, he points out that one reason for the lasting success of Defoe's novel is in the lack of specificity found in its protagonist.

Defoe expressed his views on the importance of cultural and ethnic background quite clearly in a poem entitled "The True-born Englishman," where he suggests in unequivocal terms that national identity should never be equated with a lack of change or a petrified sense of history. The poem conjures up all the various inhabitants of the British Isles, from its early days through the Roman and Saxon invasions and throwing in some Danes, Scots, Picts (a late-prehistoric/early Celtic people), Irish, and Normans. Describing "this amphibious ill-born mob" as the starting point of what would eventually come to be considered his eponymously true-born Englishman, Defoe's poem easily deflates any sense of purity or racial essence. It is this notion of multiplicity that Walcott praises in his comments on Defoe's work and that allows readers from myriad backgrounds to identify with much of *Robinson Crusoe*. Walcott emphasizes that, despite Defoe's private thoughts about colonialism and imperialist control, his Crusoe does not fully represent that dark chapter in the history of the West: "Crusoe is no lord of magic, duke, prince. He does not possess the island he inhabits. He is alone, he is a craftsman, his beginnings are humble" (37). Unlike the powerful and hierarchical figure of Shakespeare's Prospero, whom Walcott evokes in his description, Crusoe is marked by the character's simple background and nonimperialist attitude. However, many critics have faulted Defoe's spatial outline of the island as marked by the very idea of control (see, for instance, Weaver-Hightower and also

Pratt) with the view afforded from the mountaintop, positioning Crusoe at the very center of the gaze. This panoptic stance reveals that the novel does after all promote notions like control and power, ideally wielded by a European colonizer.

However, Defoe does allow room in his novel for counter-visions, markedly when he presents reality from Friday's point of view. In one scene, Defoe has Friday comment about the arrival of some European sailors and their prisoners. Even the personal witnessing of such a scene, Defoe's text suggests, does not necessarily allow those present to comprehend what they see. This is how Crusoe and Friday react:

> I was perfectly confounded at the Sight, and knew not what the Meaning of it should be. *Friday* call'd out to me in *English*, as well as he could, *O* Master! *You see* English *Mans eat Prisoner as well as* Savage *Mans.* Why, says I, *Friday, Do you think they are going to eat them then: No, no,* says I, Friday, *I am afraid they will murther them indeed, but you may be sure they will not eat them.* (*Robinson Crusoe* 211)

Friday's inaccurate assumptions about how the scene that unfolds in front of him might end smartly alert readers to the fact that one's cultural background and personal experience will influence any confrontation with other traditions and behaviors. Friday's wrongful belief that cannibalism is practiced universally serves as a foil for the same process taking place in reverse when Europeans wrongly judged other cultures. Like Michel de Montaigne (1533–1592) did before him in a famous essay entitled "Of Cannibals" (1580) that questioned the ethnic arrogance with which Europeans whitewash their own ethical shortcomings, Defoe's novel promotes a certain sense of humility in its presentation of cultural encounters as dependent on careful negotiations of linguistic and cultural translations. Written at a time when Europe was in the midst of major cultural, social, and political reshufflings, his novel resonates strongly with the Enlightenment spirit of rational, unbiased, and empirical logic. The realism that structures *Robinson*

Crusoe thus helps to justify the colonialist attitude toward other parts of the world.

Daniel Defoe also applied his talents as a travel writer to his own geographical background when, from 1724 to 1727, he published *A Tour thro' the Whole Island of Great Britain*. Defoe's project connects with the growing sense of nationalist pride and identity at the time, which made the Home Tour—that is, visits to English sites—the natural complement to the more heralded Grand Tour, which saw predominantly young gentlemen travel to Italy and other places in Europe as part of their general cultural and linguistic education. Defoe's *Tour* engages in extended discussions of the British market forces and regional products that center on London, the capital metropolis (see Marzec 18–19). Nigel Smith has offered a perceptive explanation for this change in the literary utilization of the natural landscape when he notes that subsequent to the 1660 restoration of the British monarchy (that was followed almost immediately by the establishment of the Royal Society), work had started to dominate the human-natural relationship, and therefore "the pastoral was somehow superseded or displaced in the seventeenth century by the georgic. In the pastoral eclogue, the shepherd speakers do very little except sing, but in the georgic, work (ploughing the land) is the dominant activity" (320). This development certainly intensified even further during the eighteenth century with its substantial increase in global exchange, scientific development around the Enlightenment project, and an increasingly urban and ever wealthier population on the British Isles.

While the *Tour* thus already showed Defoe to be a staunch supporter of English sentiments, his *A New Voyage Round the World* (1724) further supports this impression. The fictional account of a global trade expedition, the book promises to differ from other travel accounts. Criticizing earlier travelogues for focusing too much on technical details and facts of the kind favored by the scientific writers of the day, what Defoe dismisses as "tedious accounts of their log-work" (3), the narrator of the *Voyage* promises to concentrate instead on particular "incidents [that] have happened in such a voyage" (2). His book indeed relies on story and plot and on the development of tensions and their narrative resolution. While propagating trade may well have been the underlying rationale for the publication of *Voyage*, its portrayal of foreign lands and peoples also shows the master plotter at work, albeit frequently, by resorting to ellipsis or silence. In fact, the trope of deceit and the willingness to lie reveal the narrator to be eager to manipulate his adversaries met around the world and also his readers. In general, Defoe's *Voyage* is dominated by control. Both in the protagonist's dealings with his fellow travelers, whom he rules without giving them so much as the space on the page to voice their opinions in their own language, and in his silencing of indigenous voices, the book firmly propagates one opinion. When discussing the threat of a mutiny, the crew is presented as driven by "brutish rage" (26), a phrase that closely resonates with the kind of language later used in describing the inhabitants of various non-Western territories. The book implicitly justifies this control by the narrator's superior intellectual powers by his having the necessary "presence of mind" that allows him to argue smoothly and convince others (26). Rationality rules supreme, but the victory is easily scored in the absence of other opinions. The shipmen are "conquer'd" (43) and subsequently exposed to a written version of the new course, as if only the printed word has the final power to make an action legitimate and just. The *Voyage* thus approaches both the world and people of lower rank or with slightly flatter noses as mere objects to be spoken for by others.

While Defoe's *Voyage* can hardly count as one of his most popular publications, it nevertheless serves as a reminder that writers and readers around the beginning of the eighteenth century were still willing to rally behind the force of rhetoric when it came to promoting their own interests. Defoe's *Voyage* is most likely a good representation of how most European readers thought about the rest of world: They looked down on its human population, in particular when they perceived racial differences; and as far as its resources and produce were concerned,

Europeans tended to believe such bounty was sent from heaven exclusively for their own benefit and consumption. This attitude easily developed into the exploitative colonialist system that almost without exception placed financial gain over the well-being of the indigenous populations.

Defoe's attitude to nature and the environment as found both in *Voyage* and in *Robinson Crusoe* furthermore echoes the arguments developed by his near-contemporary John Locke (1632–1704), whose *Second Treatise of Government* suggested that ownership of land is established by working the land. This implies that any territory that is not visibly farmed or mined is up for the taking. In other words, Crusoe (and the travelers in Defoe's *Voyage*) can claim ownership of a particular territory by being the first people to invest their labor into cultivating the land. Later, this same idea would be used to rationalize the displacement by European settlers of numerous peoples in territories around the world.

While the resulting project of colonialism has been linked to the kind of formal realism found in Defoe's novels (see Hulme, "Robinson Crusoe"), the more fascinating account of this historical development connects the early novel with colonialism and the Enlightenment project. Robinson Crusoe's status as an individual whose background allows many readers to identify with him and the range of skills he brings to his island partly reflects the Enlightenment push for greater rationality, for scientific and technical advances, and for a move beyond the mythical and mystical belief systems of traditional cultures. However, while promoting values that would later be manifest in democracy-minded revolutions in North America, France, and elsewhere, the Enlightenment also saw a public discourse take shape. This discourse would eventually be used to rationalize the outright dispossession of various peoples around the world and resulted in the often brutal destruction of cultural traditions and livelihoods and the outright enslavement of a sizeable percentage of the global population serving the (Eurocentric) gods of progress, rationality, commerce, and capital gain. As Walter Mignolo and like-minded scholars have shown in their research, the very notion of the Enlightenment can thus be shown to have brought forth its evil twin, the ruthless forces of unethical exploitation that go by the name of colonialism and imperialism.

Robinson Crusoe belongs with this narrative since it also connects the positive forces of the Enlightenment—individuality, rationality, and a turn from myth to science—with its dark doppelgänger: the Eurocentric and essentially racist exploitation of less developed parts of the world. However, it is worth remembering that Crusoe does not succeed due to his superior genes or racial background but rather because he benefits from technological advancements. Crusoe's survival on the island is indeed made possible by the fact that after he was stranded during a storm, he returns the next day to the wrecked ship during calmer weather and salvages not only building materials, food, arms, and clothes, but, most importantly, tools to help him put up a shelter and farm the land. He is, accordingly, delighted when he discovers on the wreck "the Carpenter's Chest," which he rightly describes as "much more valuable than a Ship Loading of Gold" (*Robinson* 44). He returns to the ship a number of times, creating "the biggest Magazine of all Kinds . . . that ever were laid up, I believe, for one Man" (48). His subsequent success in organizing his life, creating a home, hunting for food, and feeding himself must therefore be put in perspective somewhat: Crusoe clearly did not have to start from scratch. Rather, he had ample stock of tools and utensils and of wooden boards, chests, weapons, gunpowder, bullets, and other necessities. When his quality of life is later compared positively with the barbarity of the cannibalistic inhabitants of the neighboring island, it is necessary to remember that he was given a substantial head start. Far from being thrown back to a state of nature, Crusoe in effect took numerous inventions and achievements of Western society with him. The novel nevertheless contrasts Crusoe's lifestyle and his values with those of the local inhabitants, allowing European readers to feel good about the supposed superiority of their own culture and, by implication, race.

Crusoe's success at controlling the natural environment is similarly aided by his access to European technology. Looking for animals to domesticate, he encounters goats and indeed manages to impose his rule over them. However, his relationship with goats begins through shooting them, and it is only after he "lam'd" a goat and, in his camp, nurses it back to health that he begins to start his own herd. Crusoe almost brags about the fact that he "took such Care of it, that it liv'd" and goes on to claim about the goat that "by my nursing it so long it grew tame . . . and would not go away" (65). What this engagement between man and nature shows is that far from having access to any superior skill or remarkable knowledge, Crusoe first resorts to technological violence of firearms, making the goat dependent on him, and then later claims as his achievement the apparent training of the animal. This attitude closely echoes the overall colonialist project when Europeans would (often intentionally) harm the indigenous population and then afterwards present themselves as the paternal providers of the poor locals. The cycle of control, dependency, and support that underlies Crusoe's engagement with the natural environment—here exemplified by his turning a wild animal into a domesticated provider of milk (and, eventually, meat and skin)—thus plays out on a much grander level time and again in the European attitude toward non-European places with human inhabitants frequently degraded to little more than another feature of the natural landscape in need of the Western missionary spirit.

Defoe's novel offers other examples that show that for Crusoe, non-Western people do not seem to deserve the same treatment and enjoy the same rights as (white) Europeans. Earlier in his seafaring life, Crusoe had become enslaved to the Moors, but he eventually escaped with the help of fellow slave Xury. The two are later picked up by a Portuguese ship, and it is here that Crusoe reveals some insight into his moral outlook by selling his fellow escapee back into slavery. Even though he is "loath to take" the money (30), he quickly calms his conscience by the captain's claim that he would set Xury free in ten years' time. When a little later Crusoe learns what the life of a slave in the cane field is like, he admits, "I had done wrong in parting with my Boy Xury" (31). On his island, Crusoe's attitude to Friday mirrors this earlier encounter in that the ethnic difference between the two men seems to justify the hierarchical relationship, making Crusoe the unquestioned master over somebody who is essentially treated as property to be disposed of.

While Crusoe may thus strike the modern reader as a somewhat bigoted and even racist man, he is certainly not unprincipled. In fact, it is possible to sketch a development in his character. Whereas as a young man he frequently rebelled against the powers that be, leading him to ignore his parents' wishes and become a sailor, he later comes to respect and even uphold structures of hierarchy. When, toward the end of the novel, Crusoe's island is visited by another ship, the former rebel turns conservative, overthrows the mutineers that had stranded their captain, and reinstates law and order. Without asking about the reasons for the mutiny, Crusoe aligns himself with traditional power structures, uses his firearms to overpower the mutineers, described as "incorrigible Villains" (215), and assumes control. The choice of words is of particular interest here: By describing the rebels as people who can no longer be turned into valuable members of society, Defoe takes a rather awkward position vis-à-vis the overall Christian framework of his book. Whereas Crusoe is allowed to atone for his initial sin of disobeying his parents—after all, violating one of the biblical Ten Commandments—others are not allowed to make up for their wrong-doing. Defoe's text thus implicitly differentiates between those whom God may still grant his forgiveness and those who are beyond redemption. By thus creating categories of human beings that are not all created equal, his book must be seen not only as quietly propagating the class consciousness so dominant in British culture at the time, but also as giving voice to the racist logic that would continue to propel colonialism and imperialism for centuries to come.

Such a view of a text written in the early decades of a century long passed may strike some readers as unfair as it seems to accuse an author of not sufficiently heeding the ethical debates of later generations. Yet it is less Defoe who is revealed by such arguing as unethical but the age in which he lived. That age, however, set in motion historical and political developments whose consequences continue to determine the present lives of many people around the world. It is therefore extremely important that through the study of such early modern sources, twenty-first-century readers get an opportunity to learn about the mindset of earlier generations. At the same time, reading a book such as *Robinson Crusoe* has been a pleasant experience for millions across the ages without these readers having to embrace all the cultural, historical, and racial implications brought out in this chapter. The tale of perseverance and survival in fact resonates with both younger and mature readers. In fact, Defoe's novel can now look back on a long and distinguished history of adaptations. While earlier centuries often stuck to the same format, writing novels whose strategy of retelling Robinson's story earned them the generic term "Robinsonade," more recent adaptations have moved beyond the written, as in the feature film *Cast Away* (2000), directed by Robert Zemeckis. Needless to say, the colonialist tendencies of *Robinson Crusoe* have also not gone unnoticed, and one of the most fascinating recent reworkings of Defoe's novel has come at the hands of J. M. Coetzee, the South African Nobel Prize winner, whose novel *Foe* (1986) plays with the role that Defoe played in the publication of this fictional tale, with the repression of Friday's personality and version of the story and with the gender politics at play in the all-male cast of the original novel. Hailed across the centuries as one of the first examples of the European novel, Defoe's *Robinson Crusoe*, it seems, continues to enjoy popularity, and it continues to provoke debate.

Works Cited

Adams, Percy G. *Travel Literature and the Evolution of the Novel*. Lexington: UP of Kentucky, 1983

Aravamudan, Srinivas. *Tropicopolitans: Colonialism and Agency, 1688–1804*. Durham, NC: Duke UP, 1999.

Ballaster, Ros. *Fabulous Orients: Fictions of the East in England, 1662–1785*. Oxford: Oxford UP, 2005.

Bhabha, Homi K. *The Location of Culture*. London: Routledge, 1994.

Davis, Lennard J. *Factual Fictions: The Origins of the English Novel*. New York: Columbia UP, 1983.

Defoe, Daniel. *A New Voyage Round the World by a Course Never Sailed Before*, Ed. George A. Aitken. London, 1895. *Google Book Search*. Web. 6 Jan. 2012.

_____. *A tour thro' the whole island of Great Britain*. 3 vols. London: Strahan, 1724–27.

_____. *Robinson Crusoe*. Ed. Thomas Keymer. New York: Oxford UP, 2007.

Downie, J. A. "Defoe, Imperialism, and the Travel Book Reconsidered." *Yearbook of English Studies* 13 (1983): 66–83.

Fish, Stanley E. *Self-Consuming Artifacts: The Experience of Seventeenth-Century Literature*. Berkeley: U of California P, 1972.

Frantz, R. W. *The English Traveller and the Movement of Ideas, 1660–1732*. Lincoln: U of Nebraska P, 1967.

Greenblatt, Stephen. *Marvelous Possessions: The Wonder of the New World*. Chicago: U of Chicago P, 1991.

Hadfield, Andrew. *Literature, Travel, and Colonial Writing in the English Renaissance, 1545–1625*. New York: Oxford UP, 1998.

Hulme, Peter. *Colonial Encounters: Europe and the Native Caribbean, 1492–1797*. London: Methuen, 1986.

_____. "Robinson Crusoe and Friday." *Post-Colonial Theory and English Literature: A Reader*. Ed. Peter Childs. Edinburgh: Edinburgh UP, 1999.

Hunter, J. Paul. *Before Novels: The Cultural Contexts of Eighteenth-Century English Fiction*. New York: Norton, 1990.

Kaul, Suvir. *Eighteenth-Century British Literature and Postcolonial Studies*. Edinburgh: Edinburgh UP, 2009.

Marana, Giovanni Paolo. *Letters Writ by a Turkish Spy*. [Trans. William Bradshaw.] London: Henry Rhodes, 1691–94.

Markley, Robert. "'So Inexhaustible a Treasure of Gold': Defoe, Capitalism, and the Romance of the South Seas." *Eighteenth Century Life* 18.3 (1994): 148–67.

Marzec, Robert P. *An Ecological and Postcolonial Study of Literature: From Daniel Defoe to Salman Rushdie*. New York: Palgrave, 2007.

Matar, Nabil. *Turks, Moors, and Englishmen in the Age of Discovery*. New York: Columbia UP, 1999.

Mayer, Robert. *History and the Early English Novel: Matters of Fact from Bacon to Defoe*. Cambridge: Cambridge UP, 1997.

McKeon, Michael. *The Origins of the English Novel: 1600–1740*. Baltimore: Johns Hopkins UP, 1987.

Mignolo, Walter D. "The Geopolitics of Knowledge and the Colonial Difference." *SAQ* 101.1 (2002): 56–96.

Novak, Maximilian E. *Economics and the Fiction of Daniel Defoe*. Berkeley: U of California P, 1962.

Pratt, Mary Louise. *Imperial Eyes: Travel Writing and Transculturation*. London: Routledge, 1992.

Rummell, Kathryn A. "Defoe and the Black Legend: The Spanish Stereotype in *A New Voyage Round the World*." *Rocky Mountain Review* 52.2 (1998): 13–28.

Smith, Nigel. *Literature and Revolution in England, 1640–1660*. New Haven: Yale UP, 1994.

Todd, Dennis. *Defoe's America*. Cambridge: Cambridge UP, 2010.

Weinbrot, Howard D. *Britannia's Issue: The Rise of British Literature from Dryden to Ossian*. Cambridge: Cambridge UP, 1993.

Walcott, Derek. "The Figure of Crusoe." *Critical Perspectives on Derek Walcott*. Ed. Robert D. Hamner. Washington: Three Continents, 1993. 33–40.

Watt, Ian P. *The Rise of the Novel: Studies in Defoe, Richardson, and Fielding*. Berkeley: U of California P, 1957.

Weaver-Hightower, Rebecca. *Empire Islands: Castaways, Cannibals, and Fantasies of Conquest*. Minneapolis: U of Minnesota P, 2007.

American or Postcolonial Studies?: *The Last of the Mohicans* on the Frontiers of Nation, Colony, and Empire

Craig White

Any analysis of the classic American novel *The Last of the Mohicans* in terms of the international discourse of postcolonial studies must acknowledge that James Fenimore Cooper's most famous installment in *The Leatherstocking Tales* usually finds its interpretive home in American literature and American studies. As their names indicate, these "Americanist" disciplines concentrate less on international than on national identities. *The Leatherstocking Tales*—*Last of the Mohicans* (1826) was the second in Cooper's series of five novels—are traditionally acclaimed as founding texts of US literature and culture. Specifically, the characters whose presence unifies the Tales—the frontiersman Leatherstocking (called Hawkeye in *The Last of the Mohicans*), and Chingachgook, a Mohegan chief uprooted from his homelands— are prototypes for many heroes in later American literature and popular culture, from cowboys and noble savages in westerns, to space rangers and sublime aliens in the faraway worlds of science fiction.

Postcolonial studies, originating in the British Commonwealth and former colonies of the French empire, differs from national studies like American, English, or French literature, which traditionally elevate a single cultural theme or character above others. In place of this hierarchical, self-affirming method, postcolonial studies develops dialogues between peoples or texts—even within a single individual. Students who have invested time and effort in American literary or historical studies that highlight themes and identities unique to the dominant culture of the United States may wonder if postcolonial studies represents more of a challenge than an opportunity. From before Columbus to the International Space Station, however, American and Western cultures—despite definite exclusionary qualities—have always crossed borders, coming to terms with others and changing to meet the future.

Through dialogue and storytelling, literature offers a record of such narratives and the challenges that face representative characters. Literary studies build knowledge and exercise critical thinking on problematic issues. If American studies once cultivated an idealized self-image to the exclusion of others, postcolonial studies listens to others' voices to learn how the self-image of one's culture mirrors or alters another. The United States is an extraordinarily inclusive nation, but pressure to learn techniques for managing change only grows. People increasingly live in a world without boundaries where the future of each is connected to all—much like our past, whether we knew it or not. Human nature yearns for master narratives and stand-alone characters, but postcolonial studies finds ways to keep the world's many voices talking and learning together instead of taking turns dominating and resisting.

James Fenimore Cooper, with his privileged youth, his career as the United States' first successful professional novelist, and his reputation as a "founding father" of American literature, may appear as just the sort of towering presence that might repress the voices of others, but two factors—one literary, one historical—make *The Last of the Mohicans* a favorable ground for postcolonial studies. The literary factor is Cooper's development of the prevalent genre of colonial and postcolonial literature: the novel, whose combination of narrative and dialogue and whose literary primacy since the Renaissance make it an essentially modern genre for representing and mediating the "open-ended" or "developing reality" readers find in a changing world like that of postcolonial studies (Bakhtin 39). *The Leatherstocking Tales'* historical backgrounds also sync with postcolonial studies, spanning the late 1700s when the American colonies were a battleground of empires, to the early 1800s, when the new republic of the United States began acting like an empire all its own.

Colonies, empires, and their human agents meet, assert themselves, and more or less turn into each other—such is the subject matter of postcolonial studies, though the field has traditionally concentrated on settings beyond North America and periods since the founding of the United States. Recent American studies and American literature work in terms compatible with postcolonial studies, but founding traditions in Americanist fields and nationalist elements in American culture might object to identifying the United States with "empire," or reading *The Leatherstocking Tales* as more than a nostalgic evocation of the nation's destiny to rule the continent. As familiar starting points, such interpretive traditions continue in many classrooms, while postcolonial studies' recent emergence makes the field new territory even for instructors.

Mediation of these two fields might begin by introducing postcolonial studies' types and terms through an extended dialogue between *The Last of the Mohicans* and a well-known classic in postcolonial studies, Joseph Conrad's *Heart of Darkness* (1899). This novella, familiar to many, describes a journey from Europe into an African colony in the late 1800s. Its depiction of a first-world empire's intrusion in the developing world exemplifies colonial and postcolonial characters and generates textual and intertextual dialogues that reappear in the American scenario of *The Last of the Mohicans*.

Texts associated with the British Empire offer models of postcolonial studies to American readers otherwise unfamiliar with colonial issues. American students could easily locate *Robinson Crusoe* or Shakespeare's *The Tempest* in the history of European imperialism or observe that family fortunes in *Pride and Prejudice* or *Jane Eyre* often derive from colonial enterprises. For postcolonial studies, *Heart of Darkness* has been a defining text. Though Conrad is celebrated as an author of exquisite English prose, English was his third language. Born in Poland in 1857, Conrad left his native country for the life of a sailor partly because of the Russian Empire's repression of his family and nation. Conrad based *Heart of Darkness* on his journey in 1890 to the Congo region of West Africa, then colonized by Belgium. Like Cooper's *The Last of the Mohicans*, Conrad's masterpiece takes place on a frontier where forces of European empires are advancing. For much of the twentieth century, however, *Heart of Darkness* was studied less for its colonial subject matter than as a psychological "journey into self"—much as *The Last of the Mohicans* with its very title speaks to an innate human sense that the age of heroes has passed (Guerard 326).

Later in the twentieth century, though, literary and political changes invested Conrad's novella with new meanings. First, after decades of intense formal analysis of individual texts, literary scholars began reading texts in dialogue with each other—a practice known as intertextuality, which would read *Heart of Darkness* or *The Last of the Mohicans* less as autonomous masterpieces and more as social texts. Historically, mid-twentieth-century events inspired a cultural revaluation of colonial texts like *Heart of Darkness*, particularly the African independence from colonial rule (among them the Congo) and the emergence of distinguished African fiction by authors like Chinua Achebe of Nigeria. Achebe's 1977 article, "An Image of Africa: Racism in Conrad's *Heart of Darkness*," reshaped colonial-postcolonial dialogue by challenging Conrad's "dehumanization of Africa and Africans" (344). For other critics, Conrad depicted colonialism as an equally dehumanizing experience for the colonizers whose "corruption comes not from Africans but from Europe" (Hawkins 371). Postcolonial studies' continuing debate "whether to regard *Heart of Darkness* as a daring attack on imperialism or a reactionary purveyor of colonial stereotypes" continues to shape classroom reading (Armstrong, "Reading" 430). "Achebe's own novel *Things Fall Apart* is also now frequently anthologized next to *Heart of Darkness*," and intertextual comparisons of Conrad's and Achebe's novels are "a standard assignment"—even though Achebe wrote *Things Fall Apart* in response to another colonial African novel, *Mister Johnson* (1939) by Irish novelist Joyce Cary, and the setting of Achebe's novel in the Ibo region of Nigeria is "more than a thousand miles from the upper Congo depicted by Conrad" (Hawkins 366–67). In 1979, the American film *Apocalypse Now* extended *Heart of Darkness*'s postcolonial dialogue by relocating its narrative from Belgian exploitation of the Congo in the 1890s to the US war in Vietnam in the 1960s.

The Last of the Mohicans operates in a comparable network of history and writing. Relating events contemporary with its publication in 1826, John P. McWilliams Jr. relates Cooper's depictions of Indians threatened with extinction in the American colonies to political controversies in the early United States of the 1820s and 1830s that led to The Trail of Tears, when Cherokee Indians were forcibly relocated from the Appalachian region to Oklahoma. The Cherokees, who had adopted literacy and instituted a bilingual press, opposed their removal by sending Congress petitions known as the Cherokee Memorials, while American Indian writers like William Apess (1798–1839) protested the legal and ideological basis of westward expansion.

Against this contention between American and Indian claims to North American land, *The Last of the Mohicans*, subtitled *A Narrative of 1757*, takes place in another phase of imperial expansion and conflict from two generations earlier—about as far back from the 1820s and 1830s as World War II is from the 2010s. The French and Indian War (1754–63), which involved the British Empire, its American colonies, and their Indian allies versus the French Empire, its Canadian colonies, and their Indian allies, was the North American theater of a global conflict called the Seven Years' War, which involved European empires (England, France, Spain, the Netherlands) and their colonies in the Americas, the Caribbean, Africa, Asia, and the Pacific. The Treaty of Paris that ended the French and Indian War led immediately to the American Indian resistance known as Pontiac's Rebellion, and the treaty's bar on English colonists crossing the Appalachian Mountains to settle Indian lands contributed to the American Revolution in the next decade.

Such historical and textual dialogues do not undermine the prestige of literary classics but reinforce their significance. Were it not for fiction like *Heart of Darkness*, *The Last of the Mohicans*, and other novels dramatizing Western civilization's interactions with the non-Western world, many conscientious and informed people might never know of historical entities like "the Belgian Congo," "the French and

Indian War," or their influence on current events like American Indian rights or civil wars in the Congo region. What has changed is that a classic text of national literature is not elevated to a triumphant and autonomous status in isolation from the voices of others whose land or labor supports that status. Instead, postcolonial studies uses well-known classics to initiate dialogues with writing or speech that might otherwise be neglected. Each of us may read one text at a time, but no text speaks separately from the global history in which it is written or read. These dialogues create a world map marked by crossroads where peoples of the developed and developing worlds have met and made what they can of each other. Knowledge gained from these encounters gives a fresh, if challenging, sense of how the world we share works and may work better.

Yet students venturing from American to postcolonial studies need not memorize every nation or empire in history nor learn each available constellation of classic texts. The dynamics of postcolonial dialogue may be found in a single appropriate text, and fiction's power of representation makes literary and cultural history more accessible. *Heart of Darkness* and *The Last of the Mohicans* in and of themselves embody the contending voices and mixed identities that follow first-world imperialism's penetration into local cultures like the nineteenth-century Congo or eighteenth-century America. The imperial mission described in *Heart of Darkness*—to extract elephant ivory from the African interior—is more explicitly economical than *Mohicans*'s military adventure, but in both Africa and America the action is determined by faraway powers in Europe whose representatives in the colonized continents define the theater of operations in each.

Heart of Darkness's protagonist–narrator Marlow—whose wandering, practical, gabby ways make him, like the Leatherstocking, at once a skeptical observer and an enabler of imperialism—begins his journey in Belgium at the headquarters of "the Company" managing the Congo's exploitation. An 1885 European conference in Berlin granted the Congo region to Belgian King Leopold II as his personal possession. That imperial figure remains remote from the novel's perspective, as do the emperors of England and France in *The Last of the Mohicans*. Marlow does, however, meet the director or chief executive officer of "the Company," the "great man himself" with "his grip on the handle-end of ever so many millions" (10). Another imperialist figure waits at the end of Marlow's journey, down the Atlantic coast of Africa and up the Congo River. Much as European trade and militarization destabilized Indian communities, Kurtz—"All Europe contributed to [his] making" (49)—has disrupted local African politics and economics by using violence to extort ever larger amounts of ivory for Europe's markets. (Ivory, like today's plastics made from foreign oil, provided raw material for numerous consumer products.) *The Last of the Mohicans* comparably opens with the historical British General Daniel Webb looking on as the fictional figures Cora and Alice Munro start a journey to meet their father Colonel Munro, himself an actual figure in the English army at Fort William Henry, a site in the French and Indian War that is under siege by forces of the French Empire and Indian allies led by the illustrious General Montcalm (19).

In contrast to these figures of first-world military and economic power, both novels also represent the peoples whose lands, resources, and social structures are disrupted by imperialist power. The title characters of *The Last of the Mohicans*—Chingachgook and his son Uncas—are descendents of the Mohegans, whom Cooper describes as "the possessors of the country first occupied by the Europeans in this portion of the continent" and "consequently, the first dispossessed" (6). (The fictional Uncas is theoretically descended from a historical Uncas who in the 1620s allied his breakaway tribe of Mohegans with the Pilgrims in Massachusetts.) Chingachgook and Uncas partner with Hawkeye and the English. Cooper shows less affinity for the Iroquois, who are depicted as allies of the French. But the upheaval of American Indian communities appears in the Indian camps, where traditional enemies mix, and in Magua, an Indian military leader in exile from his original northern tribe, the Hurons, following disgrace and punishment at the hands of Colonel Munro.

Marlow too witnesses, in addition to Belgium's imperial masters, the innocent victims of Europe's "fantastic invasion" of Africa (23). "Now and then a boat from the [African] shore gave one a momentary contact with reality," Marlow reports, in the form of native people who "wanted [i.e., needed] no excuse for being there" (13–14). At a "scene of inhabited devastation" where captive labor is "building a railway" alongside the Congo River, Marlow sees "[a] lot of people, mostly black and naked, mov[ing] about like ants" (15). In the two works of fiction, both Africans and American Indians also face incomprehensible changes in the law. Near the railway construction site, Marlow sees "[s]ix black men advanc[ing] in a file. . . . [E]ach had an iron collar on his neck. . . . They were called criminals, and the outraged [European] law . . . had come to them, an insoluble mystery from the sea" (15–16). Comparably in *The Last of the Mohicans*, Magua's back-story provides a motive for revenge against Colonel Munro: "'The pale-faces have driven the red-skins from their hunting grounds, and now, when they fight, a white man leads the way.'" Such changes in leadership are accompanied by new laws and punishments. Munro, Magua reports, "made a law, that if an Indian swallowed the fire-water" (i.e., liquor, unknown before European contact), he would be publicly flogged. "Justice!" Magua exclaims: "The Huron chief was tied up before all the pale-faced warriors, and whipped like a dog." No Indian could be prepared for these new perils and punishments, which leave "marks on the back of the Huron chief, that he must hide . . . under this painted cloth of the whites" (103).

These extremes of characterization—the imperialist as unreflecting tyrant, the colonized as helpless victim—render any prospect of cross-cultural dialogue unlikely beyond a cycle of oppression and revenge. However, other characters in *Heart of Darkness* and *The Last of the Mohicans* provide evidence of shared humanity and exchange. Captaining a steamboat full of European adventurers up the Congo River,

Marlow glimpses communities of African peoples. "They howled and leaped, and spun, and made horrid faces" at the alien intruders, yet despite such "ugly" appearances and behaviors, Marlow reflects, "they were not inhuman": "there was in you just the faintest trace of a response to the terrible frankness of that noise" (36). Even the frostiest imperialists provoke a detectable response from the colonized. The "Company's chief accountant" maintains a comically European look in Africa's tropical climate: "high starched collar, white cuffs, a light alpaca jacket, snowy trousers, a clean necktie, and varnished boots" (18). Yet this imperial "vision" triggers an embryonic note of protest. "'I've been teaching one of the native women about the station,'" the accountant explains. "'It was difficult. She had a distaste for the work.'"

The potential for resistance by the colonized grows in *Heart of Darkness* as other Africans learn the colonizer's language or technology and enter a dialogue with the first world's power structures. The station manager's "'boy'—an overfed young negro from the coast— [was permitted] to treat the white men . . . with provoking insolence" (22). With a climactic utterance near the novella's end, this youngster uses his new language to belittle the colonizers: "Suddenly the manager's boy put his insolent black head in the doorway, and said in a tone of scathing contempt: 'Mistah Kurtz—he dead'" (69). Postcolonial studies labels such a character a "subaltern"—a representative, in theorist Homi Bhabha's characterization, of "oppressed, minority groups whose presence was crucial to the self-definition of the majority group: subaltern social groups were also in a position to subvert the authority of those who had hegemonic power" ("Unpacking" 210). That is, colonizers require the colonized to learn their language and technologies, but those powers make the colonized dangerous as when Robinson Crusoe demonstrated to Friday the power of his gun but not how it worked. Another subaltern in *Heart of Darkness* is the "fireman" in Marlow's steamboat who learns an essential Western technology by tending the fire whose steam drives the boat upriver. *Mohicans* glimpses this relation when Hawkeye instructs Uncas in proper use of the rifle, which the Iroquois also use (70). The Mohicans and Magua can switch from Indian tongues to French or English; among the whites, only Hawkeye shares this ability.

For his part, Kurtz—comparable to Hawkeye as a white living among Indians—crosses the spectrum of colonial identities by going native. Kurtz replicates the career of Magua who, deposed from his Huron chieftaincy by colonial justice, relocates his leadership to the similarly unsettled Iroquois and finds himself desiring Cora, the daughter of his English oppressor. Kurtz, far from the power structures in which he originally rose, becomes—like Colonel Munro leading Magua's Huron tribe—a leader of displaced Africans in militias that "[ruin] the district" (57). Forgetting his fiancée in Europe and giving up the empire's prescriptive values such as purity of nation or race, Kurtz develops a relationship with a local woman, whose "wild and gorgeous apparition" Marlow associates with "the colossal body of the fecund and mysterious life" of Africa itself (60). Kurtz's transformation also resembles that of *The Last of the Mohicans*'s David Gamut, a character much like Ichabod Crane from Washington Irving's *Legend of Sleepy Hollow* (1819). Exposed to the wilderness, this instructor of Christian music increasingly takes on a Native American identity. At the Massacre of Fort William Henry, Gamut sings psalms as protection from marauding Iroquois who admire "the firmness with which the white warrior sung his death song," thus equating his performance with that of an Indian captive singing during Iroquois torture rituals as a demonstration of courage (177). Later in the novel, Gamut adopts an Indian appearance by shaving his head and painting his face (219).

Instead of completely switching out one style for another, however, characters like the "manager's 'boy'" and Marlow's fireman in *Heart of Darkness* and Cora, Uncas, Hawkeye, and others in *The Last of the Mohicans* more typically combine codes and values associated with both colonizer and colonized. Postcolonial studies calls such individually centered dialogues hybrids or examples of hybridity. Hybrid automobiles combining petroleum power with electrical battery storage make this metaphor familiar, but the hybrid concept derives from biology and genetics, where different plant or animal species are bred to produce new organisms with features from distinct sources.

Postcolonial studies applies the hybrid metaphor to persons, cultures, and languages that embody "new trans-cultural forms within the contact zone produced by colonization" (Ashcroft 118). Bhabha describes hybrid as "a dialectical power struggle between self and Other" that spawns "a mutation" in the "ambivalent space" of imperial-colonial interaction ("Signs" 34–5). As one American instance, the Cherokee Indian newspaper *The Cherokee Phoenix* (still in publication) cultivates a hybrid identity with bilingual texts in distinct alphabets, while the Cherokee Memorials—written in English around the same time as Mohicans and sent to Washington to petition against Cherokee relocation—used political tropes from the US Declaration of Independence and the Constitution along with native spoken traditions like repetition and rhetorical questions. Such hybrid signs or systems in or between characters often drive fictional narratives, with several hybrid characters propelling *The Last of the Mohicans* to "mutations" that threaten exclusive cultural norms.

For American popular culture, the titanic characters in *The Last of the Mohicans* stand as prototypes of the cowboy or western genre: solitary white men with guns, noble savages at home in nature, and damsels spunky or distressed. The hybridity of these characters' depictions and development raises Cooper's fiction to classic status. The novel opens with the Munro sisters, Gamut, and Duncan Heyward, an American major in the British army, on a wilderness journey across the Empire's boundaries to the "contact zone produced by colonization." A subsequent chapter shifts to a nearby scene where "two men"—Hawkeye and Chingachgook—are in "a dialogue" over their separate origins (28). Though they are discussing their differences, both men share signs of colonizer and colonized. Hawkeye, "descen[ded] from a European parentage," wears a costume of "nearly savage equipments," while

Chingachgook's "red skin and wild accoutrements" include a "tomahawk and scalping knife of English manufacture" and "a short military rifle . . . with which . . . the whites armed their savage allies" (29).

The process of postcolonial hybridity, advanced by these middle-aged warriors, accelerates in younger characters whose off-and-on courtships determine the novel's plot. Hawkeye, Chingachgook, and Uncas rescue the Munro sisters and their escorts from an ambush staged by Magua. The mixed group flees to a secret cavern, where their interactions grow more intimate. Hawkeye's and Chingachgook's earlier dialogue intimated the risk of such interactions. Hawkeye refers to himself as "genuine white" with "no cross in his blood, although he may have lived with the red skins long enough to be suspected," and he extends this intended compliment to his Mohican friends: "let us remember we are men without a cross" (31, 35, 76). Chingachgook in turn refers to himself as "an unmixed man" and calls his son Uncas "the last of the Mohicans" because there are none "of [his] race" with whom to marry and have children (33).

Postcolonial studies questions any notions of ethnic and cultural purity. What nations posit as pure origins (as of a single racial founder) are often only the earliest ethnic memory that serves national purposes. *The Last of the Mohicans*'s reference to the American "father of our country," George Washington, as "a Virginia boy" leading troops for the British Empire suggests that the borders and identities that divide empires, colonies, and nations are always contested (13). Such issues' sensitivity is only heightened by the threat of distinct populations fast-forwarding in a single generation to become genetic hybrids.

Cooper's attitudes toward race are complicated even for his time. Jane Tompkins finds in Mohicans "an obsessive preoccupation with systems of classification—the insignia by which race is distinguished from race, nation from nation, tribe from tribe . . . " (105). Hawkeye's and Chingachgook's concern with "unmixed" status forms a cultural puzzle—different races may work together but not have children together. As same-sex associates of different races—in the mold of

Crusoe and Friday, Huck and Jim, or contemporary "buddy movies"—the men's partnership does not threaten the racial status quo. However, members of the next generation experiment with a hybridity that, instead of remaining metaphorical or cultural, has the potential to get physical. Hiding in the secret cave with the Munro sisters, Uncas initially emerges as a cultural hybrid by giving up Indian customs, "which forbid their warriors to descend to any menial employment, especially in favour of their women," and serving a meal to Cora and Alice—"an utter innovation on the Indian customs" (56). Later, after helping Chingachgook and Hawkeye rescue the sisters a second time, Uncas "den[ies] his habits" by leaving his father busy scalping the Iroquois dead in order "to [assist] the females" (114–15). Uncas thus crosses from indigenous "habits" to those brought by empire—but such hybridity is so far only cultural. Given the novel's many references to "knight[s] of ancient chivalry," Uncas may mimic Hawkeye's courtesy to ladies—after all, the Munro sisters are daughters of an officer and a gentleman, while Uncas is a prince of the Mohican royal family (129).

Uncas's class and behavior make him bold to cross the boundaries of sexual and racial segregation. "Had there been one there sufficiently disengaged to become a close observer," the author writes, "he might have fancied that the services of the young chief were not entirely impartial." Uncas's "dark eye lingered on [Cora's] rich, speaking countenance," and his "mild and musical" voice "causes both ladies to look up in admiration" (56). Later, outside the cave when an attack by the Iroquois makes captivity imminent, Cora urges Uncas to flee rather than die. When he lingers at her side, Cora, "perhaps with an intuitive consciousness of her power," instructs him to "go to my father . . . and be the most confidential of my messengers" (79)—whereupon Uncas politely departs. Whatever Cooper's attitudes, his text here glimpses a potential union between a Native American chieftain and a lady of the British Empire in America. Cora and Uncas hereby enter the annals of such forbidden loves as Romeo and Juliet, but with greater implications for racial or national identity. Any development of Uncas's role as "messenger" to Colonel Munro is precluded by plot developments, not the least of which is Cora's repeated capture by Magua, who explicitly solicits "the daughter of the English chief [to] live in [my] wigwam for ever" (104).

What attracts the noble and ignoble savages in *The Last of the Mohicans* toward Cora—but not, say, Alice? Cora is "surpassingly beautiful" (19), and either suitor might note her adaptability to frontier conditions and her leadership in crises while her younger sister faints. Only when the novel's opening adventures slacken—after another fight with Magua's forces and the deliverance of Colonel Munro's daughters to Fort William Henry—does Cooper reveal that any courtship between Cora and Uncas would be more than a union between a dispossessed Indian prince and a lady of the British Empire. A meeting by another young marriage prospect with Colonel Munro concerning his daughters forces the revelation of Cora's remarkable identity, which even then is disclosed only obliquely. Major Heyward calls on Colonel Munro to ask for Alice's hand in marriage, but Munro mistakenly assumes that Heyward wishes to marry his elder daughter Cora, who is evidently in her early twenties while Alice is still a teen.

The personal and cultural secret revealed at that meeting implies a deeper, more conflicted history of empire whose significance to the novel, its characters, and its nation can be appreciated only by tracing how Cooper has both insinuated and concealed that secret. From its opening chapter, *The Last of the Mohicans* has differentiated the Munro sisters through a color code familiar since Shakespeare: Alice, with "her dazzling complexion, fair golden hair, and bright blue eyes," is the fair lady associated with hope and sunshine, while Cora, marked physically by a "dark eye," "tresses . . . shining and black" and a "complexion . . . charged with the color of the rich blood" fits the profile of a dark lady who knows the complications of age and the mysteries of night (18–19). Such familiar characterizations—a white or black hat for upstanding or low-down cowboys, for instance—provide audiences with a visual code for virtue and vice or innocence and experience.

This color code may appear altogether natural—doesn't the clear light of day illuminate reason and the sunny side of life? Doesn't darkness or night dim the light of reason and confuse order? The title of our postcolonial model, *Heart of Darkness*, suggests cultural factors in the color code that relate *The Last of the Mohicans* not only to colonialism but to Africa itself. In the 1870s and 1880s, the Welsh-American explorer Henry Morton Stanley led two expeditions to the Congo region that intended to end the slave trade but in fact inflicting immeasurable violence on its peoples. The second journey was financed by King Leopold II of Belgium, who used routes pioneered by Stanley to begin the despoliation described in *Heart of Darkness*. Stanley's best-selling accounts of these famous adventures, *Through the Dark Continent* (1878) and *In Darkest Africa* (1890), publicized "the Dark Continent" as an epithet for Africa. Marlow alludes to this status when he recalls Africa "becom[ing] a place of darkness" on maps indicating unexplored territories (8), but he also uses darkness as a figure for immorality, as when he styles Kurtz's specious rhetoric as "the deceitful flow from the heart of an impenetrable darkness" or refers to "the barren darkness of [Kurtz's] heart" (47, 68). The text's references to Europeans and Africans align such figures of speech with racial identities corresponding to light and darkness. In contrast to the "fair hair," "pale visage," and "pure brow" that mark Kurtz's "intended" in Europe, Marlow's overloaded descriptions of Africans reveal what Achebe calls a "fixation on blackness": "A black figure stood up, strode on long black legs, waving long black arms . . . " (345). To reduce white and black imagery to a secret code for racism is unproductive, but disregarding such factors in the color code's signification can blind readers to evidence that hybridity complicates imperialism's insistence on racial purity.

Expanding the color code to include distinct races or ethnicities is justified in *The Last of the Mohicans* by a postcolonial and personal narrative that complicates Major Heyward's and Colonel Munro's discussion about which daughter to marry. Fair Alice and dark Cora, it turns out, are half-sisters, whose distinct appearances result from their father's colonial and postcolonial wanderings. Colonel Munro's story begins in Scotland, part of Great Britain since Shakespeare's time but "curse[d] . . . by [its] unnatural union with a foreign and trading people"—i.e., the English. Like other colonized people before and since, Munro joins the imperial military and is assigned to another part of the Empire:

> [D]uty called me to the islands of the West Indies [i.e., the Caribbean]. There it was my lot to form a connection with one who in time became my wife, and the mother of Cora. She was the daughter of a gentleman of those isles, by a lady whose misfortune it was, if you will . . . to be descended, remotely, from that unfortunate class [i.e., Africans] who are so basely enslaved to administer to the wants of a luxurious people. (159)

Colonel Munro speaks with indirection worthy of Conrad, but the "luxurious people" to whom he refers are the colonizers of the Indies, and Cora, instead of being "unmixed," is "descended" from African as well as European ancestry—from the "enslaved" as well as the "luxurious." Alice is the daughter of Munro's second wife, herself a fair lady from Scotland, fulfilling the standard of ethnic purity to which Major Heyward subscribes.

The violation of empire's racial and sexual boundaries by Cora's ancestors has mixed results. Cora's mother may be part-African but she is "the daughter of a gentleman," possibly on one of the Caribbean islands where a majority-black population made such unions more commonplace—the Black Atlantic, in postcolonial theorist Paul Gilroy's phrase. For American literary and cultural studies, Cora fits the racial profile of a "tragic mulatto"—a mixed-race person tragically caught between two worlds while belonging to neither, and so disabled from finding a proper partner. Uncas and Magua as Indian men whose normal partners may be extinct or in exile face this problem from another cultural perspective. These powerful cultural narratives drive these characters to each other and, under the fictional rules of empire, to their deaths.

In contrast, Heyward and Alice survive and retreat from the frontier to "the settlements of the pale faces" (348). As D. H. Lawrence wrote in *Studies in Classic American Literature* (1923), Cora loves Uncas, Uncas loves Cora. But Magua also desires Cora. . . . So Fenimore kills them all off, Cora, Uncas, and Magua, and leaves [Alice] to carry on the race. She will breed plenty of white children to Major Heyward (58).

Any hypothetical offspring of Cora and Uncas (or Magua) would inherit early America's three major racial bloodlines: Indian, European, African. Cooper as a founding father of American fiction cannot write that future, but real life succeeds where fiction faltered. William Apess, the American Indian author who wrote against Indian removal while Cooper was writing *The Last of the Mohicans*, was the child of a European-Native American father and a mother who may have been a "Negro" (O'Connell xxvii, n17). Prior to The Trail of Tears, the Cherokees had "at least two hundred interracial (red and white) married couples" and owned more than a thousand black slaves (McWilliams 104). Uncas may have been "the last of the Mohicans" in one sense, but in Uncasville, Connecticut, the diverse Native American employees of the giant Mohegan Sun casino, home to the WNBA's Connecticut Sun, have found their own mixed ways to survive in the American empire.

"'Ha!'" Colonel Munro chides as though addressing a resistant reader from the US dominant culture, "'Major Heyward, you are yourself born at the south, where these unfortunate beings are considered of a race inferior to your own'" (159). As an affluent young man from South Carolina—for later American history, the state that starts the Civil War in defense of slavery—Heyward certainly knows African American women, but not as marriage prospects. "'And you cast it on my child as a reproach!'" Munro thunders. "'You scorn to mingle the blood of the Heywards with one so degraded—lovely and virtuous though she be?'"

"Heaven protect me from a prejudice so unworthy of my reason!" returned Duncan, at the same time conscious of such a feeling and that as deeply rooted as if it had been ingrafted in his nature. (159)

"[U]nworthy of [his] reason" yet true to his culture, Heyward find his purity "engrafted" in his American "nature" as surely as other American characters graft a hybrid identity rooted in three continents. Haltingly, incompletely, yet briefly glimpsing a "lovely and virtuous" possibility, *The Last of the Mohicans* draws the empires of Europe and the colonies of America into dialogue with the same continent whose exploitation Conrad witnessed in *Heart of Darkness*. Gilroy postulates the Black Atlantic as a frontier whose "history . . . yields a course of lessons as to the instability and mutability of identities which are always unfinished, always being remade" (xi). Colonizer and colonized from old and new worlds meet to rule or turn into each other. As a text of shifting frontiers and mixed identities, *The Last of the Mohicans* speaks in dialogue as a classic American text of postcolonial literature.

Works Cited

Achebe, Chinua. "An Image of Africa: Racism in Conrad's Heart of Darkness." *Heart of Darkness. Norton Critical Edition.* 4th ed. Ed. Paul B. Armstrong. New York: Norton, 2006. 336–49.

Armstrong, Paul B., ed. *Heart of Darkness. Norton Critical Edition.* 4th ed. New York: Norton, 2006.

_____. "*Heart of Darkness* and the Epistemology of Cultural Differences." *Under Postcolonial Eyes: Joseph Conrad After Empire.* Eds. Gail Fincham and Myrtle Hooper. Rondebosch, So. Afr.: U of Cape Town P, 1996. 21–39.

_____. "Reading, Race, and Representing Others." Armstrong, *Heart of Darkness* 429–44.

Ashcroft, Bill, Gareth Griffiths, and Helen Tiffin. *The Post-Colonial Studies Reader.* London: Routledge, 1995.

_____. *Post-Colonial Studies: The Key Concepts.* London: Routledge, 2003.

Bakhtin, M. M. The Dialogic Imagination: Four Essays. Ed. Michael Holquist. Trans. Caryl Emerson and Holquist. Austin: U of Texas P, 1981.

Bhabha, Homi K. "Signs Taken for Wonders." Ashcroft et al., *Post-Colonial Reader* 29–35.

_____. "Unpacking my Library . . . Again." *The Post-Colonial Question: Common Skies, Divided Horizons.* Eds. Iain Chambers and Lidia Curti. London: Routledge, 1996: 199–211.

Cooper, James Fenimore. *The Last of the Mohicans.* New York: Penguin, 1986.

Dictionary of Human Geography, ed. R. J. Johnston et al. 4th ed. Malden, MA: Blackwell, 2000.

Gilroy, Paul. *The Black Atlantic: Modernity and Double Consciousness*. Cambridge, MA: Harvard UP, 1993.

Guerard, Albert J. "The Journey Within." Armstrong, *Heart of Darkness* 326–36.

Hawkins, Hunt. "Heart of Darkness and Racism." Armstrong, *Heart of Darkness* 365–75.

Lawrence, D. H. "Fenimore Cooper's Leatherstocking Novels." *Studies in Classic American Literature*. 1923. New York: Viking, 1961.

McWilliams, John P., Jr. *Political Justice in a Republic: James Fenimore Cooper's America*. Berkeley: U of California P, 1972.

O'Connell, Barry. Introduction. *On Our Own Ground: The Complete Writings of William Apess, A Pequot*. Ed. Barry O'Connell. Boston: U of Massachusetts P, 1992. xiii–lxxvii.

Tompkins, Jane. "No Apologies for the Iroquois: A New Way to Read the Leatherstocking Novels." *Sensational Designs: The Cultural Work of American Fiction, 1790–1860*. New York: Oxford UP, 1985. 94–121.

A Passage to India, National Identity, and Forster's "Others"_____

Nicole duPlessis

The fictions of E. M. Forster ask questions that rarely, if ever, have definite answers; questions form the central focus of Forster's plots, and the reader no less than the characters is obligated to engage with them. *A Passage to India*, esteemed by many as Forster's greatest novel and seen alternately by late twentieth-century critics as inherently imperialist or subversive of the structures of imperialism, asks poignantly how colonialism and cultural differences influence contact between individuals. The role of national identity in interpersonal connection is a question asked throughout Forster's fiction, notable in *Where Angels Fear to Tread* and *A Room with a View*, which portray English-Italian encounters, and in *Howards End*, which defines the English identity of the Wilcoxes in opposition to the German Schlegals. An early critic, Peter Burra, whom Forster respected as an insightful interpreter of his novels (Forster, "Prefatory Note" 307–08), emphasizes dichotomous personal qualities, deemphasizing national identity as a reinforcing factor (Burra 319) and setting the tone for early critics who see India as a symbol of the individual's alienation in the modern world (Levine 19). However, even Burra recognizes the general applicability of the narrative commentary from *Where Angels Fear to Tread*: that "more than personalities [are] engaged" in Forster's novels, which can seem essentialist because of deceptively simplistic links between personality and national character, "the struggle [is] national" (Forster, *Where Angels* 58; Burra 318). In analyzing *A Passage to India*, which portrays the British colonial presence in India in the early twentieth century through the lens of English, Anglo-Indian, and Indian characters, it is useful to revisit early criticism that emphasizes individual identity, criticism Forster valued as true to his vision, while taking cues from contemporary criticism, which helps readers to identify how imperialism colonizes the individual, constructing his or her identity. In addressing the forces that inspire and prevent interpersonal relationships, *A Passage to India* transfers the impetus of *Howards End*—"Only connect"—to a foreign and imperialist setting, where relationships are more complex even than in the cultural conflicts of Forster's earlier novels.

The "outsider" perspective in the novel is provided by Miss Adela Quested, a young woman from England whose name reveals her "quest" to connect with the "real" India by meeting its people while visiting to decide whether to become engaged to Ronny Heaslop, the City Magistrate for Chandrapore. Accompanying Adela is Mrs. Moore, Ronny's mother, who is on her own spiritual quest. Though privileged by the hierarchy of Empire, which places the colonizer above the colonized, the English women's quest to discover India is trivial, proceeding from the leisurely curiosity of the "Ruling Race," and so occupies an inferior position in the hierarchy of human relationships within the novel. Rather, the novel privileges the masculine friendship between Dr. Aziz, a Muslim doctor, and Cyril Fielding, principal of the Government College, a friendship desired by both, but ultimately prevented by the circumstances of Empire. By centering on the attempts of Miss Quested, Mrs. Moore, Aziz, and Fielding to "connect," the novel asks what particular situations specific to the Indian colonial experience prevent connections between people or else facilitate near connection. Describing the role of "muddle" in *A Passage to India*, Stone remarks that "'[m]uddle' throughout the book is often a comic word, but it also describes a condition of separateness, of doubleness, that hints at everything that divides people and rives them into separate religions, races and political parties" (24). In this analysis, Stone identifies as the cause or consequence of muddle some of the major factors that prevent connection in the novel. In spite of these divisions based on imperialism, actual differences, and cultural stereotypes, there are mitigating influences such as athleticism, which provides a temporary connection between men, and more reliably, education, which stands to equalize and facilitate connection. Apart from the human social influences on relationships, natural and artificial spaces have their own power to divide or to bring individuals as close as possible before the possibility of connection is lost.

When Miss Quested asserts her desire to see "the *real* India," she is referring to something more genuine and less picturesque than the caricatures of Indians, "picturesque figures" that "pass before [one] as a frieze" (26). In addition to her quest to conceptualize India simply to know and experience something new, Adela evaluates India as the site of her potential marriage, which would exist against the backdrop of imperial bureaucracy. As she imagines the consummation of her colonialist relationship, she perceives the shortcomings of the colonial bureaucratic lifestyle:

> "Yes, Ronny is always hard-worked," she replied, contemplating the hills. How lovely they suddenly were! But she couldn't touch them. In front, like a shutter, fell a vision of her married life. She and Ronny would look into the club like this every evening, then drive home to dress; they would see the Lesleys and the Callendars and the Turtons and the Burtons, and invite them and be invited by them, while the true India slid by unnoticed. Colour would remain—the pageant of birds in the early morning, brown bodies, white turbans, idols whose flesh was scarlet or blue—and movement would remain as long as there were crowds in the bazaar and bathers in the tanks. Perched up on the seat of a dog-cart, she would see them. But the force that lies behind colour and movement would escape her even more effectually than it did now. She would see India always as a frieze, never as a spirit, and she assumed that it was a spirit of which Mrs. Moore had had a glimpse. (48)

In her imaginings, the "true India" is definable, but the definition is composed of abstracts: "colour" and "movement" animated by an unnamed "force" or "spirit." In spite of her idea that to see the "true India" is to know real Indians, she objectifies India bypassing people for "birds," "bodies," "turbans," and "idols." Adela understands instinctively that connection with India, arguably her priority during the visit, becomes impossible upon entering into a conjugal union with Empire or its representative, Ronny.

The relationship between Miss Quested and India is different from the connections achieved by tourists in *Where Angels Fear to Tread* and *A Room with a View*, who, in spite of muddle, become closer to the essence of the foreign country (Italy). Miss Quested's intended relationship with the host country is muddled because India—unlike Italy—has a spirit that evades definition and because under the influence of Empire, individuals—especially married English men and women—define personal identity with more reliance upon national identity. Nationality and personality exist on a continuum in Forster's novels: the extent to which one is classifiable as quintessentially "English" exists in inverse proportion to the strength of one's personality and the ability to have one's own opinions, to think critically, and to act unconventionally (as in the case of Fielding who has analogues in the Schlegals of *Howards End* and in the Emersons of *A Room with a View*). In the colonial context of *A Passage to India*, only Fielding, the most educated individual with the possible exception of Professor Godbole, transcends unambiguous labeling as "English," which has less to do with country of origin than with adopted colonialist attitudes that influence even trivial and recreational interactions.

In the aftermath of a play at the club, the performance and reception of the National Anthem reveal the polarizing effect of Empire, especially in India, which becomes—though part of the Empire—the antithesis of Empire. In particular, the Anglo-Indians—the Turtons, Burtons, and Lesleys who have settled in India as colonial bureaucrats—display increased nationalism and an increased need for nationalism as they listen:

Conversation and billiards stopped, faces stiffened. It was the Anthem of the Army of Occupation. It reminded every member of the club that he or she was British and in exile. It produced a little sentiment and a useful accession of willpower. The meagre tune, the curt series of demands on Jehovah, fused into a prayer unknown in England, and though they perceived neither Royalty nor Deity they did perceive something, they were strengthened to resist another day. (24)

The final line provides powerful testament to the colonialist attitudes of the Anglo-Indians who see ruling and simply existing in India as acts of resistance. As Forster's narrators are apt to do, commentary is provided while the effects of the anthem on the hearers in the club are described. The "stiffening" of faces renders the silence that the anthem inspires a stern rather than emotional silence, although the hearers feel "a little sentiment." Labeling the anthem the "Anthem of the Army of Occupation" undermines the legitimacy of their residence in India while also invoking the military strength that bolsters the English claim to rule. By reminding the hearers that they are in "exile," the anthem inspires solidarity but also separation from the native Indians, evoking the opposite of home. That the "demands on Jehovah" are "curt" speaks to the character of the colonialists, who not only feel justified in making demands of God, but do not feel the need to do so with humility. This rare invocation of Christianity becomes conspicuous against the backdrop of the major Indian religions—Islam and Hindu—both of which exhibit more genuine reverence for the deity than English religion.

Apart from the performance of the National Anthem, which presumably inspires nationalistic sentiment in England as well as abroad, colonialism causes the English to band together in ways that would be insignificant in England. Miss Quested observes of Ronny, for example, "how tolerant and conventional his judgments had become; when they had seen *Cousin Kate* in London together in the past, he had scorned it; now he pretended it was a good play, in order to hurt nobody's feelings" (40). This commentary complements a boastful anti-intellectualism in the club, "the Public school attitude" (40). The "cultural capital"—or social currency—that consists of knowing (and owning) the right books and being able to discuss them according to the unstated (but known) criteria of the intellectual, something Forster portrays with subtle criticism in *Howards End* and, less subtly, in "The Celestial Omnibus," is absent—and unnecessary—in colonial India where anthems rather than books are the markers of civilization.

The "public school" mentality surfaces again, albeit in a positive way, in the superficial connection achieved by Aziz and the British subaltern soldier on the polo field—pointing to a temporary respite permitted by "sport": "They reined up again, the fire of good fellowship in their eyes. But it cooled with their bodies, for athletics can only raise a temporary glow. Nationality was returning, but before it could exert its poison they parted, saluting each other. 'If only they were all like that,' each thought" (60). Rather than athleticism, however, education is the force that enables Fielding to resist prevalent imperialist attitudes and easily label as "English" or "Anglo-Indian" while earning the label "not pukka," meaning not "proper" or "socially acceptable" (Forster 23, *OED*). Fielding's "belief in education" fuels his unorthodox views about people—his analogies between India and Italy—and influences his alienation from the English in India (64). While imperialism changes the English who assume positions of colonial authority, as in the case of Ronny Healsop, Fielding is unable to change because of his belief in the equalizing force of education, confirming Anglo-Indian fear of education. Of Fielding, the narrator remarks that

> something in his manner . . . failed to allay the distrust which his profession naturally inspired. There needs must be this evil of brains in India, but woe to him through whom they are increased! The feeling grew that Mr. Fielding was a disruptive force, and rightly, for ideas are fatal to caste, and he used ideas by that most potent method—interchange. (65)

In this moment of narrative critique, the reader learns that the education of native Indians is suspect because of the danger of ideas; in invoking "caste," the narrator compares the separation between the colonizer and colonized to the separations within Indian society that all but disappear in the English regard for native Indians, which implies a homogeneity that does not exist. Simultaneously, by comparing the division between colonizer and colonized with caste, the narrator minimizes the apparent racial and ethnic differences between English and Indian, suggesting, as Burra suggests in his analysis of the novel, that the divisions are between people who are more similar than dissimilar (Burra 319). Like Forster himself, who taught briefly at the Working Men's College, Fielding teaches across social barriers: "He did not mind whom he taught; public schoolboys, mental defectives and policemen, had all come his way, and he had no objection to adding Indians" (64). In *Howards End*, Forster invokes in the autodidacticism of Leonard Bast the idea that education and literacy have the potential to minimize social differences, but he finds that social and often physical obstacles prevent the realization of this ideal. Similarly, Fielding's willingness to connect with Indians indicates the power of education to minimize nationality, even in a colonial situation. Instead, the power of education to "bridge" cultures, which is not accomplished by Turton's "Bridge Parties," raises suspicion because Fielding's educated attitudes preclude the reliance on nationality that imperialism (as seen in the club when the National Anthem plays) demands.

Though education allows Fielding to transcend cultural differences, the novel does not claim that the differences do not exist or that they are insignificant. Aziz, as the primary Indian character, provides the locus of Indian difference (or "Otherness") for the reader. Through Aziz, the reader learns that different conceptions of truth divide the English from the Indians, an "essentialist" labeling by an author of Empire who attributes to the colonized an inherent quality even as the narrative itself critiques stereotype. Fielding, with the insight gained through education, sympathizes with the Indian sensibility:

[Aziz] was wrong about the water, which no Emperor, however skilful, can cause to gravitate uphill; a depression of some depth together with the whole of Chandrapore lay between the mosque and Fielding's house. Ronny would have pulled him up, Turton would have wanted to pull him up, but restrained himself. Fielding did not even want to pull him up; he had dulled his craving for verbal truth and cared chiefly for truth of mood. As for Miss Quested, she accepted everything Aziz said as true verbally. In her ignorance, she regarded him as 'India' and never surmised that his outlook was limited and his method inaccurate. . . . (75–76)

This passage reveals several things, among them, the narrative treatment of Aziz, who is regarded even by the narrator as something of a novelty or curiosity. Fielding, for all of his good will, does seem to regard Aziz as somewhat of an amusement, while Miss Quested regards him as a symbol: the essence of India because he is the only real Indian she can access. Narrative analysis of Aziz's poetic inaccuracy also reveals a typology of truth and different English attitudes toward Indian untruths based on length of time in India, colonial authority, attitude toward the colonized, and education. Ronny, who is relatively "green," would wish to correct Aziz's inaccuracy, while Turton, the Collector or Burra Sahib, who has been in India longer than Ronny and has a more tolerant attitude toward interactions between the English and Indians, would refrain from reprimanding Aziz either from some combination of these factors or perhaps from a sense that to do so would be futile. Fielding, by contrast, recognizes that there is a type of truth—"truth of mood"—in Aziz's story and prefers it to "verbal" or literal truth, which Miss Quested craves and, like Ronny and Turton, assumes is the only possible truth. Reinforcing the idea that Indian truth is different, Professor Godbole becomes the focus of Aziz's self-analysis on the topic. When asked to describe the caves, Professor Godbole replies, "It will be a great pleasure," but remains silent; the narrator, anchored in Aziz's consciousness, comments on the situation:

Aziz realized that he was keeping back something about the caves. He realized because he often suffered from similar inhibitions himself. Sometimes, to the exasperation of Major Callendar, he would pass over the one relevant fact in a position, to dwell on the hundred irrelevant. The Major accused him of disingenuousness, and was roughly right, but only roughly. It was rather that a power he couldn't control capriciously silenced his mind. (80)

While both can be accused of disingenuousness from the English perspective, Professor Godbole seems to be silenced by a spiritual instinct to control expression so as to prevent communication of inadequate truth, and Aziz is prevented from locking onto the relevant detail by an emotional—even poetic—attention to the details of the situation.

As someone who bypasses literal truth himself, Aziz suspects that others are similarly representing truth according to personal whim: "In every remark he found a meaning, but not always the true meaning" (70). This suspicion becomes his downfall in his attempt to connect with Fielding, even from their earliest encounter. When Fielding greets Aziz's mention of Post Impressionism with dismissiveness, Aziz assumes that Fielding, a member of the "Ruling Race," means to disparage him and not Post Impressionism itself (70). Truth of sentiment moves the muddle toward resolution as Aziz realizes Fielding's "fundamental good will" and longs to meet it while understanding the emotional risks involved: "His own [good will] went out to it, and grappled beneath the shifting tides of emotion which can alone bear the voyager to an anchorage but may also carry him across it on to the rocks" (70). Though a sympathetic character, Fielding occupies a superior position, even if he chooses not to claim it as such. In trying to connect with Aziz, Fielding is confident while Aziz remains insecure. Aziz's consistent mistrust illustrates his inability—as a colonial subject—to transcend the colonial situation.

Truth becomes a more tangible practical concern in social interactions between Miss Quested and Mrs. Moore and their Indian hosts.

In particular, the casual treatment of appointments, a symptom of a more instinctive culture—akin to that of Italy in *A Room with a View* and *Where Angels Fear to Tread*—that privileges sentiment over literal truth, registers with the English as a violation of hospitality. The first muddle occurs when "[a]n Indian lady and gentleman were to send their carriage," but fail to do so, leaving Miss Quested and Mrs. Moore disappointed (72). Fielding explains it as a misunderstanding, but Aziz, hearing the name, blames them for being "slack Hindus" who were not sincere in their invitation because they were "ashamed of their house" (72). Though he stereotypes his fellow Indians according to their religious and ethnic identity, Aziz commits a similar blunder by inadvertently inviting the English ladies for a visit and feels the same insecurity about his house (73, 79). Realizing that Miss Quested takes him literally, he is shocked and feels that she is a "stupid girl" for "taking him at his word" (79). Like the Hindu couple, Aziz does not intend a literal invitation but a display of sentiment, and he attempts to remedy the situation by transferring the appointment to the Marabar Caves. Ronny, who wishes to protect Miss Quested from further disappointment, displays rare insight into Indian perception of Truth: "Aziz would make some similar muddle over the caves. He meant nothing by the invitation, I could tell by his voice; it's just their way of being pleasant" (89). Although he remarks dismissively that Aziz "meant nothing by the invitation," which is not true, Ronny nevertheless understands that an invitation is a form of courtesy for the Indians and not a verbal (or literal) truth.

As Fielding indicates by calling it a "muddle" (73), the greatest unknowable force in the novel is India, which is nevertheless not necessarily a mappable geographical place. Even in the green bird that Ronny cannot identify for Miss Quested, India proves ineffable, and the narrator concludes that "nothing in India is identifiable" (91). In India, Forster creates a character that lacks a centralizing unity or a concrete identity. It is impressionistic and mysterious (or muddled) rather than being a theoretically solid entity like the geographically disperse

British Empire. By portraying India in a way that stresses disunity, Forster might be seen as "colonizing" India himself through his fiction—imposing his idea of India onto India, and creating through his descriptions an India that is weak and in need of definition by an external force, whether an author or an Empire. Working against the claim that Forster "recolonizes" India by defining India in terms of the colonial relationship, Parry argues that unlike colonialist English literature—taken broadly as official, personal, and fictional texts—*A Passage to India* creates dialogue between the colonialist representation of India and an alternative (28). Explaining further, Parry identifies this kind of dialogue as a form of Modernist rhetoric and claims that in Forster's depiction of India, "the rhetoric of positivism, moral assurance and aggression is transgressed by the language of deferred hope, imponderables, and quietism" (29). In pointing to an India that cannot be pinned down, Forster—according to Parry's reading—contradicts the aggressive certainty that permits the domination of one civilization by another through imperialism. The ineffability of India—its inability to be easily defined according to anything except its tendency to divide—is less troubling to Parry than it is to the narrative. India remains a problem for the characters in the novel, notably Miss Quested but also for Aziz who struggles to unify India in his mind and define himself in reference to it and against the English and the British Empire. While Parry does not interpret Forster's portrayal as an act of colonization, India nevertheless remains a powerful force in the novel that prevents connection.

Attempts to conceptualize India replace the colonial act of mapping, and in spite of narrative efforts to "ground" it—to make it rocks and soil—India, divisive and ineffable, more closely resembles a character than a place as revealed by the anthropomorphic terms in which it is described initially. Because India cannot be pinned down, when Fielding attributes to the physical land—the *soil*—an absence of peace, the analogy between India and other physical countries breaks down: "Every one was cross or wretched. It was as if irritation exuded from the very soil. Could one have been so petty on a Scotch moor or an Italian alp? Fielding wondered afterwards" (83). Because they rely on similarities between India and other geographic locales, Fielding's analogies register as false. India differs from a "Scotch moor" or an "Italian alp," not because of its soil, but because unified India is an artificial construct defined, at least in part by the British Empire in contrast to England; in Aziz's poetry, it is not one but "a hundred Indias" (12). By contrast, both the "Scotch moor" and the "Italian alp," though perhaps reflecting an Anglocentric perspective, exist apart from an overseas Empire. Significantly, "moor" and "alp" do not relate to "Scotch" and "Italian" in the same way that "soil" relates to "Indian"—the former are features with geographical and symbolic significance and point to a truth about the national character of a geographically situated political unity. "Soil" is generic, but in Fielding's meditation it also contains the essence of India. Because the narrative establishes a false analogy, the reader must ask how the analogy might be corrected. In the narrative, the equivalent value would be the "Indian cave," as the Marabar Caves could exist in relation to India as an alp to Italy or a moor to Scotland. In this false analogy, then, Forster gives the reader a place (India) that is not one, while emphasizing the importance of place and of the places (the Caves in particular) that drive the plot.

As the accidental invitation and disastrous excursion to the Marabar Caves demonstrate, attempted connections between people happen within the constructs and situations of Empire, but also within place. Encounters occur not only within the spaces of Empire, but also in the negative space of the Caves, which are primal and primordial, and the cultured spiritual spaces of the Mosque and the province of Mau, which seem, like the epigraph to *Howards End*, to urge individuals: "Only Connect." These spaces provide a backdrop for the most significant moments in the novel, representing discord or harmony. The civil station and the club in Chandrapore—the spaces of Empire—are too trivial to inspire anything other than superficial social exchanges between Anglo-Indians based on "Othering," emphasizing the difference, or "Otherness," of the native Indians. In the initial description of the civil station, the reader is told that it "provokes no emotion":

> It charms not, neither does it repel. It is sensibly planned, with a red-brick club on its brow, and farther back a grocer's and a cemetery, and the bungalows are disposed along roads that intersect at right angles. It has nothing hideous in it, and only the view is beautiful; it shares nothing with the city except the overarching sky. (5)

The description emphasizes functional buildings and the separation between official Colonial space and "the city"—native Indian space. The narrator further uses the descriptions of the roads to symbolize British domination of India, "the net Great Britain had thrown over India" (13). In such spaces, the only cross-cultural interactions are official encounters.

Significant encounters—both the harmonious and the disruptive—occur within quintessentially Indian spiritual spaces and represent the tripartite structure of the novel: Mosque, Caves, and Temple. The mosque is the site of the first encounter between Mrs. Moore and Aziz, and the tenor of the situation depends on the Englishwoman's attitude to the sacred space. Upon seeing her in the solitary mosque in the moonlight, Aziz becomes "furiously angry," addressing her with hostility: "Madam, this is a mosque, you have no right here at all; you should have taken off your shoes; this is a holy place for Moslems" (18). Realizing that she has removed her shoes from respect and that "she was old," he attempts reconciliation (18). Mrs. Moore's assertion that "God is here" earns Aziz's approval (18), and they are able to connect based on a moment of near-misunderstanding, situated in a place that might have hosted cultural discord. Aziz perceives in Mrs. Moore the empathy necessary for connection, remarking, "You understand me, you know what others feel. Oh, if others resembled you!" (21). In the mosque, Mrs. Moore shows judgment based on impulse and feeling, a quality that Aziz labels "Oriental." This impulsive sentimentality is something Forster attributes to Italians, and though welcome in the mosque, it registers as false in English spaces like Fielding's dwelling. A moment of connection happens between Mrs. Moore and Aziz in the space of the mosque; that secular communion might be all that humans can hope to achieve given critic Benita Parry's observation that "*A Passage to India* is a novel from which God, though addressed in multiple ways, is always absent" (36).

The mosque in the first section and the temple in the third are civilized sacred spaces based in an organized religious practice; given the correct circumstances, the spaces within the mosque and surrounding the temple facilitate connection. However, when humans are precluded from sacred spaces, as in the Caves of Marabar, situations become dangerous. The Caves are constructed as "shrines [that are] are unfrequented, as if pilgrims, who generally seek the extraordinary, had here found too much of it" (136). The narrator speculates that "even Buddha, who must have passed this way . . . , shunned a renunciation more complete than his own" (136). Many critics have examined the significance of the caves, with Wilfred Stone connecting the primordial cave to Jungian and Freudian motifs. On the one hand, the Caves resemble the spaces of the unconscious, which can break into the conscious mind and, in the case of someone "not accustomed to such visitations," cause panic (Stone 21). Miss Quested and Mrs. Moore each suffer a panic-causing assault of some sort within the Caves. However, the cave also represents the Freudian *id*, the instinctive, contrary, hidden part of the personality that exists in the unconscious (Stone 22). Describing their importance to Hindu mythology, Stone explains that

the caves represent the "womb of the universe," from which, by some miracle of androgynous fertilization (*sic*), emanated all the forms of created life: first appeared a feminine principle (moon), then a masculine (sun), then the progeny resulting from the rape of the female by her offspring. There are many varieties of the myth, but basic to them all is the identification of caves with some primordial, prehistoric, nothingness from which life emerged. (20)

The Caves are not only a place that lacks identity, they are a place that defies identity. While India makes the English define themselves more strongly with reference to England and deprives the native Indians of a unified nationality, the Caves, a place for violation and suffocation that nevertheless offers a reflection, reduce all identity, spirituality, and rationality to a single syllable: "Boum" (163).

Emblematic of India and also the self, the caves are the emptiness (and confusion) within, which Parry sees as a cultural confusion, observing that "Adela Quested experiences cultural differences as a violation of her person" (35). Although the caves provide the setting and the opportunity for the alleged assault against Miss Quested, Levine argues that "[t]he caves make no *direct* claim on Adela," who is "too troubled by her personal problems" (88), specifically, her failure to connect. This interpretation implies that the attempted rape did not occur—at least in a physical sense. For Mrs. Moore, the confusion within is spiritual, and so, Levine argues, the Caves claim Mrs. Moore in a metaphysical sense. Levine further argues that the Caves are unable to claim Aziz, who is Indian and male and is rendered invulnerable (according to Levine) by the "closed system" of his religion. He is also defined by human connections (Levine 87–8). However, Aziz is "claimed" by the Caves because of his vulnerability—his reliance on human connections. The anonymity of the Caves and Aziz's trusting proximity to Miss Quested cause his arrest and trial for the assault of an English woman, as well as his own disillusionment. The Marabar Caves harm Mrs. Moore spiritually, so she no longer desires connection; they harm Miss Quested psychologically and perhaps physically, so she is no longer able to make the connection of matrimony. Both women have lost the desire to connect with India. They harm Aziz so that he distrusts the English more than before when his distrust was more a mild suspicion. As they destroy the characters, the Caves also widen the gap between the Anglo-Indians and native Indians, each of whom blames the "Other" for the insult suffered.

Like the progression of the seasons, "the Cold Weather, the Hot Weather, and the Rains," which are also represented by its three sections (Forster, "Notes" 345), the novel is cyclical and returns from division to connection in the final section, "Temple." However, Mau—a blended but primarily Hindu place—is framed by Professor Godbole's Hinduism, notably the song to Krishna that Godbole sings in the first section, in which Krishna fails to come to the milkmaiden (85). The space that offers to Aziz and Fielding the possibility of reconnection and reconciliation is also defined by a mythic failure to connect, even as Professor Godbole imitates God in a union of sorts. From his initial description, Godbole, the quintessential Hindu as Aziz is the quintessential Muslim, represents unity in his blending of Eastern and Western modes of dress; he seamlessly integrates costumes of the colonizer and colonized: "[t]urban, coat, waistcoat, dhoti, socks with clocks." Symbolic of Hinduism, he is the emblem of unity: "his whole appearance suggested harmony—as if he had reconciled the products of East and West, mental as well as physical, and could never be discomposed" (77). Along with Professor Godbole's explanation of the universal complicity and responsibility for all acts, whether good or evil (196), Forster's discussion of religion in his essay "The Gods of India" (1914) helps to explain why Hindu space can facilitate near-connection and also host inevitable division. Forster expresses the practicality but also the detachment and inadequacy of English religion, which, he writes, "is mainly concerned with conduct. It is an ethical code—a code with divine sanction it is true, but applicable to daily life. We are to love our brother, whom we can see. We are to hurt no one, by word or deed. We are to be pitiful, pure-minded, honest in our business, reliable, tolerant, brave." By contrast, "[t]he Hindu is concerned not with conduct, but with vision" (Forster, qtd. in Stone 18–19). Attempted connections and failed connections are matters of conduct, not of vision, but the Hindu vision of the universe contains them all.

Forster's India recalls Yeats: "A terrible beauty is born." There is a clash, a contrast, a contradiction—even a violence that is terrible, but nevertheless yields something awe-inspiring and beautiful as the rain and the festival of the "birth of God" converge with the reunion and reconciliation of Aziz and Fielding. However, though Fielding corrects Aziz's suspicion that he has married Miss Quested for the money that should have been given to Aziz as reparation and the two reconcile, neither the reconciliation nor the harmony of the Hindu province can permit a friendship, and their paths, which come so near to convergence, diverge. True to his emphasis on the individual rather than the politics of colonialism, Burra describes the novel's final scene: "The rocks that rise between them on their last ride together, the horses that swerve apart—they symbolize Indian differences, it is true, but differences that are not more great, only more particular, than the differences that exist between any two men" (Burra 319). In the novel, however, the differences between Fielding and Aziz are the differences of Empire—the inequality of India and England renders friendship between an Indian and an Englishman (friendship between women is not addressed in the novel) impossible. Having "thrown in his lot with Anglo-India by marrying a countrywoman," who was Mrs. Moore's daughter Stella, Fielding is "acquiring some of its limitations," becoming less "heroic" and more nationalistic (358–359). "Wrangling about politics" with Fielding, who jeers at Aziz about Indian disunity (359, 361), Aziz unambiguously claims his nationality in opposition to Fielding's imperialism by denouncing the English: "Down with the English, anyhow. That's certain. Clear out, you fellows, double quick, I say. We may hate one another, but we hate you most" (361). It is only in asserting his opposition to the "Other"—the English or Fielding—and not to his religion, which has sustained him previously, that Aziz can claim India. It is only in the future liberation of India from the English that Aziz and Fielding can be friends.

Works Cited

Beer, John, ed. *A Passage to India: Essays in Interpretation*. Basingstoke, Eng.: Macmillan, 1986. 27–43.

Burra, Peter. "Introduction to the Everyman Edition." Stallybrass, 309–26.

Forster, E. M. "Notes." Stallybrass, 343–72.

_____. *A Passage to India*. San Diego: Harvest-Harcourt, 1984.

_____. "Prefatory Note (1957) to the Everyman Edition." Stallybrass, 307–08.

_____. *Where Angels Fear to Tread*. Suffolk, Eng.: Hamondsworth, 1959.

Levine, June Perry. *Creation and Criticism:A Passage to India*. Lincoln: U of Nebraska P, 1971.

Parry, Benita. "The Politics of Representation in *A Passage to India*." Beer, 27–43.

"Pukka." *Oxford English Dictionary*. 3rd ed. Oxford University Press, 2007. Web. 03 August 2011.

Stallybrass, Oliver, ed. *A Passage to India* by E. M. Forster. London: Penguin, 2005.

Stone, Wilfred. "The Caves of *A Passage to India*." Beer, 16–26.

The Formal Artistry of
Richard Wright's *Native Son*_____

Robert Butler

When Richard Wright's *Native Son* appeared on March 1, 1940, many reviewers were quick to point out that it was groundbreaking work that introduced something radically new into American and African American literary traditions. Harry Hansen's review in the *New York World-Telegram*, for example, remarked that the book packed "a tremendous punch, something like a big fist through the windows of our complacent lives," establishing Wright as "a new and powerful novelist" (Reilly 47). Several other reviewers explained the originality of Wright's novel in terms of its strikingly new kind of central character: an embittered, undereducated black man who has been so cut off from mainstream American life that he finds a kind of psychological fulfillment in acts of terrifying racial violence. Milton Rugoff's review in the *New York Herald Tribune Books* stressed that "the first extraordinary aspect of *Native Son* is that it approaches the tragedy of race, not through an average member but through a criminal" and that such a character is developed by Wright to "connect one individual's pathology to the whole tragedy of the Negro spirit in the white world" (Reilly 52). Sterling Brown in *Opportunity* likewise praised *Native Son* as a "literary phenomenon" because it was the very first novel about black Americans that provided "a psychological probing of the consciousness of the outcast, the disinherited, the generation lost in the slum jungles of American civilization" (Reilly 95–96). Margaret Wallace's *New York Sun* review sensed a "peculiar vitality" in the book that added "something to the reader's mind which was not there before." She concluded that *Native Son* was "the finest novel written by an American Negro" and that it was likely to "father other books" (Reilly 60–61).

What all of these reviews stress is the fact that Wright's novel boldly describes a new kind of cultural encounter between a radically alienated, deeply embittered black man and a dominant white society that is unable to perceive him as a human being. Over the past seventy years many scholars and critics have confirmed this belief of the early reviewers that *Native Son* was a powerful, seminal text that not only transformed American literature but also fundamentally changed the way Americans envisioned race. Irving Howe in 1963 proclaimed that

> the day *Native Son* appeared, American culture was changed forever. No matter how much qualifying the book might later need, it made impossible the repetition of the old lies. . . . Richard Wright's novel brought out in the open, as no one had before, the hatred, fear, and violence that have crippled and may yet destroy our culture.
>
> A blow at the white man, the novel forced him to recognize himself as an oppressor. A blow at the black man, the novel forced him to recognize the cost of his submission. (Baker 63)

Keneth Kinnamon aptly observed in 1972 that "with *Native Son* Wright became one of the most important figures of twentieth century American fiction" (*Emergence* 18). Four years later, Eugene Redmond characterized Wright as "the father of the black novel" and "one of the most influential and dominant forces of American literature," praising *Native Son* as a book that "summed up the emotional and psychological history of black urban America" (224). And Arnold Rampersad's 1991 essay, "Too Honest for His Own Time" also argued that Wright's "fearlessness" in honestly depicting American racial problems in *Native Son* enabled him to chart bold new directions in African American literature. Rampersad stressed that "compared with him, some of the bravest earlier black writers seem almost timid" (3).

So Wright's reputation as a seminal writer is secure. But many critics who are quick to praise Wright's power and originality are slow to recognize his skill as an artist. As Rampersad noted, "Virtually from the day of its publication, the artistry of *Native Son* has been questioned and found wanting" ("Introduction" xx). Howard Mumford Jones's review of *Native Son*, while praising the novel's "great power" objected to its "melodramatic" plot that reduced its themes to "dull propaganda" (Reilly 47). Jonathan Daniels, while conceding that Wright's book contained "authentic powerful writing," nevertheless complained that it ultimately degenerated into a political "tract" (Reilly 50–51), which stereotypes characters and oversimplifies themes to deliver its message. Clifton Fadiman's *New Yorker* review, likewise, grants that *Native Son* is a "powerful" novel but has "numerous defects as a work of art" such as "paper thin" white characters, a melodramatic plot, and a shallow vision of life depicting human experience "solely in social terms," which fails to capture "dense, many sided, and shifting reality" (Reilly 48–50).

These complaints from the early reviews about the alleged aesthetic deficiencies of *Native Son* were amplified in important studies of the novel done in the 1950s and 1960s and continue to the present day. James Baldwin's influential analysis in *Notes of a Native Son* faulted the book for being a "protest" novel that fails to capture the full richness and complexity of African American experience. Baldwin argued that by oversimplifying Bigger's character to serve the needs of the novel's political thesis, Wright has ironically made him a kind of racial "monster" (34), reinforcing the negative stereotypes of blacks held by whites. Ralph Ellison argued that Wright's commitment to political ideology led him to practice a "harsh naturalism," which prevented him from creating an art that could express the full range of human experience that "more supple modes of fiction" (122) would make possible. Like Baldwin, Ellison strongly believed that Wright's commitment to social "protest" produced "bad writing" and "a simple failure of craft" (142) because it narrowed his vision and encouraged him to use crudely naturalistic techniques.

In recent years, the most complete attack on Wright's artistry can be found in Harold Bloom's introduction to his 2009 collection of essays on Wright. While praising Wright for his "will, force, and drive" and acknowledging him as a "pioneer" in the development of African American literature, Bloom relegates him to a very low status when applying "only aesthetic standards" to his work. He faults Wright for having "a bad authorial ear" (2) that results in graceless, imprecise diction, flat characterization, and inconsistent use of point of view. Labeling Wright as "the son of Dreiser" (1), he asserts that he "could not rise always even to Dreiser's customarily bad level of writing" (1). In an introduction to an earlier series of essays on Wright, Bloom went as far as to claim that reading *Native Son* was "not in itself an aesthetic experience" (*Richard Wright*, 3), however important the novel might be as a social document.

Donald Gibson once observed that "the difficulty most critics have who write about *Native Son* is that they do not see Bigger Thomas. They see him with their outer eyes but not their inner eyes" (729). A similar claim may be made about the ways in which the art of *Native Son* has been misperceived. Critics have been so struck by the novel's extraordinary "power" that they have been blinded to its very considerable conscious artistry. As a result, even astute readers such as Baldwin, Ellison, and Bloom have misinterpreted the novel because they have failed to perceive its subtle art that creates very complex, nuanced meanings.

For example, many false readings of *Native Son* are rooted in a failure to understand how Wright carefully employs point of view in that novel. Reviewers like Daniels who claim that "the story of Bigger Thomas is the story of a rat" (Reilly 50) or critics like Baldwin who reduce Bigger to "a monster created by the American republic" (34) fail to understand how Wright consciously uses third-person point of view in a nearly Jamesian way[1] to create a much richer, more complexly human character than most of the novel's readers are aware of. In "How 'Bigger' Was Born," Wright emphasized that the novel is filtered through a mode of narration technically known as "third person limited," which projects the novel through the author's voice but restricts itself rigorously to the central character's consciousness:

Wherever possible, I told of Bigger's life in close-up, slow motion. . . . I had long had the feeling that this was the best way to "enclose" the reader's mind in a new world, to blot out all reality except that which I was giving him.

Then again, as much as I could, I restricted the novel to what Bigger saw and felt, to the limits of his feeling and thoughts, even when I was conveying *more* than that to the reader. I had the notion that such a manner of rendering made for a sharper effect, a more pointed sense of the character, his peculiar type of being consciousness. Throughout there is but one point of view: Bigger's. This too, made for a richer illusion of reality.

I kept out of the story as much as possible, for I wanted the reader to feel that there was nothing between him and Bigger; that the story was a special *premiere* given in his own private theater. (459)

This point of view, which Henry James used brilliantly in novels such as *The Portrait of a Lady* (1881) and *The Ambassadors* (1903), not only creates "a richer illusion of reality" because it simulates the way all of us are restricted to our subjective consciousness, but it also opens up rich possibilities for irony, since it allows us some distance from the character's perspective, coming to us through the author's voice. Wright can therefore plunge us dramatically into the character's consciousness, enabling us to *experience* his mode of living, but it can also succeed in "conveying *more* than that to the reader." We thus perceive Bigger simultaneously from two angles of vision, seeing him from the inside and the outside. The novel's narrator repeatedly makes clear to the reader what Bigger is only dimly aware of, "There were two Biggers" (Wright, *Native* 252), a hardened outer self that, when pressured by environment, can explode in rat-like, monstrous violence and a softer inner self that is altogether human. As Wright makes clear in "How 'Bigger' Was Born," "Bigger, as I saw and felt him, was a snarl of many realities; he had in him many levels of life" (450). While characters like Buckley are so blinded by racial stereotypes that they see him as a "monster" (412) and the howling mob intent on lynching him in Book

3 reduce him to a "black ape" (337), Wright artfully utilizes a point of view that enables the careful reader to view Bigger as a complex human being. Although his environment treats him as an animal and a beast and this provokes him to terrible acts of violence, Wright stresses that Bigger is much more than what his environment tries to make him.

This is made clear in an early scene where he is able for a few brief moments to relax and operate independently from the intense pressures of his environment. Hanging out on the streets with Gus, Bigger demonstrates that he is not simply the "tough guy" most people. He also has a "soft" human side to his character that aspires to a better life and a more fully realized self. Although one part of Bigger resents Gus and later almost kills him in a poolroom fight, another part responds to Gus in a personal, even affectionate, way. Indeed, Bigger shares with his friend his most deeply felt longing: a desire to be a pilot and to "fly" (16) beyond the harsh restrictions ruling his life. When Gus reminds him of the ways in which white society will frustrate these hopes, Bigger does not lash out with reflexive hatred but instead jokes about the situation, transforming his pain and resentment into a complexly ironic awareness that the two of them enjoy.

Bigger can use consciousness to mitigate the effects of his severely restrictive environment. This part of Bigger possesses the normal drives of a twenty-year-old American male responding to the opportunities of American life. Leaning against a "brick wall" (15)—an obvious reminder of an environment intent on depriving him of these opportunities—he nevertheless can feel an understandable urge to transcend his narrow existence and become part of a fluid world of movement and possibility:

> Bigger took out his pack and gave Gus a cigarette; he lit his and held the match for Gus. They leaned their backs against the red brick wall of a building, smoking, their cigarettes slanting white across their black chins. To the east Bigger saw the sun burning a dazzling yellow. In the sky above him a few big white clouds drifted. He puffed silently, relaxed, his mind

pleasantly vacant of purpose. Every slight movement in the street evoked a casual curiosity in him. Automatically, his eyes followed each car as it whirred over the smooth black asphalt. A woman came by and he watched the gentle sway of her body until she disappeared into a doorway. He sighed, scratched his chin and mumbled, "Kinda warm today." (15)

This is the Bigger Thomas whom most critics fail to see because his actions violate their standard view as a stereotyped "bad nigger" or victim of society. Despite the fact that Bigger will later kill two women after his normal drives toward love have been twisted by environment, here he takes an altogether normal pleasure in watching the "gentle sway" of a woman's body as she enters a building. And whereas the novel's key scenes of violence are acted out at night during powerful snowstorms that reflect his turbulent, uncontrolled emotions, Bigger here relaxes and enjoys the "sun burning dazzling yellow" and the white clouds floating in a clear, bright sky. Rigidly trapped in confining rooms throughout the novel, Bigger at this point is given a rare opportunity to become a part of the natural, fluid world that evokes his "casual curiosity." The fast-moving cars, the drifting clouds, the gracefully walking woman touch Bigger at the core of his being, revealing a person who has all the usual instincts for a life of change and possibility.

As environmental pressures later force Bigger to act violently, Wright makes us keenly aware of Bigger's inward, human self by skillfully probing the images that flit through Bigger's subconscious mind, even as he performs these grisly acts. When Bigger amorally gloats over his killing of Mary, Wright makes us fully aware of Bigger's very moral inward nature by describing images arising from the conscience he is trying to suppress. One is the picture of Mary's severed head, something that repeatedly torments Bigger. When he gets out of bed the morning after Mary's death, he is shaken when his subconscious mind generates "an image of Mary's head lying on the wet newspapers" (99). Riding a streetcar to the Dalton house a short while later, he consciously rejects any guilt over killing Mary—"He did not feel sorry for Mary; she was not real to him, not a human being" (114)—and he actually feels "justified" (114) in killing her. But on a deeper level, his mind does respond to Mary as a person and feels profoundly troubled about killing her, for he cannot get "that lingering image of Mary's head . . . from before his eyes" (113). When Bigger arrives at the Dalton house, this image becomes even more vivid and his moral reaction becomes more explicit. He is compulsively drawn to the furnace in the basement, and when he opens the furnace door, he looks into the fire, imagining "the vision of Mary and her bloody throat" (118), all the while consumed with both guilt and fear.

Wright clearly establishes the fact that the image of Mary's head, rather than being representative of Bigger's fear of getting caught is instead a poetic image arising from Bigger's moral imagination, telling him that in killing Mary he has killed part of himself. Indeed, Wright has Bigger point imagining his own head in the same terms that he had earlier imagined Mary's. After having been questioned about the night Mary died and secretly relishing his killing of Mary because it "evened the score" (164) against the white world, Bigger falls asleep and has a dream that runs counter to his coldly amoral thoughts. He imagines himself carrying a large package in his hands while walking down a dark street. He is alarmed when he hears the "ringing of a distant church bell" (165) and panics when the bell tolls more loudly, seeming to ring "directly above his head" (165). He then runs into an alley, unwraps the package, and discovers that it contains "his *own* head . . . lying with black face and half-closed eyes" (165). The sounds of the bell get progressively louder, and when Bigger runs away to hide from its noise, he finds himself surrounded by white people. The dream concludes with Bigger throwing the severed head into the crowd of whites, cursing them and the bell.

This dream, rendered in a powerful stream of consciousness that exposes Bigger's most private self, establishes that Bigger is not a monster who wantonly kills and is incapable of feeling the implications of his actions. He not only feels guilty about having deprived Mary of life but is also aware, as the discovery of his *own* head in the package suggests, that in killing Mary he has also destroyed part of himself. Bigger's dream, which uses imagery of noise, darkness, and entrapment found in the novel's opening scenes, shows him to be more than a cornered animal; he possesses a moral imagination that is uniquely human.

Many students and scholars fail to understand how Wright's subtle use of point of view functions in *Native Son* and therefore miss many of the novel's most important ironies. They usually make the mistake of equating the narrator's views with Bigger's perceptions and thus fall into the trap of grossly oversimplifying the novel. This is particularly true in their responses to Bigger's extended meditations on his acts of violence. For example, many readers have argued that when Bigger gloats over his killing of Mary and imagines that the accident has empowered him with a "new life" (105) that Wright shares his "elation" (107). They fail to see the ironic distance between narrator and character that third-person point of view makes possible and succumb to two false images of Wright: He is a misogynist who endorses violence against women, and he is a communist revolutionary who advocates violence against the white system, which Mary represents.

Bigger's violence provides a form of rebellion that gives an illusory sense of power in a world that reduces him to paralysis. Wright does not valorize violence. Instead, he makes clear that Bigger's killing has disempowered him in two ways: It will inevitably lead to his own death, thus fulfilling his mother's prophecy that "the gallows is at the end of the road you travelling, boy" (9), and by killing Mary, Bigger has also severely harmed his innermost human self. Wright, who was strongly influenced by the works of Fyodor Dostoevsky and Joseph Conrad, sees Bigger as Conrad saw Kurtz and Dostoevsky regarded Raskolnikov, as a person who is humanly damaged by acts of violence, which he mistakenly regards as empowering.[2] And just as Conrad observed that "all Europe contributed to the making of Kurtz" (50), Wright could very well be claiming in *Native Son* that America contributed to the making of Bigger Thomas. Wright saw Bigger's violence as a kind of time bomb planted by an unjust, racist environment, and at no point in the novel does he romanticize it.

Wright deplores Bigger's violence but stresses throughout the novel that it does not derive from any innate perversity in Bigger's character but instead from the white culture that he encounters throughout his life. To dramatize the lethal effects of mainstream society on Bigger's behavior, Wright uses patterns of imagery that emphasize the separation between Bigger and the white world. Bigger perceives this world as powerful images of whiteness, coldness, and darkness that define a nightmarish experience that confuses and threatens him and drive him to reflexive acts of violence. Because he lives in a coldly segregated world, neither he nor whites regard each other as human beings. For example, when Bigger first appears at the Dalton's home to begin work for them, he sees this "cold and distant world" (44) as so strange and hostile that he carries a gun with him for protection. Wright later emphasizes that "to Bigger his kind white people were not really people; they were a sort of great natural force, like a stormy sky looming overhead, or like a deep, swirling river stretching at one's feet in the dark" (114). Most of the major scenes, therefore, take place at night while it is snowing heavily, suggesting a social world that can freeze blacks into restrictive social roles or actually deprive them of life.

A powerful epiphany of Bigger's failed cultural encounters with mainstream society comes in Book 2 when he is being questioned by reporters who then discover Mary Dalton's bones in the furnace. Sensing that he will be identified as Mary's killer, Bigger panics, bolts to his upstairs bedroom, and tries to escape by jumping out the window. He then falls into a massive pile of snow, which threatens to freeze, blind, or suffocate him:

> Snow was in his mouth, eyes, ears; snow was seeping down his back. His hands were wet and cold. Then he felt all of the muscles of his body contract violently, caught in a spasm of reflex action, and at the same time he felt his groin laved with warm water. (220)

His physical "struggle against snow" (221) symbolically represents all of his encounters with white culture that threaten him with paralysis and then trigger reflexive actions that prove to be self-destructive.

Wright also stresses that as white people encounter black culture, they are similarly blinded, confused, and forced into equally destructive behavior. No white character in the novel can adequately see Bigger as an individual person because they have been so radically separated from blacks by "walls" of physical segregation and emotional fear. The mob that wants to lynch Bigger in Book 3 regards him as a "black ape" (337), and Buckley, the prosecuting attorney, presents him as a "fiend" (407), a "half-human black ape" (408), and a "black mad dog" (409). Even his lawyer refers to him repeatedly as a "boy" (395), little realizing how insulting this term is to a young black man. And just as Bigger wants to lash out violently against a culture to which he feels no human connection, so too does white society want to "blot out" Bigger by executing him rather than humanly encountering him.

Another source of formal artistry in *Native Son* that has never been properly understood and has not received sufficient attention from critics and students is its elaborate narrative structure. Here again, the novel's enormous "power" has obscured its craftsmanship. In "How 'Bigger' was Born" Wright reveals that he had serious difficulty working out a coherent narrative shape to his novel that after four years of writing had become an unwieldy manuscript substantially longer than the completed novel that appeared in 1940. He had particularly frustrating problems writing the opening scene and drafted "twenty or thirty" (456) versions. He needed an episode that could anchor the novel by providing it with a clear, coherent principle of organization. As he reveals in "How 'Bigger' Was Born,"

> I could not think of a good opening scene for the book. I had definitely in mind the kind of emotion I wanted to evoke in the reader in that first scene, but I could not think of the type of concrete event that would convey the motif of the entire scheme of the book, that would sound, in varied

form, the note that was to be resounded throughout its length, that would introduce to the reader just what kind of organism Bigger's was and the environment that was bearing hourly upon it. (456)

In other words, he was searching for an episode that would, like the first two pages of Joyce's *Portrait of an Artist as a Young Man*, telescope the entire novel, using images, symbols, and actions that would resonate in various forms throughout the book. This "motif structure" closely resembles musical composition such as jazz, which might state themes in embryonic form at the beginning of a piece and then make complex variations on those themes, deepening and enriching the music. Wright reveals in "How 'Bigger' Was Born" that he was so frustrated with his failure to produce such an opening scene that he "sneaked out and got a bottle" (456), hoping to relieve his anxiety with alcohol. But his drinking somehow released the energies buried in his subconscious mind and he fastened on the image of Chicago being a Great Lakes city plagued with rats. He then "let the rat walk" (460) into his imagination, allowed the rat to do "his stuff" (460), and the novel's famous opening scene emerged. It was precisely what he was looking for, a "motif" that provided him with a structural principle upon which the entire book could be built. He then "reworked the book" (460) to make it consistent with the opening scene, cutting extraneous scenes and "developing themes that had only been hinted at in the first draft" (461). Significantly, "the entire guilt theme than runs through *Native Son* was woven in *after* the first draft was written" (461). Although the image of the rat initially sprang from Wright's subconscious mind, he was careful to bring it under artistic control through extremely conscious artistry, for Wright wanted to make his readers sharply aware that the novel was centered, not in a rat, but in a richly imagined human being who was treated by his society as a rat. The "guilt theme" that Wright grafts into the novel endows Bigger with a deeply human conscience.

The narrative structure of *Native Son*, therefore, can be seen as a tightly organized sequence of scenes radiating from the opening episode. The novel breaks down into three closely connected "books," each of which contains three major scenes arranged in the following order:

Book 1
Bigger's killing of the rat
Bigger's near killing of Gus
Bigger's accidental killing of Mary
Book 2
Bigger's murder of Bessie
Bigger's escape from the authorities
Bigger's capture by the police
Book 3
Bigger's conversations in his cell
Bigger's dialogue with Max in the visiting room
Bigger's final talk with Max

It is important to realize that these scenes do not mechanically repeat each other but provide variations like a musical composition that complicate and enrich the themes while deepening our understanding of the central character. Although the opening episode depicts Bigger as a trapped animal who, like the rat, lashes out against an environment intent on destroying him, later scenes portray him in more complex human terms. He finally becomes "bigger" than all of the stereotyped images and roles that his social world imposes on him. Although he begins as a naturalistic victim, he eventually attains no small measure of freedom and selfhood by existentially developing his consciousness and then using that consciousness as a basis for human action.

Threaded through all of these major scenes are networks of images that define Bigger's deterministic environment. Each incident contains physical or psychological walls that trap Bigger and most take place

---

at night when Bigger's vision is obscured and his judgment is darkened. At the beginning of the novel, for example, the Thomas family is trapped between the four walls of a cramped one-room apartment and their condition is likened to the rat who is also cornered when the lights are turned on and he is spotted. Bigger's reflexive violence in killing the rat is repeated many times in the novel when he is confined to similar dark interior spaces and, like the rat, responds with instinctual acts of violence. In Mary's bedroom, for example, he is physically and psychologically trapped when Mrs. Dalton opens the door and illuminates the room, creating "hysterical terror" (85) in Bigger. This results in his accidentally suffocating Mary and then pressing his body to "the wall" (84) so that he can avoid Mrs. Dalton's gaze. His near killing of Gus in the poolroom and his murder of Bessie in a cold, dark room of an abandoned apartment building follow the same pattern. In all of these scenes, physical walls and darkness symbolically reflect Bigger's trapped, blinded consciousness, producing terrible violence erupting from deep fears he can neither understand nor control.

Wright employs another important pattern of images in these scenes that dramatize that Bigger is not an animal hopelessly at the mercy of environment but is a human being endowed with a consciousness that can create the freely willed action he needs to construct a human identity. Ocular images are used systematically throughout the novel to dramatize Bigger's growth from a blinded victim to a person who can see himself and his world lucidly and then transcend the dehumanizing roles that a racist society has imposed upon him. In the first scene, for example, Bigger rubs his eyes to adjust his vision from total darkness to blinding light (1). Because the ensuing action takes place quickly and Bigger can see it only in a blur, he is forced to act in an unthinking, reflexive way. Bigger's vision is likewise defective in the poolroom scene, where he views Gus murderously through "the hard glint of his bloodshot eyes" (38) and also in Mary's pitch-black bedroom, where he accidentally kills her because he can neither physically see her nor mentally envision his situation. But ocular images are used for very different effect in books 2 and 3, which show Bigger becoming increasingly more able to see himself and his world so that he can eventually free himself of the environmental determinants that blinded and trapped him in Book 1. He clearly sees Bessie when he deliberately murders her, turning on the light to get a good view of her face. When he escapes from the authorities, he gradually develops a lucid vision of how he and other blacks are treated in society. Having a clear view of the world around him for the first time in his life, he can begin to gain emotional distance from and psychological control over that world. In this way, he takes crucial steps toward selfhood, planting seeds that eventually flower in Book 3. At the end of the novel, he no longer wants to "whirl and blot [people] from sight" (332) as he had wished earlier in Book 3, but instead he desires to see them and himself as human beings. He comes to see Jan as someone who "had performed an operation upon his eyes," (289) and later he looks "straight into Max's eyes" when the two engage in conversation (347). As a result, Bigger is able to dismantle the psychological walls that previously obscured his vision and separated him not only from other people but also from his own human nature. The three major scenes of Book 3, which show Bigger outwardly immobilized in jail but inwardly moving toward increased consciousness and a new sense of self, contrast sharply with the three major scenes of Book 1, which portray Bigger as physically active but visually stunned and psychologically paralyzed. By the end of the novel he might still be invisible, like Ellison's invisible man, to those who lack his inward resources, but he is no longer blind to himself or to his world.

Bigger's growth in Book 3 is vividly illustrated by his ability to relate to people in meaningful, humane ways. Whereas in the novel's first two books he was so trapped by fear and anger that he was unable to form any sustained relationships with friends or family, in the novel's final section, he breaks out of his trapped condition and achieves surprising human contact with people he had earlier wanted to "blot out." As the narrator stresses at the beginning of Book 3, "Toward no one in the world did he feel any fear now, for he knew that fear was useless; and toward no one in the world did he feel any hate now, for he knew hate would not help him" (273). Physically trapped and waiting for death, he, paradoxically, achieves the psychological liberation to achieve a "new mode of life" (275) centered in understanding and meaningful connection with other human beings.

A revealing key to this development is his desire and ability to touch others. In Book 1 he is coldly distant from his family and perversely enjoys taunting his sister by dangling the corpse of the rat before her terrified eyes. As the narrator emphasizes at the conclusion of the opening scene, he perceives his family "behind a wall, a curtain" (10) that hides his guilt over not being able to help them by assuming the role of father. He is terrified of touching Mary for fear that she will scream and identify him as a rapist and will touch her only in lust or murderous violence. He refuses to shake Jan's hand when he meets him in the street because he has been conditioned never to touch or establish eye contact with a white person. And Book 2 ends with his hands physically frozen by the water sprayed on him by the police.

But throughout Book 3, tactile images are transformed to suggest Bigger's awakened humanity. Encouraged by Jan and Max "to believe in himself" (311), he begins "holding his life in his hands" (288). Observing a fellow black prisoner being manhandled by guards, he feels a genuine "sympathy" (343) and a desire to reach out to another person: "For the first time, Bigger felt that he wanted someone near him, something physical to cling to" (344). On a broader level, Bigger is able to experience a vision of human solidarity in which all people "touch" each other:

> Slowly he lifted his hands in darkness and held them in mid-air, the fingers spread weakly open. If he reached out with his hands, and if his hands were electric wires, and if his heart were a battery giving life and fire to those hands, and if he reached out with his hands and touched other people, reached out through these stone walls and felt other hands connected with

other hearts—if he did that, would there be a reply, a shock? And in that touch, response in recognition, there would be union, identity; there would be a supporting oneness, a wholeness which had been denied him all his life. (362)

Here Bigger is no longer divided into two mutually exclusive selves. As a result of this momentary wholeness, he can tentatively reach out to the world in love rather than violence. Although Bigger's efforts to touch people will finally be canceled out by the "shock" of his being executed in the electric chair, Wright nevertheless stresses that Bigger in Book 3 achieves a range of human responses not possible for him previously.

Clear evidence of this development is Bigger's changed view of most of the people he had earlier wanted to "blot out." He finally overcomes the feelings of shame and resentment he had previously felt toward his mother and at the end of the novel asks Max to tell her "not to worry none" because he is "all right" (428). Listening to Jan reveal his deepest feelings about Mary, he grasps Jan's humanity and feels genuine remorse for hurting him: "For the first time in his life a white man became a human being to him; and the reality of Jan's humanity came [to him] in a stab of remorse" (289). He likewise identifies with Jan as he is baited on the witness stand by Buckley, sensing a basic kinship with Jan as an outsider to American society. And part of him comes to realize that his killing of Bessie and Mary is no cause for pride. Rather, he begins to understand that his acts stemmed from his own "blindness," which resulted in his harming other people and himself:

Another impulse rose in him, born of desperate need, and his mind clothed it in an image of a strong blinding sun sending hot rays down and he was standing in the midst of a vast crowd of men, white men and black men and all men, and the sun's rays melted away the differences, the colors, the clothes, and drew what was common and good toward the sun.

Had he killed Mary and Bessie and brought sorrow to his mother and sister and put himself in the shadow of the electric chair only to find out this? Had he been blind all along? (362)

Bigger's human awareness is never adequate fully to resolve all his problems because he is never given sufficient time to sustain and develop such an awareness. But Wright does portray him as moving away from the dehumanized violence and impoverished consciousness that characterized his point of view in Books 1 and 2. Through the depth of his own suffering and genuine contact with other people, Bigger is able to "see" much of what he was earlier blind to. He comes to understand that his mother, Jan, Bessie, and Mary are victims of the same society that has brutalized him, and he responds to them with compassion rather than defensive hatred. He also realizes that he killed two people not out of any heroic motive but simply because he was "scared and mad" (354). Moreover, he consciously tries to reconcile his blind feelings with an existential consciousness that can assimilate, transform, and direct those feelings: "He felt he could not move again unless he swung out from the base of his own feelings; he felt he would have to have light in order to act now" (311). Because he makes such a conscious attempt to move from "blind impulses" to "understanding" (361), he begins to live in "a thin, hard core of consciousness" (360).

Although Bigger's newly developed consciousness never quite becomes the same as Wright's implied consciousness as third-person narrator, the distance between the two diminishes considerably by the end of the novel. As this diminishing happens, the authorial voice and the central character's perspective collaborate to produce a vision of life that can be described as both affirmative and ironic. Bigger's final conversations with Max, Jan, and his mother clearly establish that he has developed a balanced, humane point of view. But his "faint wry bitter smile" described in the novel's final paragraph also reveals that he is fully aware of the ironic gap between his own humane vision and the way society continues to operate, for he knows society will execute him precisely at that point in his life where he has achieved human self.

Perhaps the novel's most pointed irony stems from the fact that Bigger dramatically develops as a human being but the static society in which he lives remains a coldly dehumanizing world. The novel's ending bristles with painful ironies stemming in part from the fact that society has wrongly convicted Bigger of first-degree murder when in fact Mary Dalton's death was clearly accidental. Moreover, Bigger did in fact murder Bessie Mears but, because she was black, the legal system did not consider her death significant enough to bring to a court of law. Moreover, Wright ironically links society's execution of Bigger with his earlier killings of Mary and Bessie. All three deaths take place when intimate human activity is initiated but is then aborted by environmentally induced fear and hatred. Just as Bigger's and Mary's lovemaking is inverted into killing when Mrs. Dalton strikes terror into Bigger's heart, Bessie is murdered when Bigger's attempts to "love" her are overcome by his fear that she will somehow reveal his whereabouts to the police. In a comparable way, the serious conversation begun by Bigger and Max at the end of the novel is cut off by Max's terror, Bigger's incomplete understanding, and society's fear that real human bonds might eventually develop between two such hated people. *Native Son* therefore concludes with the same brutal irony that has vibrated throughout the novel: Death comes precisely at the threshold of our most deeply human experiences. This finally becomes Wright's most terrible revelation of a social world that encourages and even necessitates fear and hatred but violently blocks love and understanding wherever it emerges. Bigger Thomas's cultural encounters with mainstream society result in his own human growth but, ironically, produce no change in the static, rigidly segregated white world.

Because *Native Son* is a carefully crafted work of art and not a dated period piece providing dusty footnotes to a bygone era, it continues to speak vitally to us today. This is true for two reasons. First, our current society has not overcome the racism, poverty, and injustice so vividly depicted in the novel as many thousands of Americans continue to inhabit the teeming racial ghettoes of our urban centers. Although much social and racial progress has been achieved since *Native Son* appeared in 1940, we are far from being a "post racial society." Second, *Native Son*, because it is a work of art and not a sociological document, achieves the universality that enables it to address problems and articulate values that transcend the times in which it was written. As Wright stressed in a 1955 interview when asked why he devoted himself to writing:

> Writing is my way of being a free man, of experiencing my relationship to the world and to the society in which I live. My relationship to the society of the Western World is dubious because of my color and race. My writing therefore is charged with the burden of my concern to that society. The accident of race and color has placed me on both sides: the Western World and its enemies. If my writing has any aim, it is to try to reveal that which is human on both sides, to reveal the essential unity of man on earth. (Kinnamon and Fabre 163)

Brilliantly describing the particular conditions of black America during the Great Depression, *Native Son* also distills broader human meanings that relate to all times and places. This is what Wright meant in "How 'Bigger' Was Born" that his central character was not only a unique individual caught up in very specific cultural circumstances, but that he was also a "meaningful and prophetic symbol" (44) of mankind alienated from traditional sources of human meaning, trapped in a world whose "fundamental assumptions could no longer be taken for granted . . . a world whose metaphysical meanings had vanished" (446). Because of this, Bigger's resonant story "transcended national and racial boundaries" (443) and he becomes like Faulkner's Joe Christmas, Camus's Meursault, and Dostoevsky's Raskolnikov—an archetypal figure. As the inscription to *Native Son* makes clear, Bigger's story is as old as Job's whose "stroke is heavier" than his "groaning" (xxiii).

But Bigger's narrative is also as new as the growing number of school killings carried out by young American men who, like Bigger, express their alienation and anger with equally terrible and self-destructive acts of violence.

NOTES

1. Wright was strongly influenced by Henry James's artful use of point of view in his major novels, and he carefully studied James's *The Art of the Novel* when he was living in Chicago in 1934 and was writing *Uncle Tom's Children* while also preparing preliminary notes for *Native Son*. Wright reread James's prefaces discussing point of view after he moved to Brooklyn in 1938 and was deeply immersed in the writing of *Native Son*. Like James, Wright consciously employs point of view to deeply probe the inward life of his central character and also to provide his novel with an important source of formal unity.

   Wright also studied how point of view is used in the fiction of Joseph Conrad to create irony and thematic complexity. He was introduced to Conrad's work in 1927 when he read H. L. Mencken's *A Book of Prefaces*. Mencken praised Conrad as "a craftsman of the utmost deftness" (30) who used multiple points of view brilliantly to explore the "subjective impulses" (200), the shadowy depths of his central characters. Throughout his career Wright cited Conrad as an important influence. In a 1940 interview published just a few months after the appearance of *Native Son*, he cited Conrad, along with Dreiser, Joyce, and Dostoevsky as one of the "literary influences" (Kinnamon and Fabre 32) shaping his work.

2. Several critics have examined the close relationship between *Native Son* and Dostoevsky's *Crime and Punishment*. Dorothy Canfield Fisher's introduction to The Book of the Month Club edition of *Native Son* drew strong parallels between these novels. See Magistrale for an excellent extended study of this matter. Wright often acknowledged Dostoevsky as an important influence. In *Black Boy: American Hunger*, for example, he listed the Russian novelist as one of the writers who catalyzed his imagination, providing him with "new ways of looking and seeing" (294). In a 1960 interview, shortly before his death, Wright claimed that "Dostoevsky was my model when I started writing" (Kinnamon and Fabre 241).

WORKS CITED

Baker, Houston A. *Twentieth Century Interpretations of Native Son.* Englewood Cliffs, N.J.: Prentice-Hall, 1972.

Baldwin, James. *Notes of a Native Son.* Boston: Beacon Press, 1963.

Bloom, Harold. *Richard Wright.* New York: Chelsea House, 1987.

_____. *Richard Wright: Modern Critical Views, New Edition.* New York: Infobase Publishing, 2009.

Conrad, Joseph. *Heart of Darkness.* New York: Norton, 1971.

Ellison, Ralph. *Shadow and Act.* New York: New American Library, 1966.

Gibson, Donald. "Wright's Invisible Native Son." *American Quarterly* 21 (Winter 1969), 729–38.

Howe, Irving. "Black Boys and Native Sons." *A World More Attractive.* New York: Horizon, 1963.

Kinnamon, Keneth. *The Emergence of Richard Wright.* Urbana: U of Illinois P, 1972.

Kinnamon, Keneth, and Michel Fabre. *Conversations with Richard Wright.* Jackson: UP of Mississippi, 1993.

Magistrale, Tony. "From St. Petersburg to Chicago: Wright's Crime and Punishment." *Comparative Literature Studies* 23 (Spring 1986): 59–70.

Mencken, H. L. *A Book of Prefaces.* New York: Knopf, 1924.

Rampersad, Arnold. "Too Honest for His Own Time." *New York Times Book Review* (December 29, 1991), 3.

_____. "Introduction to the Restored Text of *Native Son.*" New York: Perennial, 1998.

Redmond, Eugene. *Drumvoices: The Mission of Afro-American Poetry.* Garden City, NY: Doubleday, 1976.

Reilly, John. *Richard Wright: The Critical Reception.* New York: Burt Franklin, 1978.

Wright, Richard. *Native Son: The Restored Text.* New York: Perennial, 1998.

_____. "How 'Bigger' Was Born" In *Native Son: The Restored Text.* New York: Perennial, 1998.

_____. *Black Boy: American Hunger.* New York: Harper, 1993.

Cultural Contact, Modernization, and Imperialism in *One Hundred Years of Solitude*_____

Juan E. De Castro

Toward the end of *One Hundred Years of Solitude*, Amaranta Úrsula, the great-granddaughter of José Arcadio and Úrsula Buendía, the founders of Macondo, returns from Brussels to her native town. While Macondo, the setting of Gabriel García Márquez's masterpiece, can be read as a representation of the Latin American hinterlands, even of Latin America as a hinterland,[1] Amaranta Úrsula is described in terms that contradict this setting: "She was . . . spontaneous . . . emancipated . . . a free and modern spirit" (378).

Amaranta Úrsula's modernity gainsays the center/periphery models that were in vogue at the time of the novel's publication and which García Márquez's depiction of Macondo seems to closely replicate in other respects. In fact, *One Hundred Years of Solitude* clearly delineates the cultural subordination of the periphery to the center and the underlying international economic hierarchy, which, in principle, is manifested in the monotonous and slavish repetition of whatever novelty originates in the center. Moreover, the presence of the US-based banana company serves to represent, with imagination and verve, the practices and abuses characteristic of imperial capital in Latin America.

Despite the novel's overall fidelity to center/periphery models and the clarity with which international economic and cultural hierarchies are presented, Amaranta Úrsula is an exception to this subordination. Instead she is presented as having achieved a sense of parity with the cultural centers.

> When she received pictures of the most recent fashions in the mail, they only proved that she had not been wrong about the models that she designed herself and sewed on Amaranta's primitive pedal machine. She subscribed to every fashion magazine, art publication, and popular music review published in Europe, and she had only to glance at them to realize

that things in the world were going just as she imagined they were. It was incomprehensible why a woman with that spirit would have returned to a dead town burdened by dust and heat. (379)

The scope of this "spirit," is such that Amaranta has achieved a full and equal belonging to the modern world from which her fashion, art, and music magazines originate. What she imagines on her own corresponds to the latest trends developed in the European and US centers. In the case of Amaranta Úrsula, modernity no longer resides outside in a distant center: It has been fully internalized.

Moreover, in this case, the time lag between center and periphery, the consequence of the existence of innovations originating in the center and being slowly disseminated towards the periphery, has completely disappeared. One must remember that at the time set in the novel in which Amaranta Úrsula appears, air transport is only in its infancy and, therefore, the speed of cultural dissemination is limited. (In a characteristic García Márquesian touch, Amaranta's Belgian husband, Gastón, "conceived the idea of establishing an airmail service" for Macondo, alas, frustrated because the plane "was delivered to the scattered tribe of the Makondos" in Tanganyika [406]). While presented as another whimsical example of García Márquez celebrated magical realism,[2] the fact is that Amaranta Úrsula's modernity permits her to be fully in sync with European developments, the eternal goal of Latin American and other peripheric artists. Latin America's always obsolescent modernization is replaced with full simultaneity with the center's innovations.

Amaranta Úrsula's consanguinity with modernity, while exceptional, is not a wholly isolated case in *One Hundred Years of Solitude*. The novel traces this "modern spirit" throughout the female members of the Buendía clan. In fact, her sister, Renata Remedios, is described as also having a "modern spirit" (273). However, unlike Amaranta Úrsula, Renata Remedios's modernity is ultimately truncated by her tragic fate. (After the discovery of her romance with the mechanic Mauricio

Babilonia, which led to the birth of the last Aureliano, Renata Remedios was placed by her archconservative mother Fernanda in a nunnery for the rest of her life.)

The novel also explicitly connects Amaranta Úrsula with her great-grandmother Úrsula:

> With Úrsula's death the house again fell into a neglect from which it could not be rescued even by a will as resolute and vigorous as that of Amaranta Úrsula, who many years later, being a happy, modern woman without prejudices, with her feet on the ground, opened doors and windows in order to drive away the rain, restored the garden, exterminated the red ants who were already walking across the porch in broad daylight, and tried in vain to reawaken the forgotten spirit of hospitality. (345–46)

Despite the differences between Úrsula, whose activity was exercised within the limits of a traditional patriarchal society, and Amaranta Úrsula, whose modernity, as the quotation makes clear, implicitly rejected any limiting gender roles, they are linked precisely in that their agency was directed toward hospitality. *Hospitality* is defined by the *Oxford English Dictionary* (OED) as "the act or practice of being hospitable; the reception and entertainment of guests, visitors, or strangers, with liberality and goodwill." In other words, underlying Úrsula's and Amaranta Úrsula's hospitality is precisely an opening to strangers and otherness and, therefore, cultural contact. Given that it enables looking outside one's own culture, hospitality is, in *One Hundred Years of Solitude*, an opening to the possibility of modernization. It is a possible antidote to the solitude that García Márquez presents as the central curse that both threatens and defines Macondo.

However, what differentiates Amaranta Úrsula from Renata Remedios or Úrsula is the extent of her contact with modernity. Her stay in Brussels permits her to internalize the values of modernity, which, as we have seen, is identified with Europe and the United States. It may be relevant that as her mother, the ultraconservative Fernanda points out, "Brussels was so close to Paris and its perdition" (351); but Paris was not only the capital of perdition but also of modernity[3] (and, one can add, modernity is for Fernanda perdition). It is true that residence in Europe is not in *One Hundred Years of Solitude* a guarantee of modernity. Amaranta Úrsula's brother, José Arcadio, who was sent by Fernanda to Rome to become pope, is a case in point, even if his sexual preferences—he may be a pederast—break the strict heterosexual norms of Macondo. Nevertheless, Amaranta Úrsula is shown as having fully embraced Western modernity at its most progressive not only when it comes to culture—that is, fashion, art, or music—but also when it comes to gender issues and sexual mores. However, while *One Hundred Years of Solitude* clearly presents progressive values as linked to the West, García Márquez does not turn a blind eye toward the dark side of modernity: imperialism and ecological destruction.

An Obsolete Modernization

One of the earliest examples of this search for modernization in *One Hundred Years of Solitude* is, in fact, linked to one of its best-known and most peculiar recurring group of characters: the gypsies. As García Márquez notes: "Every year during the month of March a family of ragged gypsies would set up their tents near the village, and with a great uproar of pipes and kettledrums they would display new inventions. First they brought the magnet" (1). Other "inventions" they would bring to Macondo include "a telescope and a magnifying glass the size of a drum, which they exhibited as the latest discovery of the Jews of Amsterdam" (2).

The gypsies, despite their reputation as soothsayers—that is, as being linked to premodern beliefs and practices—are presented as (failed) purveyors of modernity. It is not accidental that García Márquez describes the magnet as a "new invention." All inventions imply a criticism of traditional modes of doing things and are, therefore, necessarily linked to modernity—that is, to an attitude based on the rational analysis of all existing practices and values.[4] Inventions are modern in that they imply doubting earlier practices and attempting to find better, more rational ways of doing things.

Be that as it may, the fact is that these "new inventions"—the redundancy stressing the "modernity" of the inventions, as well as being part and parcel of García Márquez's humor so often based on exaggeration—are anything but new. Magnets, for instance, have been well known since the ancient Greeks, even though it was only in the early seventeenth century that a scientific theory of electromagnetism was proposed by William Gilbert. Likewise the telescope was invented by the Dutch lens maker Hans Lippershey in 1608. In other words, the isolation and backwardness of Macondo make even its most enlightened citizens see centuries-old innovations as the latest scientific trends and the gypsies as merchants of the new.

However, *One Hundred Years of Solitude* plays with temporality by presenting a triple chronology. The novel is simultaneously set when "the world was so recent . . . many things lacked names" (1), "from the . . . later sixteenth century to approximately mid-twentieth" (Bell-Villada 39), and from the mid-nineteenth century to the mid-twentieth— that is, the titular "one hundred years."[5] In fact, much of the "magical realist" effect in the novel consists in the estrangement achieved by the concurrent belonging of characters, things, and events to parallel chronologies. Thus, the Macondo at the beginning of the novel is at the same time an Edenic "happy village where no one was over thirty years of age and where no one had died," set in a pre-Adamic "when the world was so recent many things lacked name,"[6] a city founded by the grandchildren of characters who were contemporary with Francis Drake (his attack on Riohacha dates back to 1596); and, at the same time, contemporary with a "government" that is implicitly identified with that of independent Colombia (nineteenth century).

This presence of simultaneously incongruous chronologies can itself be seen as a literary expression of the concept of uneven and combined development. In other words, the fact that Macondo has its particular chronology—beginning with its own Eden—does not imply a full isolation from the rest of the world and larger national and international chronologies, which are different from that of local origin. Since Leon Trotsky, the experience of social incongruity of uneven and combined development is especially characteristic of peripheric capitalism. Thus Macondo is again presented as representative of Latin America as a (neo) colonial peripheric space.[7]

The time lag in the dissemination of innovations from the center, which is one of the central traits of peripheric modernization, is generally present in Macondo's relationship with the scientific and cultural innovations of Europe. This chronological lag is made explicit when Melquíades—a representative sage and gypsy—celebrates José Arcadio Buendía's discovery that "the earth is round like an orange" (4).

The whole village was convinced that José Arcadio Buendía had lost his reason, when Melquíades returned to set things straight. He gave public praise to the intelligence of a man who from pure astronomical speculation had evolved a theory that had already been proved in practice, although unknown in Macondo until then, and as a proof of his admiration he made him a gift that was to have a profound influence on the future of the village: the laboratory of an alchemist. (5)

While the passage can be interpreted as belonging to two of the three alternative chronologies presented in the novel, it only yields its greatest paradox if one assumes the episode takes place during the nineteenth century.[8] (One can also point out the characteristic García Márquesian irony of having this "scientific" achievement be rewarded with the "laboratory of an alchemist." Alchemy is a premodern and prescientific activity and is the stereotyped domain of gypsies.)

The magnitude of José Arcadio's failure can be seen in that his individual rediscovery of the shape of the earth originates not only in an attempt at appropriating the scientific method that he correctly, from the point of view of the novel, sees as necessary for social progress, but also at communicating Macondo with other cities and regions in Colombia. After José Arcadio fails at finding routes connecting the town with other cities and regions in Colombia—this failure leading him to the belief that Macondo was surrounded by water—the novel notes:

> The idea of a peninsular Macondo prevailed for a long time, inspired by the arbitrary map that José Arcadio Buendía sketched on his return from the expedition. He drew it in rage, evilly, exaggerating the difficulties of communication, as if to punish himself for the absolute lack of sense with which he had chosen the place. "We'll never get anywhere," he lamented to Úrsula. "We're going to rot our lives away here without receiving the benefits of science." (12–13)

What makes this passage particularly tragic is José Arcadio Buendía's awareness of the need for modernization. (One can also note that here García Márquez is again linking modernity, represented by science, one of its defining activities, with contact with the exterior.) Significantly, it is Úrsula who will be able to establish connections with other communities. In fact, if José Arcadio represents a frustrated attempt at incorporating modernity intellectually, to a great degree due to his peripheric condition, his wife Úrsula can be seen as reflecting a potentially positive action uninformed by any intellectual consideration. However, it may be significant that José Arcadio's attempt to communicate Macondo with the outside world fails while Úrsula accidentally succeeds while looking for her son José Arcadio who had escaped with the gypsies:

> Suddenly, almost five months after her disappearance, Úrsula came back. She arrived exalted, rejuvenated, with new clothes in a style that was unknown in the village. . . . They were men and women like them, with straight hair and dark skin, who spoke the same language and complained of the same pains. They had mules loaded down with things to eat, oxcarts with furniture and domestic utensils, pure and simple earthly accessories put on sale without any fuss by peddlers of everyday reality. They came from the other side of the swamp, only two days away, where there were

towns that received mail every month in the year and where they were familiar with the implements of good living. Úrsula ... had found the route that her husband had been unable to discover in his frustrated search for the great inventions. (36)

Úrsula's contact brings to Macondo some of the benefits of modernity: mail and "implements of good living." Nevertheless, the limitations of this contact are made clear: Rather than coming face-to-face with a fully modern other, the new settlers who arrive in Macondo are "men and women like them, with straight hair and dark skin, who spoke the same language and complained of the same pains." This break from cultural solitude is thus limited. The potential for modernization implicit in the contact with Europe or North America is not present in the incorporation of Macondo into an unevenly developed Colombia that has only incorporated some aspects of modernity but not those leading to emancipation.[9]

Colonialism and Its Aftermath

Nevertheless, the tragedy of Macondo is laid not at the feet of Úrsula or José Arcadio Buendía, but rather at those of Fernanda, who is presented as not only destroying the potential for modernity represented by Renata Remedios, but any possibility of Macondo evolving into a modern, emancipated, and free space. With characteristic exaggeration, García Márquez identifies with the vice-regal colonial past: "She had been born and raised in a city six hundred miles away, a gloomy city where on ghostly nights the coaches of the viceroys still rattled through the cobbled street" (205). (One can add that this city is clearly Bogotá, once the capital of the viceroyalty of Nueva Granada.) Moreover, she is presented as personally descending from "royalty." After seeing a ghost who resembles an older version of herself, her mother tells her "it was your great-grandmother the queen" (206). More dramatically, her last Christmas gift from her father symbolizes the novel's implication of colonial heritage:

On the tenth Christmas . . . the enormous box from their grandfather arrived earlier than usual, nailed tight and protected with pitch, and addressed in the usual Gothic letters to the Very Distinguished Lady Doña Fernanda del Carpio de Buendía. While she read the letter in her room the children hastened to open the box. They broke the seals, opened the cover, took out the protective sawdust, and found inside a long lead chest closed by copper bolts. Aureliano Segundo took out the eight bolts as the children watched impatiently, and he barely had time to give a cry and push the children aside when he raised the lead cover and saw Don Fernando, dressed in black and with a crucifix on his chest, his skin broken out in pestilential sores and cooking slowly in a frothy stew with bubbles like live pearls. (213–214)

In *One Hundred Years of Solitude*, the colonial inheritance received and represented by Fernanda and her family is nothing but a rotting corpse.

Moreover, given the association of Fernanda and her family with Bogotá (not only the capital of the viceroyalty but later Colombia's capital), the survival of useless colonial traditions into the present (Fernanda's great skills are speaking Latin, playing the clavichord, practicing falconry, and having mastered apologetics, 206)—is presented not as an individual trait but, rather, as a national one. Moreover, Fernanda's and Bogota's identification with this past implies a willful closing to the outside world. "Until puberty Fernanda had no news of the world except for the melancholy piano lessons taken in some neighboring house" (205). This ultimately destroys any potential for modernity or progress found among the Buendías and, more generally, Macondo, and the national space, despite its (uneven) embrace of aspects of modernity, is therefore weighed down by a colonial deadweight it is unable to overcome.

The novel explicitly contrasts Fernanda's closing off of the Macondian mind with the replacement of Úrsula by Fernanda as the Buendía matriarch. In fact, when Úrsula recovers her sanity lost during the almost five-year rain, she attempts to open the house to visitors and other foreigners:

> "Open the windows and the doors," she shouted. "Cook some meat and fish, buy the largest turtles around, let strangers come and spread their mats in the corners and urinate in the rose bushes and sit down to eat as many times as they want, and belch and rant and muddy everything with their boots, and let them do whatever they want to us, because that's the only way to drive off rain." But it was a vain illusion. She was too old then and living on borrowed time to repeat the miracle of the little candy animals, and none of her descendants had inherited her strength. The house stayed closed on Fernanda's orders. (336)

The aging Úrsula is not able to contradict the retrograde colonial isolation imposed by Fernanda. And the consequence is the apocalypse.

Banana Imperialism

While the cultural values celebrated in Amaranta Úrsula originate in Europe, *One Hundred Years of Solitude* does not idealize the European and US centers. As indicated above, García Márquez is fully aware of the inequalities in the relations between center and periphery and clearly delineates them in his novel. In fact, British colonialism underlies the origin of Macondo. As we have seen, the earliest historical event mentioned in the novel is the sacking of Riohacha by the British pirate in 1596 (19). In this manner, Britain's predatory behavior toward the Americas is highlighted.[10]

But the main example of imperial behavior in the novel is precisely that of the US, or, better said, the banana company. (This is a thinly veiled representation of the United Fruit Company, which had numerous plantations throughout the Caribbean.) Ironically, the arrival of the company originated in an act of hospitality. Mr. Herbert, one of the company's experts and a "captive-balloon" entrepreneur, was invited to stay at the Buendía home where he tried the bananas of Macondo:

No one had noticed him at the table until the first bunch of bananas had been eaten. Aureliano Segundo had come across him by chance. . . . When they brought to the table the tiger-striped bunch of bananas that they were accustomed to hang in the dining room during lunch, he picked the first piece of fruit without great enthusiasm. But he kept on eating as he spoke, tasting, chewing, more with the distraction of a wise man than with the delight of a good eater, and when he finished the first bunch he asked them to bring him another. Then he took a small case with optical instruments out of the toolbox that he always carried with him. With the suspicious attention of a diamond merchant he examined the banana meticulously, dissecting it with a special scalpel, weighing the pieces on a pharmacist's scale, and calculating its breadth with a gunsmith's calipers. Then he took a series of instruments out of the chest with which he measured the temperature, the level of humidity in the atmosphere, and the intensity of the light. (225–26)

This lengthy quotation presents Western traits in a different light from the passages analyzed previously. If the rise in rationality in the West led to the questioning of patriarchy and hierarchy and, therefore, to progressive values embraced by Amaranta Úrsula, it also led to the transformation of bananas from a source of food or "delight" into a quantifiable object, as Garcia Márquez implies, not different from diamonds or any other merchandise or commodity. To put it in Marxist terminology, with which the Colombian writer would surely have been familiar, Herbert was at first attracted to the bananas for their use value, then concentrates exclusively on its potential exchange value.

The example is at some level absurd. However, the behavior of the banana company toward Macondo reflects precisely an exclusively utilitarian perspective and is one in which even people's intrinsic value is overlooked. The famous description of the massacre of the striking Banana workers is a clear case in point. According to the novel, as José Arcadio Segundo wakes up after the massacre:

He realized that he was riding on an endless and silent train and that his head was caked with dry blood and that all his bones ached. He felt an intolerable desire to sleep. Prepared to sleep for many hours, safe from the terror and the horror, he made himself comfortable on the side that pained him less, and only then did he discover that he was lying against dead people . . . and those who had put them in the car had had time to pile them up in the same way in which they transported bunches of bananas. Trying to flee from the nightmare, José Arcadio Segundo . . . saw the man corpses, woman corpses, child corpses who would be thrown into the sea like rejected bananas. (306–07)

García Márquez's comparison of people to bananas is, of course, the point here. As is the case regarding bananas, the company has interest only in the profit they may extract from them. The dark side of modernity, its instrumentalization of reason for economic ends, is clearly presented in *One Hundred Years of Solitude*. Rather than emancipation and freedom, the great promises of the enlightenment and of modernity, the banana company brings the valuation of people as things that can be "thrown into the sea like rejected bananas."

But this instrumental reason, this inability to value anything not directly in the benefit of profit is linked to a development of science, not only as an understanding of reality, but also as the possibility of modifying it at will. The nearly five-year rain, which hastens the decline of Macondo, is clearly produced by the banana company for its own business interest:

The proclamation also stated that the union leaders, with great patriotic spirit, had reduced their demands to two points: a reform of medical services and the building of latrines in the living quarters. It was stated later that when the military authorities obtained the agreement with the workers, they hastened to tell Mr. Brown and he not only accepted the new conditions but offered to pay for three days of public festivities to celebrate the end of the conflict. (309)

The banana corporation's ability to manipulate the truth—the proclamation was clearly a lie and explicitly denied the massacre, a denial that the population would accept as true—is matched by its ability to manipulate reality: It rains for almost five years and the minimal compromise made to the union is never fulfilled. Macondo no longer was of any economic value for the banana company, and it could be discarded to ecological destruction and solitude.

Conclusion

One Hundred Years of Solitude concludes in an apocalypse. In a dark ironic twist, Amaranta Úrsula's emancipation from absurd gender roles and norms enables her to leave Gastón for Aureliano who, unbeknownst to her, is Remedios's son with Mauricio Babilonia. This coupling between an aunt and her nephew—which resembles that of the founders José Arcadio and Úrsula who were cousins—brings to fruition the curse feared throughout the novel: giving birth to a child with a pig tail. Even more tragic, fulfilling prophecies written by Melquiades, this leads to Amaranta Úrsula's death at childbirth, the child's own death, and the ultimate destruction of Macondo.

The end of Macondo is linked in part to the inability of the inhabitants of Buendía and Macondo to break free from the colonial inheritance associated in the novel with Fernanda. In fact, it is Fernanda's absurd morality and hypocrisy that lead to the death of Mauricio Babilonia, the interment in a nunnery of Remedios, and the erasure of Aureliano's lineage, which in turn causes Aureliano's and Amaranta Úrsula's ignorance of their kinship. The survival of colonial structures and mores leads to destruction.

But what is surprising is that Amaranta Úrsula's modernity is unable to stop Macondo's decadence. Even though Amaranta Úrsula has incorporated the most progressive social and cultural values of European modernity, *One Hundred Years of Solitude* is clear about the limitations of her emancipation. Although Amaranta Úrsula is able to anticipate "the models" in fashion in Paris, she still sews them "on

Amaranta's primitive pedal machine." Despite Amaranta Úrsula's embrace of modern values, Macondo, as a society, is still "primitive," still mired in economic and social backwardness. Personal emancipation is not a guarantee of social emancipation. However, modernity is not only progressive. It has a dark side illustrated by the banana company. Despite the emancipatory promise of modernity, in *One Hundred Years of Solitude*, capitalism and its economic expression lead to an even more complete repression and subjugation than that previously experienced under the warped (neo)colonial society of independent Colombia. Moreover, precisely due to its modernity, the banana corporation is able to extend its control into areas unimaginable before: individual minds (no one remembers the massacre) and nature (it is able to manipulate the weather at will). Instead of freedom, the banana company brings oppression. Instead of establishing the value of the individual, an individual is only valued for whatever profit brought to the banana company. Even the labor union formed in response to the banana company's abuses fails to assert the progressive values of modernity. With the massacre, the possibility of social emancipation is snuffed from Macondo. Neither reform nor revolution is presented as an option for social improvement. Given that Macondo represents Colombia and Latin America, one cannot but conclude that underlying *One Hundred Years of Solitude* is a profound pessimism regarding the region's chances of achieving modernization, emancipation, and freedom.[11] The ominous final phrase "races condemned to one hundred years of solitude did not have a second opportunity on earth" can be read as implying that there are races *not* condemned to solitude who possess second and perhaps more opportunities (417). These benighted "races," fortunate in that they are free from solitude, apparently inhabit the center where emancipatory modernity has been achieved. Despite the celebration of Úrsula's hospitality and Amaranta Úrsula's personal emancipation, Macondo is trapped in a labyrinth of solitude from which neither individual nor collective action offer an exit.

Notes

1. As critics have often noted, *One Hundred Years of Solitude* presents a fictionalized version of Latin American history. As Gene Bell-Villada notes, this linking of the novel's plot with the region's history is not accidental, since "García Márquez builds his narrative around the larger blocks of Colombian (and by extension Latin American) history: the early process of Spanish colonization and inland settlement, the bloody wars of the nineteenth century, the repeated instances of illusory prosperity based on a single product, and the hegemonic power of the US economy in our time" (47).

2. Despite its widespread use, *magical realism* is a particularly slippery term to define. However, one can begin by noting the presence of both magic and realism. Not only are supernatural events or objects—such as the gypsies' magic carpets—easily accepted by the characters as real, a trait shared with fantasy narrative such as Tolkien's, but the representational claims characteristic of realistic literature—the idea that the world of the narrative closely resembles reality—are still maintained. Thus Macondo is not only a location where the marvelous takes place, but at some level it is also seen as representing Colombia and Latin America. Thus *One Hundred Years of Solitude* is both magical and realist.

3. The centrality of Paris for twentieth-century Latin American writers is legendary. Carlos Fuentes, alluding to a then unknown Gabriel García Márquez's brief encounter with Ernest Hemingway in Paris in 1957, makes clear the centrality of Paris to Latin American writers in the 1950s: "And even though Hemingway said that the good Americans go to Paris to die, García Márquez could have said that the good Latin Americans go to Paris to write" (25). (My translation.)

4. The *Oxford English Dictionary* defines the "chief current sense" of the verb *to invent* as "to find out in the way of original contrivance; to create, produce, or construct by original thought or ingenuity; to devise first, originate (a new method of action, kind of instrument, etc.)." Likewise the relevant definition of *modernity* is given as "spec. An intellectual tendency or social perspective characterized by departure from or repudiation of traditional ideas, doctrines, and cultural values in favor of contemporary or radical values and beliefs (chiefly those of scientific rationalism and liberalism)."

5. Bell-Villada simplifies the complexities of the novel's chronology. In fact, the earliest historical reference is to "when the pirate Sir Francis Drake attacked Riohacha in the sixteenth century" (19) (the actual date of the attack is 1596); the history of Macondo, from its founding to its destruction, is also apparently set for the so-called one hundred years.

6. The lack of names echoes Genesis 2:19: "And out of ye ground the LORD God formed every beast of the field, and every foule of the aire, and brought them unto Adam, to see what he would call them: and whatsoever Adam called every living creature, that was the NAME thereof."

7. In his *The Revolution Betrayed*, Trotsky writes about this "law of combined and uneven development . . . the history of recent decades very clearly shows that, in the conditions of capitalist decline, backward countries are unable to attain that level which the old centers of capitalism have attained. Having themselves arrived in a blind alley, the highly civilized nations block the road to those in process of civilization. Russia took the road of proletarian revolution, not because her economy was the first to become ripe for a socialist change, but because she could not develop further on a capitalist basis. Socialization of the means of production had become a necessary condition for bringing the country out of barbarism. That is the law of combined development for backward countries" (5). While Trotsky, at least in this passage, is more concerned with pointing out how the Russian revolution was forced to work out "bourgeois tasks"—such as eliminating feudalism—the main point is clear: "Backward countries" (i.e., colonial and semi-colonial) participate in the "world system" in a different manner than "Europe and [North] America." Not only social, but also cultural and economic, modernization is frequently lacking. In the case of the Soviet Union, Trotsky points out that it found itself "with the task of 'catching up with and outstripping'—consequently in the first place catching up with—Europe and America. She has, that is, to solve those problems of technique and productivity which were long ago solved by capitalism in the advanced countries" (5).

8. It's worth mentioning that the passage implicitly refers to Columbus's "discovery" of America, which "proved in practice" that the earth is round. Therefore, the passage in *One Hundred Years of Solitude* can belong to either the late sixteenth-/early seventeenth-century chronologies or the nineteenth-century chronologies.

9. *One Hundred Years of Solitude*, for all its incorporation of "non-Western" magical points of view, slights the indigenous population in Colombia's cultural makeup. While there are a few indigenous characters, they are clearly secondary. Underlying García Márquez's novel is a vision consistent with Darcy Ribeiro's well-known characterization of Colombia (together with Brazil, Venezuela, and Cuba) as a "pueblo nuevo" ("new people"). According to Ribeiro, "Their main characteristic is to be people who have lost their Indianism, Africanism, or Europeanism to become a new ethnic entity." However, despite this "newness," the fact is that, as Ribeiro notes, "it is true that in the configuration of each new people, thanks to cultural hegemony, the European, who gave them her language and a degraded version of the Iberian culture, predominated" (27; translation mine). Thus the limited presence of indigenous cultures in *One Hundred Years of Solitude*, as well as the presentation of a relatively homogenous Colombian culture, is compatible with Ribeiro's ideas.

10. Curiously there is little reference to Spanish colonialism in the novel, perhaps due to the fact that the majority of the Macondians have an unproblematical relationship with their own past and, in fact, exhibit a very limited historical sense. Also see note 9.

11. *One Hundred Years of Solitude* was published in 1967, during the heyday of Latin American revolutionary optimism, and many readers have had difficulty grasping the depths of the novel's political pessimism. Thus Gerald Martin in an influential interpretation of *One Hundred Years of Solitude* has argued that "this is not so much a literary narration of Latin American history as a deconstructionist reading of that history. Once some characters become able to interpret their own past, the author is able to end on an optimistic note. The apocalypse of the Buendías is not—how could it be?—the end of Latin America but the end of primitive neocolonialism, its conscious or unconscious collaborators, and an epoch of illusions" (233). Although Martin admits that "the novel does not actually say this" (233), however, he still insists that this is the only reading compatible with García Márquez's often stated belief in progressive political action.

Works Cited

Bell-Villada, Gene. "The History of Macondo." *Gabriel García Márquez's* One Hundred Years of Solitude: *Bloom's Modern Critical Interpretations*. Ed. Harold Bloom. New York: Bloom's, 2009. 39–62.

Fuentes, Carlos. "Para darle nombre a América." *Cien años de soledad y un homenaje*. Carlos Fuentes and Gabriel García Márquez. Mexico D. F.: Fondo de cultura económica, 2007. 15–29.

García Márquez, Gabriel. *One Hundred Years of Solitude*. Trans. Gregory Rabassa. New York: Harper, 2006.

Martin, Gerald. *Journeys through the Labyrinth: Latin American Fiction in the Twentieth Century*. London: Verso, 1989.

Ribeiro, Darcy. "La civilización emergente." *Nueva sociedad* 73 (July/August 1984): 26–37.

Trotsky, Leon. *The Revolution Betrayed*. Trans. Max Eastman. Mineola, NY: Dover, 2004.

In the Shadow of Yeats: Tradition, Reaction, and Renewal_____

Jon Curley

Inevitably, national literature assumes a declared continuity and tradi-tion, an assumed authoritative canon, and a narrative of development both coherent and codified. Such a notion is necessary, for it allows the reader to assess a region as a understandable totality, an amassed expression of literary arts throughout the ages for which organization into neat types and groupings can be furnished for comparative analy-ses. There is also a paradox rooted in this formula as every national lit-erature depends just as much on the fractures, differences, reactive tis-sues, contradictions, unexpected connections and disconnections, and disparate natures between the works embedded in this tradition. Irish poetry in the twentieth century is no exception, and any survey of its exemplary poets needs to be pressurized into complexity, acknowledg-ing that literary heritage is emboldened by its irreducibility to a simple, streamlined history of characterization.

That Ireland in the last century migrated from the colonial status of a dominion of the British Empire to an independent Republic confers significant political and poetic implications to a conception of a nation-al literature in terms of strategic fissures, fruitful transformations, and relentless thematic underpinnings. These dynamics are best embodied by W. B. Yeats (1865–1939), the most important Irish poet of his cen-tury, who casts on himself and his forbears a splendid, difficult shadow of poetry innovation and invention, pursuant of tradition and experi-ment, demonstrating the search for a personal means of invoking and expressing a broader cultural and national idiom of poetic identity. In this effort, he fosters a lineage of poets grappling with their obligations to national heritage and poetic self, a fraught and fascinating transac-tion that has produced some of the most accomplished poetic voices in world literature and has complicated our understanding of national, colonial, political, and personal representation.

W. B. Yeats began his career as a student and advocate of both English and Irish romantic poetry, Irish mythology, and the expansive canon of native Irish poetry that was suppressed and abandoned for decades. He also affirmed the wealth of Irish poetry written in an array of languages: Latin, Old Norse, Anglo-Irish, and Anglo-Norman French. The purveyors of this verse across centuries were pagans, missionaries, monks, colonial agents, Catholics, Protestants, Irish and Anglo-Irish, ardent native nationalists, and intransigent loyalists to the British Crown under which Ireland was a colony until the early twentieth century. The dynamism of diversity pervades the inventory of this multifaceted poetry.

Yeats's early poetry reflected preoccupations with Irish nature, history, and mythology and parallels what is termed the Celtic Revival, a movement and period in which antiquarians, historians, and writers began assessing, popularizing, and adapting past Irish literature. A famous example of early Yeats and the cultivation of a romanticized Irish landscape and sensibility is "The Lake Isle of Innisfree":

> I will arise and go now, and go to Innisfree,
> And a small cabin build there, of clay and wattles made:
> Nine bean-rows will I have there, a hive for the honey-bee,
> And live alone in the bee-loud glade.

Supernatural and mythological persons and patterns are enduring subjects throughout his career, among them early representations of faeries, Cuchulain (mythical warrior), the superman-warrior, and Fergus, Poet-King of Ulster in the Ulster Cycle of Irish Tales: "Who will go drive with Fergus now, / And pierce the deep wood's woven shade, / And dance upon the level shore?" What soon emerges in middle Yeats is a complication of theme, interests, and identities. Writing as a Anglo-Irishman with roots in the minority Protestant Ascendancy and enthusiasm for the wider native, Catholic culture, he soon reflects the hybridization and cross-hatches of colonial and later postcolonial experience: an affection for English literature and an advocate of a native tradition to be recuperated to rival it in richness; a frustration with both colonial English and independent Irish politics; as mystic and materialist, artist and politician; radical innovator in poetry and conservative defender of tradition and authority, even while espousing liberal social legislation.

Interest and identity led Yeats to question the role of a poet, and this constant questioning of responsibility quickly navigates from purely aesthetic concerns—first outlined in "Adam's Curse" (1904)—to determining the political and civic duties of a public poet. In fact, the crucible of this acknowledgment of commitment and playing a central role in poetically recording various political and historical developments is enshrined in the title of his 1914 collection:

Responsibilities. This volume is a watershed in Yeats's evolution of poetic identity, written just two years before the failed Easter Rising that would precipitate a larger militant anticolonial movement leading to the Anglo-Irish War (1919–1921) and, finally, with independence and the founding of the Irish Free State (1922). "September 1913," the signal poem of the volume, rings with a tenor of menace and remarkable prophecy, especially in relation to political developments ahead: "Romantic Ireland's dead and gone, / It's with O'Leary in the grave." As political upheaval gives way to an imminent change in Yeats's approach to poetry, he adopts a documentarian and visionary perspective, seeing prevailing Irish history in terms of historical spiritual, and, at times, personal cataclysm.

Yeats once wrote, "We make out of the quarrel with others, rhetoric, but of the quarrel with ourselves, poetry" (Yeats 331). This notion of personal conflict extends to others, particularly those Irish nationalists who lost their lives in battle or who were executed in April 1916. "Easter 1916" announces an invigorated poetic voice seeking to both assess the merits and limits of those who died, undertaking an elegy that combines reproach with commemoration, testifying to the distillation of individual experience in much more diffuse, indecipherable historical forces: "All changed, changed utterly, / A terrible beauty is born." The poem's ability to be both tribute and judgment demonstrates a clear-eyed vision that is not ideological, instead becoming a genuinely sympathetic multi-portrait of his national kinsmen. He establishes himself as a national poet, speaker of the people, a role that in itself generates a political gesture as the core affinity that sets him in relation to the colonized; in Edward Said's formulation, he becomes "the indisputably great national poet who articulates the experiences, the aspirations, and the vision of a people suffering under the dominion of an offshore power" (69).

This kind of dedication poem privileges the ultimate role of the poet as collective memoirist so that the poet-commentator who might dispute the actions and intentions of the persons he describes becomes a secondary feature. First questioning whether their insurgent zeal compromised their thinking through of personal and political consequences, he then sides with his mission as master-dedicator:

> Too long a sacrifice
> Can make a stone of the heart.
> O when may it suffice?
> That is Heaven's part, our part
> To murmur name upon name,
> As a mother names her child
> When sleep at last has come
> On limbs that had run wild.

Several lines later, the roll-call reaches its climax in the invocation of these martyrs by name, concluding with the refrain of the seeming oxymoron of "terrible beauty," itself a register of world-changing repercussions encircling much smaller human endeavors:

And what if excess of love
Bewildered them till they died?
I write it out in a verse—
MacDonagh and MacBride
And Connolly and Pearse
Now and in time to be,
Wherever green is worn,
Are changed, changed utterly:
A terrible beauty is born.

This poem was published in 1921 during the Irish Civil War, a conflict sparked by a faction of Republicans disaffected by the Treaty with Britain that ceded six counties of the country to Northern Ireland, a statelet under British sovereignty. Included in *Michael Robartes and the Dancer*, "Easter 1916" should be understood as an exemplary micronarrative fused to poems with more universal concerns of historical disruptures. Nonetheless, both varieties are shadowed by a sense of highly sensitive apprehension, impending doom, even apocalypse. Seamus Deane translates this tendency as being expressive of the deep effect that current events had on him and the shape of history he had formed:

His vision of the Irish past became a rationale for his version of the Irish future. But his apocalyptic sense, always easily ignited anyway, was consumed by the spectacle of the Great War and the Irish struggle of 1916–1922. (46)

Equally a menacing portrait of Ireland, in particular, and the world in general, "The Second Coming" reverberates with a temperament and theme similar to fellow modernists like T. S. Eliot in *The Waste Land* or Ezra Pound in *The Cantos*, expressing anxiety and terror about the broken, lost modern world where tradition, ritual, and authority have all been vanquished. The opening lines of the poem are a barometer of Yeats's feverish, fearful take on the state of global and national affairs:

Turning and turning in the widening gyre
The falcon cannot hear the falconer;
Things fall apart, the center cannot hold;
Mere anarchy is loosed upon the world,
The blood-dimmed tide is loosed, and everywhere
The ceremony of innocence is drowned;
The best lack all of conviction, while the worst
Are full of passionate intensity.

Yeats insisted on the relentless shifting of opposing historical cycles and the gyre is a geometric symbol of the historical and mythological transformations that affect the stability of civilizations; in Yeats, the natural and the supernatural are superimposed on human society so history is a collision of their essences and impacts.

Throughout the 1920s, Yeats made a steep-grade immersion into the political sphere, both as poet and short-term senator, in the newly founded Dail. His desire to help foster and mobilize an Irish poetry movement was fraught with the demands of pivoting between the pressures of personal and public kinds of poetry, an intolerant Irish Censorship Bill, and the vexed situation of overseeing an Irish literary culture that could capably integrate its various elements into a singular national literature:

Irish history since 1916 had taken a direction which threatened to marginalize and make redundant their enterprise of creating a common culture that would be pluralist, avant garde, English-speaking, yet distinctively Irish. But for WBY, this simply made it all the more imperative for his generation to claim their rightful place. (Foster 141)

In the process of attaining some kind of balance between personal and public poetry, Yeats consistently embraced in his methodology a nuanced synthesis of historically astute and mythologically sublime subject matter. The effort proved exhaustive; writing about his poem "Nineteen Hundred and Nineteen," he notes:

> I am writing a series of poems all making up one poem on the state of things in Ireland and am now in the middle of the third. I do not know what degree of merit they have or whether I have now enough emotion for personal poetry. (Foster 193)

Still, the poems published in *The Tower* (1928) are powerful, deeply felt orchestrations of local, national, and personal conditions. "Sailing to Byzantium" contemplates the immortality of art and the wishes for the artist to join it in its eternity while the eponymous poem imparts an inventory of personal recollection, fable, and vision. These poems contribute to the Yeatsian dialectic of stitching the personal to the political and mythic in order to generate an integrative system of sensory perception and poetic expression. When Yeats alights on political events it can be full of candor or unmitigated fury. In the sequence "Meditations in Time of Civil War," he can adopt the guise of arch moralist, looking at the ethical dimension of human conflict:

> We had fed the heart on fantasies,
> The heart's grown brutal from the fare;
> More substance in our enmities
> Than in our love; O honey-bees,
> Come build in the empty house of the stare.

In "Nineteen Hundred and Nineteen," he observes that "days are dragon-ridden," and indicts the actions of unnamed English soldiers— "a drunken soldiery / Can leave the mother, murdered at her door, / To crawl in her own blood, and go scot-free"—but partisanship dries up with a broader incrimination: "We pieced our thoughts into philosophy, / And planned to bring the world under a rule, / Who are but weasels fighting in a hole."

Unlike much politicized poetry that seeks for its object the colonized Other, Yeats rarely confronts the specific character of the English in Ireland or in relation to its postcolonial state, opting instead for embodying the Irish in all their dimensions. One rare occasion in which he does address the English, "The Ghost of Roger Casement," is a memorial to an Irish patriot executed in 1916 for gun-smuggling for the Rising. The atmosphere is eerie, politically and supernaturally so: *"The ghost of Roger Casement / Is beating on the door,"* the refrain reads, putting John Bull, the symbol of England, on warning that in his demise the spirit of insurrection will prevail. At this late stage in Yeats's career, the political and personal are interfused so that during the Easter Rising, Irish rebel Padraic Pearse can be flanked by the mythological hero Cuchulain along with some other greater presence and energy as in "The Statues": "When Pearse summoned Cuchulain to his side, / What stalked through the Post Office?"

Ultimately, politics is etherealized in Yeats, becoming less a workaday civic operation than a legend rooted in the collective psyche of the Irish people. His final extended meditation on the relationship of the political sphere to the personal self is the posthumously published "Under Ben Bulben." Its massive accounting of world history and art, Irish politics and society, poetry-making and the new Irish nation, the spiritual world and human history, are ultimately distilled into the person of the poet himself who fashions his own epitaph and, in a sense, shapes his own demise: "Cast a cold eye / On life, on death. Horseman, pass by!" That horseman is meant to be a supernatural rider and, in his wake, the body and presence of Yeats are preserved both materially and metaphorically.

In the wake of W. B. Yeats comes the colorful legacy of his work and reputation. Typically, it is difficult or wrongheaded to pin an entire artistic tradition to any individual. However, Yeats as producer, arbiter, and advocate of a distinctly Irish poetry born out of a multitude of ethnic, religious, generic, and structural forms surely deserves credit for such achievement. It is an achievement that Seamus Heaney, born in the year of Yeats's death and generally regarded as the finest poet of his generation, recognizes when he writes, "The longer we think of Yeats, the more he narrows the gap which etymology has forced between mystery and mastery" (Heaney 108). Yeats's formidable cultural and poetic accomplishment is as both rescuer and inventor of a tradition. The Irish version of the English language, which he helped facilitate, becomes a constructive colonial and postcolonial model: "He found in Hiberno-English that elusive style, that presence of individual personality and that shared joy in free expression which was not available in official sources" (Kiberd 163). He is at once a national and nationalist poet, the latter designation less a programmatic stance than an advertisement for his shaping of Irish poetic identity. Robert Garratt notes that while nationality is not consistently foremost in Yeats, that through

> the early Revival work and the later poems celebrating the Protestant Ascendancy—Yeats not only treated but emphasized Irish material, attempting in the process to define and shape versions of an Irish poetic tradition. In doing so, he invited those who followed him to read him as a nationalist poet. (20)

Those who followed him, the lineage of contemporary Irish poetry, have worked under and against the formidable shadow of Yeats. Regardless of their various trajectories, Irish poets in three-quarters of a century after him have all dedicated themselves to mapping, reconciling, and relocating the disparate cultural materials that embody and energize the nation.

The flowering tree that descends from Yeats is multi-branched and encompasses wide-ranging offshoots. During Yeats's lifetime, contemporaries and descendents emboldened by the Celtic Revival explored traditional folklore and folksongs, offering modern echoes of old themes and forms. Better known as a playwright, John Millington Synge (1871–1911) cultivated short lyrics, often about wandering the countryside, while A. E. (George Russell, 1867–1935) explored supernatural domains and Irish ecologies. Padraic Colum (1881–1972) and Austin Clarke (1896–1974) first embraced the Yeatsian version of poetry—exuberant, declamatory, visionary, at times personal and very oratorical—only to abandon the master's influence incrementally: Colum for more rhapsodic, rambling hymns to agrarian life and Clarke for social realist narrative poems concerning guilt, repentance, and stifled sexuality in a repressive and conservative Catholic atmosphere. "Tenebrae" and "Martha Blake at Fifty-One" are tremulous, blistering hymns to human doubt and despair.

Of course, all poetic movements have their counter-reactions and other inspirations far beyond the dominant direction of the national poetry, and even in Yeats's lifetime there were contrapuntal movements. Post-independence Ireland not only invited a serious cultivation of Irish subjects and concepts about the creative and cultural definition of its postcolonial environment, it also opened up a view to the international literary avant-garde. The poems of some 1930s Irish practitioners, including Samuel Beckett (1906–1989), Thomas MacGreevy (1893–1967), Brian Coffey (1905–1995), and Denis Devlin (1908–1959), were not so much Anti-Revivalist as Non-Revivalist, reflecting in much of their work a focus on surrealism, science, and philosophy. For them, experimentation in form and divergent matter were preferable to any consideration of Irish identity.

Despite this group's divergence from the constellation of Irish poetry with the signature of Yeats or painstaking fidelity to Irish topics, they should be read seriously as explorers of a new cultural poetic that range in inflections about the cross-currents of cultural, national, and global heritage. They expose an experimental wing of Irish poetry, often neglected or simply negated by mainstream criticism. In turn, some of their protégés will generate important, underappreciated work throughout the twentieth and twenty-first centuries.

Yeats did act as a salutary irritant to a coming generation of poets, most notably Patrick Kavanagh (1904–1967), who rejected romanticism, nostalgia, and what was becoming a cliché-ridden cottage industry of calcified tropes, symbols, and stale representations. His 1942 long poem *The Great Hunger* visits the spiritual and sexual desolation of a middle-aged farmer, a vital existential exercise in disenchantment, a correction to idealizing depictions of rural life.

> October creaks the rotted mattress,
> The bedposts fall. No hope. No lust.
> The hungry fiend
> Screams the apocalypse of clay
> In every corner of this land.

Kavanagh made an important distinction between provincialism and parochialism, the former the preserve of those anxious for cosmopolitan approval and the latter producing a preferable body of work that treats locality with a universalizing sensitivity. The various deployments of Irish poetry after Yeats will undertake sustained studies of regionalism and internationalism, especially as an increasingly globalized awareness will facilitate notions of interconnections as well as national distinctions.

The process of Irish poetry's diversification from the consolidation of a recognizable idiom to an eclectic array that defied easy identification with one model begins in the World War II era, a time when Ireland was in fact neutral.

> Poetry in Ireland during the first forty years . . . was characterized essentially by romanticism and Yeatsian abstraction, both of which combined to conjure up an Ireland of the mind. After 1940, in an effort to cultivate their individuality, post-Yeatsian poets rooted their art in Joycean realism, the bedrock of everyday experience. (Garratt ix)

Personalizing experience does not diminish a remarkable, insistent historical attentiveness, encircling subjective voice with larger social and sometimes political pressures. A fundamental poet of the

---

post-WWII generation, Thomas Kinsella (b. 1928) manages a new psychic sensorium that grafts extravagant Yeatsian vision to a precise recording of the poet's venturing in the world. One of his most acclaimed poems, *Nightwalker*, is a cycle calibrating phenomena around the Dublin cityscape and its reverberations in his consciousness:

> the pulse hisses in my ear—
> I am an arrow piercing the void, unevenly
> As I correct and correct, but swift as thought.

This type of poetry is far from the multi-hyphenated elements of Irish history, society, politics, and languages that early modern Irish poets would have explored and struggled to address. However, grappling with the alphabet of identity irrevocably focuses on political concerns as the partition of Ireland and Northern Ireland in 1922 led to civil conflict, commonly referred to as the Troubles, in the North. The entire landmass has produced exceptional poets, but Northern Ireland (a region also known as Ulster, its name as an ancient province) has over the years brought some of the most ardent, memorable voices to Irish poetry.

The forerunners of the multi-generational contemporary Northern voice are most notably Louis MacNeice (1907–1963), John Hewitt (1907–1987), and W. R. Rodgers (1909–1969), all from Protestant backgrounds, negotiating their ambiguous status in a predominantly Catholic nationalist dominion. The kind of cultural and personal invention on which Yeats relied is here registered in terms of thinking of difference, affiliation, loyalty, and the liability of sectarian thinking. In "Carrickfergus," MacNeice describes his separateness from the native Irish with almost despondency: "I was the rector's son, born to the anglican order, / Banned forever from the candles of the Irish poor." In the book-length *Autumn Journal*, he implies sectarian disaffection while writing about the young country to the south, satirizing the allegiances to nationalisms of any kind. On the other hand, John Hewitt combines a sense of alienation with an insistence on his right for his people, the colonizing Protestant English who settled Ulster beginning in the mid-seventeenth century, to claim the land as much as the native Irish, even admitting a prejudice while also acknowledging their oppression:

> I know their savage history of wrong
> and would at moments lend an eager voice,
> if voice avail, to set the tally straight.

Shorn of the mythological associations ascribed to space by Yeats, Hewitt embraces the contours of territory with a desire for material and metaphorical possession, personal legitimacy, and rendering the authenticity of one's heritage—a major influence on Seamus Heaney (b. 1939), recipient of the 1995 Nobel Prize for Literature and many believe the most significant Irish poet since Yeats.

A later forerunner, John Montague (b. 1929) describes his upbringing in County Tyrone, Northern Ireland and interlaces personal and national history, reflecting on the stress-points between sectarian communities from a culturally Catholic perspective. Montague studied and taught in the United States and the influence of the Beat Generation, the Black Mountain School, and less formalized cadence of the American example became an important, early Irish import.

Montague is roughly a decade older than the members of the Ulster Group, an unofficial epithet for the poets who gathered under Professor Philip Hobsbaum at Queen's University, Belfast, in the 1960s and that included Heaney, Michael Longley (b. 1939), and Derek Mahon (b. 1941), a triumvirate critically and popularly acclaimed. Despite their proximity and friendship, their poetry is highly distinctive, radiating various courses of insight that attempt different strategies for securing vibrant, original representations of lived and imagined experience. Heaney's first collection, *Death of a Naturalist* (1966), dwells deep down in his native County Derry, surveying the countryside and its depths, his upbringing in a farm family, and his relationship to nature and history, which is at once mundane, majestic, and myth-making. In "Digging," he uses his family's farming heritage as a link and point of departure for his vocation and self. Although he will not take up farm implements, he will nonetheless plumb the depths by other means, searching for buried truths, notions, possibilities, and histories:

> Between my finger and my thumb
> The squat pen rests.
> I'll dig with it.

During the high point of the Troubles, Heaney devoted himself to extended ruminations on the relationship of political violence, tribal instinct, bodily atrocity, and the ethics of historical and personal responsibility. In what are known as the "Bog poems," Heaney links contemporary communal strife in Northern Ireland with sacrificial victims of the Iron Age discovered in Scandinavia. Poems like "The Grauballe Man," "The Tollund Man," and "Punishment" parallel past and present and the North and elsewhere in questioning communal identity and allegiances. "Punishment" describes in intricate detail an ancient female body and imagines her as a contemporary Irish Catholic punished for fraternizing with British soldiers. He condemns the humiliation and desecration, past and present, but acknowledges the pressures of communal/sectarian loyalty in imagining his complicity:

> I almost love you
> but would have cast, I know,
> the stones of silence.

Rather than aestheticizing violence and beautifying its aftermath in poetic lushness, Heaney complicates the process of identification, off-loading received cultural, historical, and ethical meanings by inquiring into their determinants and illustrating them so as to understand them. Heaney has written that poetry is about the intersection of politics and transcendence—a notion with which Yeats would certainly agree—and later work features pilgrimages encountering the dead in *Station Island* (1984) and spiritual notions of the poetic imagination, beyond religion, as in *Seeing Things* (1994). More recent work has revisited childhood and early life as a poet, Irish mythology, various international literary legacies (he is a noted translator of Ancient Greek, Old English, and Middle Scots), but always returning to the crucial occupations of place, displacement, and the poet's role. Like many of his contemporaries, he has come to rely on Ulster idiom as a necessity poetic speech. Neither unique in it characteristics nor sprouting directly from the provenance of Yeatsian sensibility, Heaney does represent a continuation of his acknowledged forbear's dedication to probing extensively the powers of poetry to unlock the mysteries and energies of state and self.

Michael Longley and Derek Mahon are not in the shadow of Heaney because their exquisite repertoire restlessly invents patterns amenable to radical alterations and reenvisioning of their poetic vehicles. Longley has evolved from being a dexterous formalist into an artist allergic to constraint or consistency except in the surprise he evokes. Allusions to Greek mythology, classical Chinese poetry, and modern photography allow for witty and poignant commentaries on culture, Northern Ireland post-Troubles, and his relationship to nature and family. "Ceasefire," written just after the Troubles, casts Achilles and Priam as early referents for establishing a hopeful future for the Catholic/Republican and Protestant/Unionist communities. It has become a much-quoted hallmark of hope in both Ireland and Northern Ireland. Derek Mahon's work has deliberated spaces or zones of aesthetic license or ruin. Whether through paintings, landscapes, or, most notably, in "A Disused Shed in Co. Wexford," which blends a site-specific domain in the Irish countryside with collective human history, his work shows devastations, nightmares, and possible renovations through the construction of memory. In recent years, Mahon's verse can be both whimsical and pungent; he emerges as a Northern Irish Jonathan Swift with an effervescent wit.

Seamus Deane (b. 1941) and Tom Paulin (b. 1949) are important Ulster voices, bringing the depth-charge of polemic and criticism about the state of Northern Ireland but also the atavistic repetitions of war in general. Beginning with *The Irish for No* (1976) and establishing a new sense of language as punctuation and explosion in *Belfast Confetti* (1987), Ciaran Carson (b. 1948) is a tireless innovator, working within different modes and themes that seem less miscellany than sustained poetic replenishments. He is also paired with Medbh McGuckian (b. 1950) and Paul Muldoon (b. 1951), presiding articulators of an oblique, riddling poetry emphatically original and difficult. McGuckian's work tackles Irish history, the vulnerability of the human body, and the feminine aura and content that animate interior lives and are subterranean guarantors of logic and redemption. Muldoon has generated some of the most beguiling verse, intermittently tied up with Irish issues, and always resonant in wild rhyme schemes dealing with love affairs and improbable voyages (some modeled after ancient Irish voyage narratives called *immrama*). These three Northern poets do not impart any Yeatsian sage-like quality (Muldoon in fact satirizes Yeats in his long poem *7, Middagh Street*), but their probing of form and theme suggests an enduring protean capacity for maneuvering poetry around astonishing new formats and formulations; this fits largely with Ezra Pound's dictum to "make it new" and Yeats's revivalist interest in retuning the language.

By "language," it is taken for granted that what is meant is some variant of Anglo-Irish. But especially since the early seventies, Irish-language poets have emerged who either translate their own poetry or have other poets do so throughout Ireland and Northern Ireland. With the founding of the journal *Innti* in Cork in 1970 by Michael Davitt (1950–2005), a group of young poets emerged that included Nuala Ní Dhomhnaill (b. 1952), perhaps the most visible modern poet working in Irish. Her poems are characterized often by humor, sexual innuendo, and references to mythology and the language issue. Her work in translations comes across as potent, alluring, and never fusty or overly classical:

There came this bright young thing
with a Black & Decker
and cut down my quince-tree.

Other notable Irish language poets include Biddy Jenkinson (b. 1949); Michael Hartnett (1950–2005), whose 1975 collection *A Farewell to English* is a riposte to the imposed colonial tongue and denounces the influence of Yeats on Irish poetry; Cathal Ó Searcaigh (b. 1956), whose work runs the range of dealing with travel, lament, and the trials and loves of a gay man; and Frank Sewell (b. 1968). This nativist recuperation of the language stands as a later instance of the living archival work Yeats conducted beginning in the late nineteenth century and continues to thrive amid and despite a globalized, English-centered Western Europe.

The Irish language poets have now only an unfortunate academic cache, but the blossoming of their work shall have wider reverberations, as seen in the more internationalist and experimental leanings of Michael Smith (b. 1942) and Trevor Joyce (b. 1947), founders of New Writers Press, who share more than a passing kinship with the vanguard of American postmodern poetry, and Randolph Healy (b. 1956), whose work morphs and moves and is hinged to mathematical, scientific, and sometimes philosophical considerations. Although outside the mainstream, their poetry deserves merit for the plurality of its reaches and as one incandescent chain of development in enlarging the scope of the national poetic language.

Arguably, critical groupings of an anthological bent are by nature defective, and categorizing by region, gender, or any other criteria can result in a fixation on superficial affinities. However, taking stock of such a dense inventory of post-Yeatsian poetic development requires recourse to such simplification, which is a necessary weakness any vigilant reader should bear in mind along with possible inadvertent or compromised exclusions. Long the subject of poems, but not often enough poets in their own right over centuries, female poets in Ireland have flourished over the past five decades, an indispensable canon of achievement. The work of poets like Eiléan Ní Chuilleanán (b. 1942), Eavan Boland (b. 1944), and Paula Meehan (b. 1955) are sites of contestation and reconsideration, being correctives to the invisibility of a female poetic presence for so long. Their reckonings with feminine roles in Irish history, mythology, and family (frequently glosses and commentaries on prior male ascriptions) expand the bounty of Irish poetic enterprise formidably. Frank representations of sexuality, violence, death, history, and memory convey testaments to the social and cultural changes of Ireland over the span of the last century.

Many of these poems also testify to a nuanced cosmopolitan, sometimes even suburban, voice, providing a barometer for calibrating Ireland in its ever-changing dynamism. Paul Durcan (b. 1944) suffuses a trickster mentality to his many odes to urban life, while Dennis O'Driscoll (b. 1954), for years a civil servant in Dublin, has brought into view the quotidian experience of office work, bureaucratic drudgery, and the need for the imagination to nourish the rhythms of everyday life. At a period where for Ireland and Northern Ireland can hardly be considered colonial or postcolonial—cultural critic Richard Kearney has argued for transnational status for each—the notion of any secure, stable Irish poetic subject or identity must be relativized and studied carefully so as to do justice to its primary, perennial concerns and the inexorable shifts in focus, taste, and matter that occur.

How the youngest generation of Irish poets establish their position beneath, beyond, or away from Yeats's shadow of influence or any of their many forebears is still too difficult to determine. But abiding poetry and history is the perpetual sculpting of forces and tendencies both recognizable and beyond conventional. As Norman Vance notes that in Ireland

a sense of cultural dislocation, or insecurity, or reviving national pride, or willed identification of colonizer and colonized, has at different times inspired different perceptions and constructions of Irish literary tradition. (3)

The colonial dimension might have subsided, but power and possession, powerlessness and dispossession can be redrawn through subtle or sensational cultural, political, and world economic conditions. The younger poets will be sure to capture the spirit of coming times with precision and power. A few of the most notable poets would be Vona Groarke (b. 1964), Sara Berkeley (b. 1967), Conor O'Callaghan (b. 1968), Justin Quinn (b. 1968), David Wheatley (b. 1970), Sineád Morrissey (b. 1971), Alan Gillis (b. 1973), Leontia Flynn (b. 1974), and Nick Laird (b. 1975), each with an eye on history and modernity, the presence and erasures of social and political change, and national and international references and areas of interest particularly in pop culture, media, and technology. In a contemporary world where the project of revitalization for Irish poetry undertaken by Yeats might seem distant, the insistent drive to envision and, at times, be visionary and to reflect on the many forces and cultural encounters home and abroad is nonetheless a trademark of this tradition and is its birthright and eternal legacy.

Works Cited

Deane, Seamus. *Celtic Revivals: Essays on Modern Literature 1880–1980*. Winston-Salem, NC: Wake Forest UP, 1987.

Foster, Roy F. *W. B. Yeats, A Life Volume II: The Arch-Poet 1915–1939*. Oxford, Eng.: Oxford UP, 2003.

Garratt, Robert F. *Modern Irish Poetry: Tradition and Continuity from Yeats to Heaney*. Berkeley: U of California P, 1986.

Heaney, Seamus. "Yeats as an Example?" *Finders Keepers: Selected Prose 1971–2001*. New York: Farrar, 2002.

Kiberd, Declan. *Inventing Ireland: The Literature of the Modern Nation*. London: Vintage, 1996.

Said, Edward W. "Yeats and Decolonization." *Nationalism, Colonialism, and Literature*. Eds. Terry Eagleton, Fredric Jameson, and Edward W. Said. Minneapolis, MN: U of Minnesota P, 1990.

Vance, Norman. *Irish Literature: A Social History*. Oxford: Blackwell, 1990.

Yeats, W. B. "Per Amica Silentiae." *Mythologies*. New York: Macmillan, 1959.

Derek Walcott and the Idea of Postcolonial Globalization_____

Maik Nwosu

The privileging of the special inheritance of the black or the multicultural literary imagination is central to African and Caribbean postcolonial literature, a nativistic traveling sign that primarily points to a return to the origins of a traditional mythic code. But, while also rooted in a native or base mythic code, some writers represent instances not of postcolonial nativism but of postcolonial globalization in which a conversation across cultural-ideological imaginaries is expansive. The difference is essentially a matter of intensity or orientation. While not fundamentally a throwback to a prenation/language era or a forward leap to a postnation/language phase, postcolonial globalization emphasizes the fact and nature of cultural intersections more than is the case in postcolonial nativism with its major focus on the fact and nature of a pristine traditional imaginary. In his poetry, *Omeros*, Derek Walcott ultimately returns to the origin, Africa, but through a route rich with differing cultural-ideological histories. He foregrounds a contextually new signifying field in his re-envisioning of the world.

Walcott himself presents an interesting instance of Caribbean assimilation or synthesis. His grandfather emigrated from England to Barbados, where he married a mixed-race woman, Christiana Wardrope. Derek Walcott's father was "thought a perfect English Barbadian, helpful, socially impeccable, quiet. He listened to recordings of opera, loved gardening, and was a gifted amateur in many arts. He had a library including a set of the complete works of Dickens, read English classics and modern novels, wrote verse, was a draughtsman and a watercolourist" (King, 9). He was a Bajan, that colonial creation that was "more British than the British." Warwick married Alix, Derek's mother, who was also of mixed race.

Walcott once owned a British passport as a citizen by birth, but when his father moved from Barbados to St. Lucia, the move brought about a feeling of cultural dislocation. While Barbados had always been a British colony, St. Lucia was then one of the few French-speaking Caribbean islands. St. Lucia, regardless of its small size, was one of the most contested Caribbean islands, in part because of its alluring environment, and it changed "ownership" fourteen times in all. The family's relocation to St. Lucia also meant that Walcott, who had been raised a Methodist, suddenly found himself in a predominantly Roman Catholic environment. "Coming from a Methodist minority in a French Catholic island," he says, "we [the Walcott family] also felt a little beleaguered. The Catholicism propounded by the French provincial priests in St. Lucia was a very hidebound, prejudiced, medieval, almost hounding kind of Catholicism" (Plimpton 269). Methodism remains one of the legacies of his upbringing that Walcott cherishes. The others are poetry, painting, and the English language. On his religion he has said, "In a private way, I think I still have a very simple, straightforward foursquare Methodism in me. I admire the quiet, pragmatic reason that is there in a faith like Methodism, which is a very practical kind of conduct. I'm not talking about a fanatical fundamentalism" (274). But his religion, or spirituality, transcends foursquare Methodism: "I have never separated the writing of poetry from prayer. I have grown up believing it is a vocation, a religious vocation. What I described in *Another Life*—about being on the hill and feeling the sort of dissolution that happened—is a frequent experience in a young writer" (272).

Walcott's colonial education formally introduced him to Shakespeare, Dickens, and Latin, and it opened the door to an appreciation of great literature and art that included T. S. Eliot, James Joyce, Hart Crane, Cézanne, and Vincent van Gogh. Walcott notably invokes Van Gogh in his "Self Portrait" published in the *Caribbean Quarterly* (1980): "The loneliness of Van Gogh / The humbleness of Van Gogh / The terror of Van Gogh." The "terror" of Van Gogh, which is also Walcott's, evokes the fiction of the self, the Walcott that has "no nation but the imagination." But it is paradoxically a convertible terror that eases Walcott across class and racial divisions. Clara Rosa de Lima sees in Walcott's (and

Van Gogh's) artist "a revolutionary, the dissenting voice that refuses to be cowed by conventional wisdom or the fashionable view, insisting on the importance of the individual talent while acknowledging the power and dignity of the un-politicized peasant and the 'theatre of the poor'" (181–82). This imagery explains Walcott's fascination with Daniel Defoe's *Robinson Crusoe* (1719). Crusoe (the character) represents for him the possibility of recreating the world or experience, not as an imperial project on a fantasy of an "empty" paradise, but as a remodeling of the sign at the interstices of connecting cultures. In "Crusoe's Island," the Crusoe-like "bearded hermit [who] built / [h]is Eden" upon a rock is "[t]he second Adam since the fall," the "[c]raftsman and castaway" with "[a]ll heaven in his head" but whom a fundamental need sends "howling for a human voice" (Walcott, *Collected Poems* 68). Bruce King has gone even further to claim that "[t]he Crusoe image became in Walcott's imagination mixed with that of Adam in Eden, with civilization as well as sex being the fruit of knowledge offered by the serpent" (24).

Walcott's Adamic consciousness links him to the Walt Whitman tradition in poetry, the secular "uniter of the here and hereafter" (in "Out of the Cradle Endlessly Rocking"), whose *Leaves of Grass* is modeled more on the concept of a transcendental unity between man and other forms of nature than on the Bible of orthodox Christianity. Whitman's vision is essentially that of a new Adam trying to invoke a lost enlightenment. *Leaves of Grass*, to him, was what John Irwin references as "the Great Construction of the New Bible" (31), a feat that Whitman likens to Champollion's decoding of the Rosetta Stone. The Whitmanesque bible of image and sound, with its stress on the sonic aspect of poetry in an attempt at a fusion of thought and sound (the spoken sign), is a literary return toward the original form of the hieroglyph and its harmony of meaning and sign. Walcott had been introduced to Whitman's poetry at the age of eleven. But he would later object to Whitman's lack of a "sense of guilt," feeling that "the widespread compassion found in Whitman came too easily; there was no confession of guilt and no engagement in a dialogue with the rest of the world" (King

446). For Walcott, reconciliation or healing requires more than such simple compassion; it requires the rigor of an inventorying or reflective process such as in his detailed narration of the Middle Passage and the massacre of Native Americans in *Omeros* (1990).

Walcott's relation to the English language and English literature has also involved reflection or reckoning. He sees imitation as part of the evolution of art and the artist, including the imitation of Western forms. "As early as a minor *Trinidad Guardian* review in 1966," notes Robert D. Hamner, "Walcott advised 'Young Trinidad Poets' that in order to establish their own voices it is first necessary to evolve through the acquisition of 'other voices'" (11). Walcott has never understated his love of the English language, and his concept of "other voices" in this case certainly prioritized English/Western literature. But as he also says, "I am primarily, absolutely a Caribbean writer. The English language is nobody's special property. It is the property of the imagination: it is the property of the language itself" (Plimpton 279). But if language belongs to the imagination, what are the reference points or signposts of that imagination? And if the language belongs to the language, how can it in fact be a language? Walcott's statement, possibly an infelicitous phrasing not unusual in interviews, may be understood to mean that the imagination, operating at the crossroads of the colonizer and the colonized, has reinvented the *Englishness* of the language. Paula Burnett writes: "For Walcott as a St. Lucian, there is a heritage of two indigenous vernaculars, English and French Creole (or patois), as well as the standard European languages, in a constant interplay with one another and not surprisingly producing new and unique meanings between them" (135). Walcott interactively relates each national or regional literature to the other (such as considering Caribbean poetry as also being in competition with English poetry) and conceives the English language common to all of them as "nobody's special property" but a linguistic sea into which the rivers of all the different "national Englishes" flow.

Walcott's "love of the English language" has led to what he describes as "a lot of provincial criticism: the Caribbean critic may say, 'You are trying to be English,' and the English critic may say, 'Welcome to the club.' These are two provincial statements at either end of the spectrum" (Plimpton 281). Dathorne cites the Walcott-Brathwaite dichotomy, according to which Walcott supposedly only manages to achieve "on the surface" a cultural invocation of the Caribbean, while Kamau Brathwaite does so at a deeper level: "Brathwaite handles dialect with ease, whereas Walcott is extremely cautious in his use of Caribbean English" (236). To Dathorne, Brathwaite "is part of the process of the invention of [a] new [Caribbean] culture (the second synthesis), whereas Walcott is still wary of the merging. For Walcott, it seems that poetry will remain a fashionable literary ailment, voluntarily contracted" (243). But both Brathwaite and Walcott are engaged, differently, in a project of synthesis—the difference being that Brathwaite's is primarily conceived as a recovery (or nativistic) mission, while Walcott's is as recuperative as it is projective (or global).

Selwyn Cudjoe adds a new angle to the misreading of Walcott's literary art. He refers to Walcott as one instance—others being John Hearne and Orlando Patterson—of an "anti-democratic and nihilistic Naipaulian tendency" (272). Cudjoe defines the "democratic sentiment" in Caribbean literature as the representation of the struggle for (postcolonial) democracy, with the masses as the catalytic agents. But V. S. Naipaul's view of the West Indies, especially his statement that "history is built around achievement and creation; and nothing was created in the West Indies," underscores his self-positioning ideologically alongside the James Froude that he cites in the epigraph to *The Middle Passage*: "There are no people there [in the West Indies] in the true sense of the word, with a character and purpose of their own" (9). Walcott is certainly not Naipaulian; he has famously satirized the pessimistic Naipaul as "V. S. Nightfall." Instead of a Naipaul*ian* tendency in relation to Walcott, there is a Walcott*ian* vision that has recast Naipaul's statement in this manner: "Perhaps it should read that 'Nothing was created *by the British* in the West Indies'" (Plimpton 281). Walcott's Caribbean project in *Omeros* is markedly different from what Cudjoe categorizes as a "Naipaulian tendency." Walcott in fact creates a rich history out of a Naipaulian "nothingness," a reprojection that positions the Caribbean not only as a place (to be) politically affected but as a place capable of affecting other geographies and histories. In *Omeros*, Walcott takes the reader on a revelatory journey that is often relatable to the fate of his native Caribbean. He reimagines the Western form of the epic within a postcolonial context, although Walcott himself prefers not to describe *Omeros* as an epic because of the distance that the term apparently suggests.

As a postcolonial epic rooted in the Caribbean, *Omeros* may be read as an imaginative discourse on colonization that references Homer's *The Iliad*. It uses some characters from *The Iliad* as symbolic figures. For instance, Helen, a maid, represents the island of Gros-Ilet especially because of her attractiveness to Europeans (such as Major Plunkett). Two local fishermen, Achille and Hector, fight over her. Walcott's Philoctete, a fisherman inflicted with an ancestral wound, is comparable to Homer's Philoctetes (who also bears a wound, by snakebite). The voyage in *Omeros* starts in Gros-Ilet. The poem then points out the fate of the island as it narrates the Battle of the Saints in 1782—that is, the struggle between Britain and France for the "ownership" of some Caribbean islands. When the setting of the poem changes to New England and the United States, it focuses on the personal tribulations of the wandering poet-persona and the plight of Native Americans. Seven Seas, previously presented as a wise, old man in Gros-Ilet, appears in this part of the narrative as a Ghost Dancer. The return of the poet-persona to the Caribbean ends the narrative trajectory of *Omeros* as an odyssey. The healing of Philoctete's ancestral wound by Ma Kilman toward the end of the poem is a symbolic act that signposts not simply individual recuperation but communal rejuvenation.

Besides its main setting and trajectory, the thematic orientation of *Omeros*—its focus on healing—sets it apart from the European epics that preceded it. While José María Pérez Fernández notes formal similarities (such as the use of the *terza rima*) between Walcott's *Omeros* and Dante's *Inferno*, he points out, "For Walcott [unlike Dante, whose *terza rima* was a representation of transcendental divinity], the pilgrimage is that of the narrator, who acquires a richer dimension by means of his partial replication in other characters that undergo similar healing processes. *Healing* is Walcott's equivalent of Dante's *conversion*" (74).

The anti-imperial inclination of Walcott's *Omeros* is clear from the very beginning: the opening scene includes the fishermen's "murder" of trees and the "resurrection" of the cut trees as canoes. In Homer's *The Iliad*, Virgil's *The Aeneid*, and Lucan's *Pharsalia*, for instance, the cutting of trees is differently contextualized. *The Iliad* portrays the transformation of trees into genealogically significant scepters. For example, Agamemnon envisions "the royal scepter of his fathers" as possessing a "power [that] can never die" (101). Aeneas's fleet in *The Aeneid* is shaped or constructed with the aid of cut timbers from Phrygian Ida. Cybele, the Great Mother Goddess of Phrygia, appeals to Jove (or Jupiter) on behalf of Aeneas: ". . . let your mother's plea avail / In this: that those ships' timbers not be breached / Or swamped on any course by any storm" (262). As this scene suggests, the Great Mother Goddess subordinates nature to the imperial project. In *Pharsalia*, Caesar decimates a sacred grove ("a grove from a bygone age, / never ravaged," 71) in the course of his imperial venture: "Leaving the blade sunk deep in the ravaged bole, / he intoned: / 'lest any of you hesitate longer / to overthrow / a wood, assign *me* the sacrilege'" (73). Historically, Julius Caesar wins—not loses—the Battle of Pharsalia.

Contrastively, the "murder" of trees in *Omeros* is presented as a genocidal act that recalls the plight of the native population in the Caribbean prior to transatlantic slavery. Another significance of the "murder" of trees and their "resurrection" as canoes is the way it prepares or equips the fishermen to "farm" the sea, an occupation that disposes them, like Walcott, more or less to wandering. Walcott's poetry makes problematic "the representation of the Caribbean as paradise and [draws] attention to the true place of origin in Caribbean culture: the shore" (Farrier 23). This vision is evident in a key Walcottian image: "the image of the poet declaring the names of his culture on the shoreline, as around him men turn trees into canoes. . . . [H]e is the Antillean second Adam, naming his landscape; he resembles the itinerant fishermen of *Omeros*, for whom the point of arrival is also, crucially, a chiastic arrangement, a point of departure" (24).

Omeros somewhat registers as a dialogue between the sea and the land. This land and sea interconnection of experience and memory is suggested in one instance by Achille's "voyage" back in time—specifically, a slave-raiding scene temporally set in a prior era in Africa. As the narrator notes, "Time is the metre, memory the only plot" (Walcott, *Omeros* 129). The sea figures as living history as well as the locus of memory (because of the Middle Passage and all those who perished at sea) that "recalls" what happens to the earth. The journey of the poet-persona to New England and other parts of the world also points to sea-based connectivity. Notably, Homer's name is reimagined as constituted by fragments of sea sounds: "and *O* was the conch-shell's invocation, *mer* was / both mother and sea in our Antillean patois, / *os*, a grey bone, and the white surf as it crashes" (14). The sea is the passageway through which the poem travels beyond its main Caribbean setting. And this movement is important. It evidences the poem's diasporic context or the motioning of African bodies away from their homelands by transatlantic slavery.

In its postcolonial globalization of Caribbean history, *Omeros* focuses on the interrelated Native American, European, and African semiospheres. This narrative circumference informs Walcott's interrogation of aspects of Caribbean history. The disruptive 1493 *padroado* by Pope Alexander VI that shared the world into East (for Portugal) and West, including the Caribbean (for Spain) is referenced as "Alexander's meridian" (193): "Once the world's green gourd was split like a calabash / by Pope Alexander's decree" (191). This division sanctions colonialism and other acts that ultimately occasion the transformation of such a "natural" place as Iounalao to an artificial tourists' haven named Hawannorra, "the gold sea / flat as a credit-card, / extending its line / to a beach that now looked just like everywhere else, / Greece or Hawaii" (229).

In between this reconstructed transformation, *Omeros* examines the refiguration of the Caribbean by forces such as exploration, conquest, slavery, and tourism. The erosion of memory by slavery figures in the scene where Achille's father, Afolabe, asks him the meaning of "Achille," with the explanation that he no longer remembered the name that he gave him "many years ago." Achille replies that he had also forgotten. Both the passage of time and the new reality imposed on the slaves have contributed to this amnesia: "Everything was forgotten. You also. I do not know. / The deaf sea has changed around every name that you gave / us; trees, men, we yearn for a sound that is missing" (137). That "deaf sea" void has been intensified by acts including the imposition of new names, with the apparent purpose of recharacterizing the slaves' identity as individuals. John Figueroa notes a practice by Caribbean slave masters "of giving slaves grand names: Pompey, Phoebe, Chloe and Caesar" (212). The instantiation of this practice in *Omeros* may be both a historical reference and a revision of its underlying assumption in that many of the characters in the poem actually live individuated or differentiated In Figueroa's thinking, these acts of renaming, by slave masters, privileges "feats performed not least of all in the European wars which then took place in the Caribbean" (212). In addition, such acts of renaming could indicate a measure of narcissism by slave masters who thus make themselves not just masters of African slaves with "incomprehensible" names but masters simultaneously of reinvented legendary or iconic figures.

The second focal experience in *Omeros* is the fate of various Native American tribes as a result of the actions of invaders and colonizers. This part of the narrative is sometimes emphasized by systemic similarities. For instance, the "Aruacs / falling to the muskets of the Conquistador" (162) has its structural correspondence in "the ice-cream paradise / of the American dream, like the Sioux in the snow" (175). Both images address the decimation of the native population by Spanish conquistadores and the suppression of the Sioux (in the United States) by white colonialists at Wounded Knee. The figure of Catherine Weldon appears as a historical negotiator of the differences between white and Native American worldviews. But Weldon's mission is a depressing one in the context of the poem, hence her attempt at the substitution of grief or pain: "When one grief afflicts us we choose a sharper grief / in hope that enormity will ease affliction, / so Catherine Weldon rose in high relief" (181).

The sociopolitical history of the conquerors of the Caribbean—including the "implacable Caesars" and "Melville's Bible"—is the third main focus of *Omeros*. This aspect of the narrative centers around Major Plunkett and his wife, Maud. Walcott's vision of history is evident in the observation that "the furthest exclamations / of History are written by a flag of smoke, / from Carthage, from Pompeii, from the burial mound / of antipodal Troy. Midden built on midden" (99). An example of this "flag of smoke" is a metonymic image of the Caribbean remains of imperial France as "two brass regimental buttons" (99). Another example is the image evoked by the contents of Major Plunkett's tea-chest: "Provinces, Protectorates, Colonies, Dominions, / Governor-Generals, black knights, ostrich-plumed Viceroys, / deserts, jungles, hill-stations, all an empire's zones, / lay spilled from a small tea-chest" (261). This sort of perspective was obviously not a significant aspect of the imperial logic that explains the heedless battles for fragments of the Caribbean. Those battles, though over, left behind some continuing conflicts. For instance, Major Plunkett does not blame the war—he in fact perceives it "like original sin," even with an "old wound in his head"—but he is drawn to the "natural" world of the Caribbean, which he has discovered to be therapeutic:

England seemed to him merely the place of his birth.
How odd to prefer, over its pastoral sites—
Reasonable leaves shading reasonable earth—

The loud-mouthed forests on their illiterate heights,
these springs speaking a dialect that cooled his mind
more than pastures with castles! To prefer the hush

of a hazed Atlantic worried by the salt wind!
Others could read it as going 'back to the bush,'
but harbour after crescent harbour closed his wound.
(61)

The three main experiences that constitute the interconnected foci of *Omeros* reflect the history of the Caribbean. The relative absence of Native Americans is telling both as a historical indicator of their extermination and as a semiotic prefiguration of the fate (physical or spiritual decimation) that the blacks have to fight against. The narrative of these three main experiences runs through seven "books" or sections. Collectively and cumulatively, the focal orientation and progression of *Omeros* highlight the necessity for intercultural healing.

Seven Seas, a single character who is capable of plural or multiple signification, points in this direction of intercultural healing or cross-cultural reimagination. Although he is blind, the fluidity of this character is such that he can defy or transcend time and space to appear in unlikely places. He is also able to interpret events in an insightful manner, such as his explanation of Achille's "voyage" before his return. Seven Seas embodies the idea of a reinvention or a kineticization of culturally static meanings. He is both the Walcott who has "no nation but the imagination" and, arguably, the blind Milton that authored *Paradise Lost*. Right from his "The Voice of St. Lucia," his first published poem, which he describes as "Miltonic" (Plimpton 275), Walcott had found Milton interesting. He saw himself at the age of nineteen as "legitimately prolonging the 'mighty line' of Marlowe and Milton" (275). He does so in *Omeros* by expanding the literary epic beyond the theological confines of Milton's *Paradise Lost*. Milton's Christian frame broadens into Walcott's inclusive spirituality. In a sense, Seven Seas is at the center of this and other intersections in *Omeros*. He possibly signals an alternative Caribbean history as well as prefigures the affective healing toward which the poem's narrative trajectory purposely progresses.

The healing in *Omeros*—of Philoctete's wound specifically—is finally accomplished by Ma Kilman, the "obeah-woman" who interestingly is also a communicant. Walcott's presentation of the ants that aid the healing by lending their "language" to the healer as the "ancestors of Achille" (*Omeros* 239) possibly refers to the 1519–1521 ant invasion in the Caribbean (Benítez-Rojo 91). Ma Kilman's "apotheosis" (*Omeros* 243) commences with her removal of her church dress:

Ma Kilman unpinned the black, red-berried

straw-hat with its false beads, lifted the press
of the henna wig, made of horsehair, from the mark
on her forehead. Carefully, she set both aside

on the coiled green follicles of moss in the dark
wood. Her hair sprung free as the moss. Ants scurried
through the wiry curls, barring, then passing each other

the same message with scribbling fingers and forehead
touching forehead. Ma Kilman bent hers forward,
and as her lips moved with the ants, her mossed skull heard

the ants talking the language of her great-grandmother,
the gossip of a distant market, and she understood,
the way we follow our thoughts with any language,

why the ants sent her the message to come to the wood
festering for centuries, reeked with corrupted blood,
where the wound of the flower, its gangrene, its rage

seeped the pustular drops instead of sunlit dew
into the skull, the brain of the earth, in the mind
ashamed of its flesh, its hair
(243–44)

She receives the communication of the ants in the church but eventually follows "the vine / of the generations of silent black workers" (244) into the woods. The potency of nature, previously evidenced by Major Plunkett's Caribbean "salvation," is again suggested. Notably, the ants invoke a "distant market" of memories, thus bridging the spatiotemporal difference between the Africa of a previous era and the modern Caribbean.

The idea of bridging or of spatiotemporal transcendence is a key part of the healing in *Omeros*. As in other parts of the poem, this bridging also involves the intersection of history and myth—a relationship that Ted Williams describes as "at once mutually constitutive and radically nullifying. One may not, in other words, simply choose between the opposed meanings of history and mythology in the poem, as the logic underwriting one mode of representation always implies the logic underwriting the other" (277). The role of the ants may also be part of the poem's suggestion—already discernible in its characterization—that the reinvention of meaning or values is not necessarily dependent (only) on extraordinary persons or deeds.

The healing has profound psychological consequences including the metaphorical uprighting of the "curled heads" in *Omeros* (37) with the infusion of positive energy: "Feel the shame, the self-hate / draining from all our bodies" (245). The existential dynamics have changed. Philoctete has been transformed into a new man (or Adam); he is given an Edenic bath by Ma Kilman. "So she threw Adam a towel. / And the yard was Eden. And its light the first day's" (248). The "yard" images the communal structure of social life in the Caribbean. So, Philoctete's healing signifies communal kinesis or redemption. Consequent on the healing, a new dynamism is infused into the narrative as is illustrated by Achille's notion of having been unchained and of having become "his own epitaph, / his own resurrection" (273) and the portrayal of Helen's pregnancy as "not only the curved child sailing in her / but Hector's [funeral] mound" (275). In these two examples, *Omeros* fuses two different or contrastive signs—repression and liberation, life and death—into a new "I" that registers as a plural singularity. This unity-in-diversity reflects the vision of a New World through fusion and distillation (or synthesis) that is an important aspect of Walcott's postcolonial globalization. This vision is not of an already perfected world or an aspiration toward stasis but of a work in progress or an ongoing refiguration characterized by healing and kinesis.

Works Cited

Benítez-Rojo, Antonio. *The Repeating Island: The Caribbean and the Postmodern Perspective*. Trans. James E. Maraniss. Durham: Duke UP, 1992.

Burnett, Paula. *Derek Walcott: Politics and Poetics*. Gainesville: UP of Florida, 2000.

Cudjoe, Selwyn R. *Resistance and Caribbean Literature*. Athens: Ohio UP, 1980.

Dathorne, O. R. *Dark Ancestor: The Literature of the Black Man in the Caribbean*. Baton Rouge: Louisiana State UP, 1981.

Farrier, David. "Charting the 'Amnesiac Atlantic': Chiastic Cartography and Caribbean Epic in Derek Walcott's *Omeros*." *Journal of Commonwealth Literature* 38.1 (Mar. 2003): 23–38.

Fernández, José María Pérez. "Terza Rima, the Sea and History in *Omeros*." *Approaches to the Poetics of Derek Walcott*. Eds. José Luis Martínez-Dueñas Espejo and José María Pérez Fernández. Lewiston: Mellen, 2001. 53–79.

Figueroa, John. "Omeros." *The Art of Derek Walcott*. Ed. Stewart Brown. Chester Springs, PA: Dufour, 1991.

Hamner, Robert D. *Epic of the Dispossessed: Derek Walcott's* Omeros. Columbia: U of Missouri P, 1997.

Homer. *The Iliad*. Trans. Robert Fagles. New York: Penguin, 1990.

Irwin, John T. *American Hieroglyphics: The Symbol of the Egyptian Hieroglyphics in the American Renaissance*. New Haven, CT: Yale UP, 1980.

King, Bruce. *Derek Walcott: A Caribbean Life*. New York: Oxford UP, 2000.

Lima, Clara Rosa de. "Walcott: Painting and the Shadow of Van Gogh." *The Art of Derek Walcott*. Ed. Stewart Brown. Chester Springs, PA: Dufour, 1991.

Lucan. *Pharsalia*. Trans. Jane Wilson Joyce. Ithaca, NY: Cornell UP, 1993.

Naipaul, V. S. *The Middle Passage: Impressions of Five Societies—British, French, and Dutch—in the West Indies and South America*. New York: Vintage, 1981.

Plimpton, George, ed. *Writers at Work:* The Paris Review *Interviews*. 8th series. New York: Penguin, 1988.

Virgil. *The Aeneid*. Trans. Robert Fitzgerald. New York: Vintage, 1983.

Walcott, Derek. *Collected Poems 1948–1984*. New York: Farrar, 1986.

_____. *Omeros*. London: Faber, 1990.

_____. *What the Twilight Says: Essays*. New York: Farrar, 1999.

Williams, Ted. "Truth and Representation: The Confrontation of History and Mythology in *Omeros*." *Callaloo: A Journal of African Diaspora Arts and Letters* 24.1 (2001): 276–286.

Zoppi, Isabella Maria. "*Omeros*, Derek Walcott and the Contemporary Epic Poem." *Callaloo: A Journal of African American and African Arts and Letters* 22.2 (1999): 509–528.

Representing the Self: Ntozake Shange's *for colored girls who have considered suicide / when the rainbow is enuf*_____

Frank P. Fury

Ntozake Shange's *for colored girls who have considered suicide / when the rainbow is enuf* (1974) is a literary work that is fundamentally concerned with representation. As it is both a theater production—that is, the result of collaboration of playwright, producer, director, stage designers, stagehands, and of course actors—and a sequence of interrelated monologues that compose the very intimate, almost confessional, work of a skilled poet, its very composition is a political statement by its author. If, as one may discern from the nature of these monologues, Shange writes predominantly of the young African American woman's struggle for identity and independence in contemporary America, to frame the play according to traditional dramatic conventions of the Western world (domestic realism, melodrama, mimesis, the well-made play are just some examples) would be to contradict the very nature of the statement Shange attempts to make through her work. At the same time, traditional verse poetry is similarly insufficient to capture Shange's conception of her unique sense of African American female identity, which indeed constitutes both the subject and the structure of *for colored girls.* The need for physical, as well as verbal, expression to realize fully the emotional state that provides the spirit of this play manifests itself in the performative aspects of the work-as-text, and thus itself transcends the status of mere "text."

Following perhaps the lead of Cornel West, who has written extensively of the misrepresentation of identity that plagues the existence of the African American in the United States, Shange depicts the fragmented nature of African American identity not only through the content of the monologues that in essence comprise the play's "script," but also through the very structure and form of the play itself. West has argued that the twin problems of "invisibility and namelessness" are grounded in "blacks' relative lack of power to represent themselves to themselves and others as complex human beings and thereby to contest the bombardment of negative, degrading stereotypes put forward by white-supremacist ideologies" (128). Shange's choice to make her "characters" seven women known only according to the color dresses they wear—brown, red, blue, purple, orange, yellow, and green— seems a dramaturgical literalization of West's critique of Western culture. While none of the characters are named, per se, Shange seems to suggest that the ladies in red, blue, purple, orange, yellow, and green are less fully realized human individuals and more the "versions" or "selves" of the lady in brown, who is struggling toward a reintegration of the self after ostensibly harrowing experiences (abortion, rape, etc.). The lady in brown frames *for colored girls* as she speaks the play's first and last monologue. These references to being "colored" of course align with the title of the piece, and, for Shange, is likely an allusion to the common term "colored folks" that has often been applied derogatorily to African Americans. In ways that demonstrate how discursive practices become intertwined with ideology and power, Shange appropriates potentially harmful language applied in racist contexts and uses such terms to depict the very manner in which subjectivity and reintegration may be achieved.

To continue the discussion of the play's concern with representation—in this case, having a voice and letting that voice be heard—it is worth noting that the play begins with an apt and striking metaphor. The stage directions at the outset of the play are as follows: "*The follow spot picks up the lady in brown. She comes to life and looks around at the other ladies. All of the others are still. She walks over to the lady in red and calls to her. The lady in red makes no response*" (3). The "lady in brown," a central performer/poet of the play, speaks the play's first words:

dark phrases of womanhood
of never havin been a girl
half-notes scattered
without rhythm / no tune
distraught laughter fallin
over a black girl's shoulder
it's funny / it's hysterical
the melody-less-ness of her dance.
don't tell nobody don't tell a soul
she's dancing on beer cans & shingles
this must be the spook house
another song with no singers
lyrics / no voices
& interrupted solos
unseen performances (3)

The feelings of dislocation that a young African American woman feels in contemporary America are akin to a performer whose dance no one sees and whose song no one hears. Shange here projects the problem of female blackness as being *without* audience (again, to use the theater metaphor). To return to West, if the central problem of blackness in contemporary times is not having the means to demonstrate to others that the black individual is a complex being, capable of profound thought and emotion, then if there is no audience to witness such demonstration the protestation becomes worthless. The enterprise of *for colored girls,* then—if we assume that the work has political in addition to personal, creative motivation—concerns infusing *voice* in the African American female subject and staging it.

"Voice" has long been a central trope of critical theory, particularly in its application toward those who have been marginalized by social and political oppression. Michel Foucault, for instance, argued that subjectivity—the concept that the individual self possesses agency to act, speak—is grounded in and made possible via discursive production.

That is, for an individual to have subjectivity, it must be processed through language. Shange's *for colored girls*—in both its content and its form—is an *enactment* of subjectivity via discursive production. It is therefore important to recognize the generic form Shange employs. She refers to *for colored girls* as a "choreopoem," quite clearly combining the terms *choreography* (dance) and *poem* (verse). The invention of the genre was very much an intentional and revolutionary conception of Shange's, though certainly not altogether novel. Dance had been an integral component of drama for thousands of years with its roots in the ancient Greek theater. The Greek dithyrambs were ecstatic, ritualistic performances of song and dance that gave honor to the gods, most specifically Dionysus, the god of fertility, among other things. The dithyrambic production was collective, communal; it both celebrated the idea of civilization and in a very real sense—in the mind of the Greek citizens who participated in it and attended it—allowed civilization to continue. Indeed, the theater, in its most ancient sense, was the site at which humankind could express creatively that it understood the universe in life-affirming manner, and song and dance were the media the people used to pledge devotion to the gods to ensure a good harvest (i.e., the continuation of life).

Shange's project retains the spirit of life affirmation and civilization, especially through song and dance, but in very different ways. Rather than, as the ancient Greeks had, engage in primitive, ritualistic acts in order to ensure the society's subsistence by satisfying the basic needs of humankind (e.g., food via the harvest), Shange is interested in a different sort of survival. In her preface to a collection of her plays, *Three Pieces,* she writes:

> the fact that we are an interdisciplinary culture/ that we understand more
> than verbal communication/ lays a weight on afro-american writers that
> few others are lucky enough to have been born into. we can use with some
> skill virtually all our physical senses/ as writers committed to bringing the

world as we remember it/ imagine it/ & know it to be to the stage/ we must use everything we've got. (x)

Shange use of the collective pronoun *we* refers to all African Americans who would consider expressing their creativity in innovative, yet rooted and organic, ways. In essence, Shange identifies a sort of psychic survival for African Americans: the need for the African American artist to turn attention inward and, in her estimation, to use "everything we've got" reflects her recognition that the survival not only of the African American individual was at stake but also of the African American community. In *for colored girls* she depicts the struggle for survival specifically through African American women banding together in support of the shamed or somehow needful member of the community.

Shange's "choreopoem," then, in its adoption of that invented generic term and specifically through the prefix *choreo* (at once suggesting both "chorus" and "dance"), builds upon and indeed transcends the tradition practiced from antiquity of the communally directed exercise of a people's collective will. And just as theater was used by the ancient Greeks as a way to channel the gods and commune with divinity, Shange also conceived of theater in terms of its capacity to bring about metaphysical redemption. In her preface to the published edition of *for colored girls*, she states that the project began in California in very late 1974 as a series of readings, the "force" of which was "to become evident as we directed our energies toward clarifying our lives—& the lives of our mothers, daughters, & grandmothers" (x). Moreover, in judging the content of the play, it is also clear that Shange understood the nature of the problem of her existence and her aesthetic project in universal terms and attempted to address them as such dramatically. The lady in yellow, in a monologue Shange entitles "no more love poems #4," states: "but bein alive & bein a woman & bein colored is a metaphysical / dilemma" (45). The line recalls Harlem Renaissance poet Countee Cullen's oft-anthologized poem "Yet Do I Marvel," which ends with the well-known couplet "Yet do I marvel at this curious thing: / To make a poet black and bid him sing!" Cullen finds incongruity in his status as "black poet" and suggests his existence—his personal store of experiences—has been contradictory to that which is capable of engendering beauty through words. Though Shange's lady in yellow does not include "poet" in her catalog of identity markers, *for colored girls* demonstrates that subjectivity—i.e., individual identity and hence survival—for the African American woman is also dependent upon one's capacity to sublimate personal experience aesthetically into poetry.

What is remarkable about the contrast between the way in which Cullen, some fifty years before, and Shange similarly express a common concern is the generic format each uses to do so. Cullen was known for his adherence to traditional—and arguably patriarchally rooted—poetic forms, most notably the sonnet, of which "Yet Do I Marvel" is a prime example. Though Shange herself was operating within a dramatic tradition that was by centuries older than the sonnet form, through her idiosyncratic and vernacular use of language and in her innovative dramaturgical approaches, she was able to depict through the form and structure she uses in *for colored girls* the very nature of the problems of fragmented identity and fractured community she intends to address in her choreopoem. Closely following the lady in yellow's recognition of the "metaphysical dilemma" of being alive, female, and "colored" comes her strong assertion that her spirit is "too ancient to understand the separation of / soul & gender" and that her love is "too delicate to have thrown back on [her] face" (45). The lady in yellow begins to exit the stage after repeating this line, and, as she does, the other ladies of color, who had been previously "frozen" on stage begin to "come to life" and enact a repetition of the lady in yellow's line that each in succession follows but with a replacement of the word "delicate"; the lady in brown's love is too "beautiful," for instance, to have thrown back in her face, while the ladies in purple, blue, orange, red, and green possess love that is too "sanctified," "magic," "saturday nite," "complicated," and "music," respectively, to have thrown back in their faces (46–47). Following this improvisational riff, the lady in yellow returns, and the ladies collectively chant:

> *everyone (but started by the lady in yellow)*
> delicate
> delicate
> delicate
> *everyone (but started by the lady in brown)*
> and beautiful
> and beautiful
> and beautiful
> *everyone (but started by the lady in purple)*
> oh sanctified
> oh sanctified
> oh sanctified (48)

The chant continues in this way until each of the words that the ladies inserted in place of the word "delicate" gets repeated three times, with the exception of "complicated," which is intoned eight times. That the word *complicated* is chanted the most recalls Cornel West's observation that black individuals in the contemporary era are afflicted by a lack of power to represent themselves as "*complex* human beings." Young black women, Shange suggests, are too wonderfully complex to be summarized in just one color.

Shange's invocation of the chant resonates in the conventions of ancient Western drama. *Catharsis*, from the Greek for "purging" or "cleansing," is a concept derived from Aristotle's *Poetics*, in which he theorized that characters onstage, but more so playgoers, would achieve emotional release upon experiencing the horrifying and pitiful effects of a tragedy. The cathartic effect is ultimately liberating, allowing the audience of a particularly harrowing theatrical production to affirm essentially the good in leaving the theater and moving forward constructively with their lives minus the fears that had been purged via the playgoing experience. The chant is thus Shange's confirmation of the cathartic effect communal theater can have, which is evident in the stage directions following the repeating of the word "complicated" eight times: "*The dance reaches a climax and all of the ladies fall out tired, but full of life and togetherness*" (49). It is worth noting again that the title of the poem that includes the "my love is too delicate to have thrown back in my face" intonation is "no more love poems #4," a title that negates one of the oldest and most revered forms of poetic expression: lyric poetry. The title, the chant, and the performance all contribute to Shange's rejection of an implicitly patriarchal—that is, European American—creative tradition that, according to the content of another of her non-love poems—"no more love poems #1"—affords no lyric space for "someone callt / a colored girl an evil woman a bitch or a nag" (42).

True to Shange's poetics and dramaturgy in *for colored girls*, however, her utilization of the chant—an example of her aesthetic movement away from traditional mimetic forms of representation within the "world" of the play—is not simply an appropriation of the communal, life-affirming, and cathartic spirit that infused ancient Greek drama. Such adherence to convention would be antithetical to the purposes of Shange's overtly political theater. Instead, we may view her use of improvisation as indicating a use of jazz forms that, in the footsteps of Langston Hughes, who, during the Harlem Renaissance, used the blues form as a replacement of more conventional poetic forms, amounts to what Houston A. Baker Jr. referred to as the "black aesthetic," encompassing a need to assess a work produced by a black artist from within the accepted parameters of black culture that holds different standards of artistic creation in comparison to more traditional—i.e., white, patriarchal—modes of expression. Jazz was dependent not upon Old World musical cadences or forms, but rather enabled the individual performer to invent as s/he goes. The preceding example from "no more love poems #4" is an apt illustration of Shange's penchant for integrating the opportunity for improvisation into her work, fitting the fluidity of the unique composition of her choreopoem.

The improvisational qualities of *for colored girls* are embedded in the very constitution of Shange's work. In her own preface to the published edition of the play, she writes of the emergent nature of *for colored girls*' stage history:

> I had never imagined not doing *for colored girls*. It waz [*sic*] just my poems, any poems I happened to have. Now I have left the show on Broadway, to write poems, stories, plays, my dreams. *for colored girls* is either too big for my off-off Broadway taste, or too little for my exaggerated sense of freedom, held over from seven years of improvised poetry readings. Or, perhaps, the series has actually finished itself. Poems come on their own time: I am offering these to you as what I've received from this world so far. (xv–xvi)

From these comments alone one perceives that *for colored girls* is always in the process of becoming, even when it is enacted onstage as the ostensible "finished product." This is of course even more evident in the performative elements of the work. A pertinent illustration of the text-as-performance is the "Sechita" episode. Sechita is not a character necessarily in the choreopoem, but rather a persona—or more accurately a sub-narrative of the play—acted out by the lady in green. The lady in purple enters the stage alone, amid "*soft deep music*" with "*voices calling 'Sechita' com[ing] from the wings and volms*" (23), and prefaces the Sechita tale with a very story-book quality scene-setting:

> once there were quadroon balls / elegance in st. louis / laced
> mulattoes / gamblin down the mississippi / to memphis / new
> orleans n okra crepes near the bayou / where the poor white trash
> wd [*sic*] sing / moanin / strange / liquid tones / thru the swamps / (23)

At this point the lady in green joins the lady in purple on stage; "*she is Sechita*," the stage directions inform us, "*and for the rest of the poem dances out Sechita's life"* (23). If Sechita's "life" exists for the audience in the forty-four lines of poetry Shange devotes to her, then one imagines the need for a virtuoso physical performer to enact it. Consider the challenge for a performer of embodying—quite literally—the following: "sechita / goddess / the recordin of history / spread crimson oil on her cheeks / waxed her eyebrows / n unconsciously slugged the last hard whiskey in the glass" (24); or "she made her face like nefertiti / approachin her own tomb" (25); or the perhaps the ultimate performing challenge:

> sechita / goddess / of love / egypt /
> 2nd millennium / performin the rites / the conjuring of men /
> conjuring the spirit / in natchez / the mississippi spewed
> a heavy fume of barely movin waters / sechita's legs slashed
> furiously thru the cracker nite / & gold pieces hittin the
> makeshift stage / her thighs / they were aimin coins tween her
> thighs / sechita / egypt / goddess / harmony / kicked viciously
> thru the nite / catchin stars tween her toes. (25)

That a playwright such as Shange would trust a performer to enact the preceding passages according to individual interpretation is a testament to her unique conception of theater both as a fluid process—a new, emergent theater with the conception of the play-as-becoming—but also as a true collaboration in every sense of the word. In order for a play such as *for colored girls* to achieve the sort of communal catharsis Shange suggests is necessary for a reintegration of spirit and identity, not only must the content of the play—its language, images—be consistent with such a project, but the very production of the work itself must cohere with such assumptions of the nature of theater.

Shange's privileging of innovation, interpretation, and improvisation registers her beliefs in a new sort of dramaturgy that in effect resists the suffocating traditions of a long male-dominated theatrical scene. Women playwrights had certainly been writing and producing plays for decades prior to the staging of *for colored girls* in 1974. Consider just a few examples: Susan Glaspell in the 1910s and 1920s in her participation with the Provincetown Players; Lillian Hellman and her plays of the Depression and post–Depression eras; and Lorraine Hansberry with her ground-breaking treatment of race and social class in *A Raisin in the Sun* in 1959. These women and many others staged popularly and critically successful plays, but none did so within the auspices of an entirely newly conceived theater that Shange was refashioning in the early 1970s. The need for the various avant-garde theater movements of the 1960s—with which Shange could herself claim kinship—arose from a sense of the limitations of theatrical conventions that implicitly propagated a patriarchal agenda. We may return to the notion of a "politics of representation" to appreciate more properly the manner in which playwrights of color and women playwrights in the late 1960s and early 1970s strove to reimagine what theater could do. It was not sufficient to change the message, in other words. Playwrights who truly sought to make a statement must change the rules of the game. That is, they had to reconceive how a play could be brought to the stage, and Shange was a major player in this new game.

In this sense, Shange's dramaturgy—the ways in which she sought to "represent" a new piece for performance on the stage—is overtly oppositional. That she chose theater as the medium for her aesthetic portrayals of the struggles for identity of young black females is consistent with the notion of theater as a public sphere and the need to project resistance not in a private—i.e., purely poetical—sphere but where others (an audience) may witness the change. Because of its history of male domination, the theater of the Western tradition had become a socially constructed space where gender and racial assumptions were not so much explicitly stated but rather subtly coded and embedded over time. The forms of protest theater that arose in the 1960s were aimed at deconstructing such long-entrenched assumptions that informed the conventions of American theater. In this sense, theater for Shange became a locus for resistance and opposition. To truly *represent* the "metaphysical dilemma" noted earlier, the *form* of representation had to align with the *content*. Thus, for Shange, as Chris Barker observes, "representations [were] always matters of contestation" (414).

Many have remarked on the more blatantly confrontational elements of Shange's theater. Shange had positioned her own work within a theoretical framework that envisions and utilizes a poetics of resistance. Indeed, Shange herself acknowledged that her work has "combat breath," a term she borrows from the postcolonial theorist and cultural critic Frantz Fanon. In *Three Pieces*, Shange writes of Fanon's influence on her work and personal politics:

> in everything i have ever written & everything i hope to write i have made use of what Frantz Fanon calls "combat breath." although Fanon was referring to francophone colonies, the schema he draws is sadly familiar: "there is no occupation of territory, on the other hand, and independence of persons on the other. It is the country as a whole, its history, its daily pulsation that are contested, disfigured, in the hope of final destruction. Under this condition, the individual's breathing is an observed, an occupied breathing. It is a combat breathing." (xii)

For the poet who breathes combat, representation—and indeed *self*-representation—is of crucial importance. As Deepika Bahri notes, "The absence or unavailability or the perspectives of women, racial minorities, and marginalized cultures," or this "lack of representation," as she terms it, is most evident in how "those 'other' to the dominant discourse have no voice or say in their portrayal; they are consigned to be 'spoken for' by those who command the authority and means to speak" (204). Though the very notion itself of representation has been critiqued by other postcolonial theorists—most famously by Edward Said, for instance, who reconceives representation as a "re-presence" (21)—it nonetheless remains a locus of power. Representation can be said to have double meaning for Shange: it involves both the "presentation" of a statement through communal participation—i.e., "staging" one's beliefs in the public sphere—and a "standing in" or a speaking for those whose voice has been silenced.

Each staging of *for colored girls* can thus be seen as a political act, a bold and charged *enactment* of beliefs in a more malleable and receptive theater that provides a forum for voices of all classes, races, and backgrounds to be heard. Indeed, this enactment of resistance and opposition can be seen not just in the genre and the form of the work, but also in the images, language, and allusions in the poetry of the piece. The monologue in the choreopoem that best registers the poet's stance of (political) struggle toward freedom of identity is "toussaint." The "toussaint" monologue is performed by the lady in brown, who recounts becoming fascinated by the figure of François-Dominique Toussaint L'Ouverture, the military leader of the Haitian Revolution, which took place during the last decade of the eighteenth century. L'Ouverture appears to be a figure of immense power for the young lady in brown, who confesses that she "found" him in "the ADULT READING ROOM" (26) of the library into which the children were not supposed to wander. Toussaint becomes many things to the young lady in brown. Consider the impact he has on her: He was "a blk man a negro" and "didnt low no white man to tell him nothing" (26); he was "the beginnin uv reality for [her]" (26); he became her "secret lover at the age of 8" (27); finally, and perhaps most significantly,

> TOUSSAINT
> waz layin in bed wit me next to raggedy ann
> the night i decided to run away from my
>   integrated home
>   integrated street
>   integrated school (27)

That the young lady in brown links Toussaint to her "integrated" existence bespeaks the irony of his significance to her. He exists powerfully as a model of *segregation*, as one who would not be subject to the oppression of patriarchy and who, for the lady in brown, "dont take no stuff from no white folks / & they gotta country all they own / & there aint no slaves" (30). The irony lies in the segregation that the lady in brown observes in the figure of Toussaint leads to an *integration* of a much different sort: "i am TOUSSAINT JONES" (30) she declares, and, though she feels his presence "sorta leave me" by the end of the monologue, she nonetheless has borrowed and appropriated his spirit of brave resistance and struggle: "toussaint jones waz awright wit me / no tellin what all spirits we cd move" (30). Survival—both in the individual and in the communal sense—requires self-identification and, at times, reidentification.

As important as the prefix "*choreo-*" is to the aesthetics of *for colored girls*—that is, as indicator of its performative, interpretive, improvisational, and generally non-verbal elements—of equal importance is its language. In published editions of *for colored girls*, the "table of contents" is an index of "poems by title," beginning with the first performed poem of the piece—the aptly titled "dark phrases"—and ending with the healing "a laying on of hands." That she organizes the play by its succession of poems stresses the choreopoem's attention to its own discursive practices, which though it might seem at odds with its more communal, ritualistic qualities, emphasizes the very personal, intimate nature of Shange's work. It also alerts the reader to the reality of this play: that though there are numerous "lady" characters in the play, from a certain viewpoint we may see them as various "versions" of the lady in brown who, as suggested in the color Shange ascribes her, is the central and indeed the only "character" in the play. The "ladies of the rainbow" are symbolic in this reading. Consider again that the lady in brown was the speaker of the "toussaint" poem, one of the choreopoem's monologues that deals intimately with the young African American woman's groping toward an articulation of identity. Here we find again a preeminence in the lady in brown's status in the choreopoem, a focal point for the reintegration through which the women of color may unite. They constitute, perhaps, elements of the lady in brown's personality and makeup so that by the play's end the various distinctive elements of her identity—though fragmented and unresponsive at the beginning of the play—have now collectively exorcised the pain and grief toward a harmony that allows for integration—integrated within itself and within its community through the supportive network of other African American women. Evidence for this lies in how Shange has the lady in brown begin and end the play; whereas in the opening monologue-poem she speaks of "the dark phrases of womanhood" and of having "no voice(s)" (3), by the play's end she victoriously asserts, "& this is for colored girls who have considered suicide / but are movin to the ends of their own rainbows" (64). Both the initial moments of the physical and verbal action of the play depict a lack or nothingness that makes for the primary "subject" of the enterprise. Shange forces her central lady—the lady who comprises the other ladies of color in the play—to speak her mind before any of the other ladies participate. The implication here is that there is the promise of renewal and reconstitution in the exploration of the divided self and dislocated existence with the hope that one may recognize the assistance of community in defining the self. One must still achieve that individually, however.

It is no surprise that identity—the representation of the individual self to the world as one may describe it—was of crucial concern to a woman who herself demonstrated the importance of identity through her own renaming. Born Paulette Williams in Trenton, New Jersey, Shange herself fittingly was a product of the very same sort of recoding of identity—empowering the self through language and shared experience—in adopting the name *Ntozake,* translated as "she who comes with her own things," *Shange*, translated as "walks with lions." The word *things* from the translation echoes the word *stuff* in the humorous yet poignant monologue from *for colored girls* entitled "somebody almost walked off wid alla my stuff." Though "stuff" remains vague in everyday usage as a catch-all term for items, things, or just amorphous matter, Shange invests the word with metaphysical resonance—the sort of metaphysical resonance necessary to help cope with the "metaphysical dilemma" of which the lady in yellow speaks in "no more love poems #4." In "somebody almost walked off wid alla my stuff," consistent with the ever-changing paradigms and perspectives of *for colored girls*, the lady in green turns the spotlight on the choreopoem's author:

> honest to god / somebody almost run off wit alla my stuff /
> & i didnt bring anythin but the kick & sway of it
> the perfect ass for my man & none of it is theirs
> this is mine / ntozake 'her own things' / that's my name /
> now give me my stuff (50)

Thus the choreopoem may ultimately belong to the theater, the performances may belong to the actors, and the inspiration for the work may belong to the black community, but the words—in all their agrammatical, slangy, and sometimes abbreviated glory—are all the property of the playwright of *for colored girls who have considered suicide / when the rainbow is enuf*. Ntozake Shange, in a moment of literary revolution, found a new mode of representation in her "choreopoem," delivering her art, herself, and her community to the stage as a representation of her own unique vision of the world.

Works Cited

Bahri, Deepika. "Feminism in/and Postcolonialism." *The Cambridge Companion to Postcolonial Literary Studies*. Ed. Neil Lazarus. Cambridge, Eng.: Cambridge UP, 2004. 199–220.

Barker, Chris. *Cultural Studies: Theory and Practice*. 2nd ed. Thousand Oaks, CA: Sage, 2003.

Said, Edward. *Orientalism*. New York: Pantheon, 1978.

Shange, Ntozake. *for colored girls who have considered suicide / when the rainbow is enuf*. New York: Scribner, 1997.

_____. *Three Pieces: Spell #7, A Photograph: Lovers in Motion, Boogie Woogie Landscapes*. New York: Penguin, 1982.

West, Cornel. *The Cornel West Reader*. New York: Basic, 2000.

The Limits of Culture and Community in Monica Ali's *Brick Lane*

Dave Gunning

Even before its publication in June 2003, Monica Ali's *Brick Lane* was considered a major work. On the basis of the manuscript alone, the author was named by the literary magazine *Granta* as one of the twenty best young British writers, in the third installment of their list that appears once every ten years and aims to identify writers who will go on to shape British literature. Also on the list were Zadie Smith and Hari Kunzru, signaling that the *Granta* editors believed these Oxbridge-educated, mixed-race writers could make a vital contribution to British writing. Perhaps the editors were also echoing a major literary concern of the era: there was the need to understand the nature of cultural encounter in a Britain where the aftermaths of migration from South Asia, the Caribbean, and elsewhere had led to a thoroughly multicultural nation despite the fact that the relationships between cultural communities were often disharmonious.

Ali was born in Dhaka, Bangladesh, in 1967 to a white English mother and a father from a well-off Bengali family. She migrated to Britain at a young age and was mostly raised in Bolton, a town in the north of England. She later attended Wadham College, Oxford University, and has lived all her adult life in London. Her debut novel, *Brick Lane*, similarly deals with Bengali immigrants in London but who come from a very different background. Brick Lane is a major street in East London and borders some of the poorest neighborhoods in the city. For centuries, this area has been a key site for the settlement of immigrants, and by the late twentieth century it had become synonymous with South Asian culture, especially that of migrants from the Sylhet region of Bangladesh. Ali had initially wanted to call her novel *Seven Seas and Thirteen Rivers,* but her publisher, Doubleday, suggested that *Brick Lane* had "lots of relevant connotations" (Maxey 229). Again, even before publication, the novel was positioned as making an important statement about the nature of British–Asian culture, perhaps beyond what its contents might actually provide.

Although a few key events do take place in Brick Lane, most of the narrative is set in the tower blocks of the fictional Dogwood Estate in nearby Tower Hamlets. At the center of the novel is Nazneen, who is just eighteen when she marries the much older Chanu Ahmed and is taken from her small village in rural Bangladesh to live with him in London. Chanu had emigrated to London a decade earlier, and he is overweight and ugly and is increasingly revealed as inept. A graduate of Dhaka University, he has struggled to establish himself successfully in Britain and has been working at a job with few prospects while always believing he deserves better. Chanu never manages to achieve his promotion and eventually quits, taking on a series of doomed jobs before eventually becoming a taxi driver. The novel is set during two key periods of Nazneen's life. The first, from 1985 to 1988, details her initial impressions of life in London and comes to an end with the birth and tragic death of the couple's first child, Raqib. Her story resumes in 2001 when she is the mother of two daughters, Shahana and Bibi. The profound isolation she experienced in the earlier section at first seems to have continued into the later period, but her life radically changes when she takes on home sewing work and begins an affair with Karim, the young British-born Bengali who brings the garments for her to work on. Karim is also involved in local political organization among the Bengali community, which further brings Nazneen into contact with a broader community. The novel ends with Chanu deciding to take his family back to Bangladesh but Nazneen instead choosing to stay in London with her daughters. She also chooses to end her relationship with Karim and begins to work in a garment-manufacturing cooperative with other Bengali women from Dogwood.

Perhaps not surprisingly, given the hype that accompanied *Brick Lane*'s publication, its reception was very lively. Ruth Maxey has documented how much of the initial reaction to the novel was "polarised" between the praise given to it by a mostly-white mainstream literary community who applauded its ability to represent a world rarely presented in British writing, and the negative response often coming from South Asians who felt the text was simplistic and inaccurate and often offensive to the communities it represented. A community organization called the Greater Sylhet Welfare and Development Council was particularly inflamed by it, feeling that it pandered to negative stereotypes of the area and its inhabitants and publicly calling for the novel's 2007 adaptation into a film to be called off.

Recent studies of what was at stake in this divided reception have examined the issue of who had the right to lay claim to representing the Brick Lane area. Both sides of the debate have called attention to significant contemporary arguments about cultural ownership and the status of minority communities among their participants and as instrumental elements within an often triumphalist or celebratory mainstream British multiculturalism (Ahmed; Brouillette). This focus on the novel's reception does not always allow for full exploration of the text's own consideration of culture and community. At the heart of *Brick Lane* is the question of how an individual thousands of miles from where she was raised might find a sense of belonging when "culture" and "community" are not only contested terms, but often fail to offer any practical guidance as to how one should live and understand one's place and that of one's family.

Rehana Ahmed sees the claustrophobic presence of the novel's Dogwood Estate as contributing to its inability to offer a productive sense of the predicaments of East London Bengalis, and she argues that "the extent of [this] territorialisation . . . forces a break between community and context, fragmenting the former and blurring the socio-spatial relations within which it is embedded." However, Ali's close focus on Nazneen's perceptions of herself and her environment seem precisely intended to show that this fragmentation of community is exactly the experience of a young woman placed within the profoundly alienating space of this estate. Nazneen feels herself to be without grounding and has little opportunity to understand the deeper currents of British political and economic culture that have led to her to where she is. It is with this notably partial knowledge that she must struggle to eke out some form of survival and flourish.

Nazneen in 1985 is confined within her small flat, alone and separate from the world. She hears through the walls the sounds of neighboring flats but is disturbed by the realization that this is the first time in her life that she has ever truly been alone (Ali 18). The noises serve only to reinforce her sense of the walls that divide her from her neighbors. The only contact she has with English society is in the form of the Tattoo Lady, who sits all day smoking and drinking in a window opposite Nazneen's own. The Tattoo Lady functions both as a metonym for the life from which Nazneen is excluded—the young bride imagines walking over with a friendly gift of samosas or bhajis, but realizes the only English she knows is "sorry" and "thank you" and that this is impossible (13–14)—but also increasingly as a mirror for Nazneen herself, who is frustratingly passive and immobile: "How can she just sit and sit? What is she waiting for? What is there to see?" (70)

For Chanu, however, the flat is a space to assert his belonging whether through the collection and display of his often-meaningless certificates of qualification or in his huge collection of tired and broken furniture. He tries to make this bleak space into a home through possessions that speak of his ownership of British space. Nazneen too is intended to serve as a component of his identity as a successful migrant. A "totally unspoilt" village girl (17), she is positioned as a link back to the culture he has left behind, but, given Nazneen's extreme solitude, it is unclear whether she can be said to possess any culture at all at this point in her life.

To make some mark against the dominance Chanu exercises over her life, Nazneen begins a campaign of "small insurrections" such as not washing his socks and slipping with the razor when cutting his corns (50). Most often, however, she rejects the confines that Chanu has placed her by taking an imaginary retreat to Bangladesh either through her memories of her village childhood in Gouripur or, more directly, through the letters she receives from her sister Hasina. It becomes increasingly clear that the memories rarely offer much that is useful to her. Jane Hiddleston has convincingly argued that the stereotypes that proliferate in many of the early accounts of Bangladesh seem to show Ali's unsettling, straightforward representation (61–62). It may be that such recourse to stock images is intended to show the unrealistic nostalgia with which Nazneen imagines the place of her birth. However, these reveries increasingly fail to function as nostalgia when instances of brutality and death come to dominate her memory. Hasina's letters also offer little comfort, since tales of her economic and sexual exploitation leave Nazneen worried for her sister and sceptical about the quality of life available in Bangladesh, even if return were possible.

Nazneen attempts to perform small acts of self-assertion such as when she walks westward beyond Brick Lane and into the financial heart of London, but her experience, however, is overwhelmingly marked by fear. For Nazneen, the promise of expressing agency is always tied to the danger of the destruction of what little she has. Indeed, she seems to believe at times that free will can only be exercised in the act of self-destruction. When she reflects on the story of a woman who has fallen from a neighboring tower, she is sure that it was deliberate: "A big jump, feet first and arms wide, eyes wide, silent all the way down and her hair wild and loose, and a big smile on her face because with this single everlasting act she defied everything and everyone" (31). The only way to assert herself, this suggests, is to destroy everything she is; there is no positive alternative imaginable.

The birth of Raqib allows for a respite from Nazneen's loneliness as she is able to withdraw from the strain of failing to connect with the world outside and instead can justify an inward focus on herself and her baby. Even during his illness (which is not named but seems to be meningitis), she retains this comfort of not needing to seek validation within the wider world. Her relationship with Chanu even improves greatly. In a family room at the hospital, she recognizes that this inward focus seems to play out for others in the same way: Other families are described as "refugees," somehow separated from the national and subnational cultures outside and instead like "stateless people, where the rules were unknown and in any case suspended" (97). Raqib's death, however, brings an end to this interlude in Nazneen's maddening isolation.

The time between the baby's death in 1988 and the story's continuation in 2001 is marked by a series of letters from Hasina in Bangladesh. Hasina's story can seem depressingly repetitive: She repeatedly finds reason to hope for a happy outcome to her life, but she is always frustrated and instead forced into situations of greater misery. As stated above, this has the effect of offering a bleak counterpoint of life in Bangladesh set against that in London, but it also serves a further function. Unlike Nazneen, for whom imagining the possibility of agency is always accompanied by the foreboding of disaster, Hasina never gives up hoping or trying to improve her life. In an early letter she describes a disabled beggar, *"like a big big foot press on her back,"* who nevertheless struggles to assert her freedom. Hasina's reaction can seem surprising: *"I like to watch this woman. She have courage"* (46–47), but the sense of needing to act for oneself even against seemingly insurmountable obstacles is significant for Hasina, and eventually for Nazneen also.

When Nazneen's story resumes, the central focus is the new sense of freedom that she finds in her relationship with Karim. While the loving attention with which he is described suggests a strong physical attraction, it is noticeable that his "Western" dress of tight jeans and rolled-up shirtsleeves seems as much a focus of desire as the young body within it. Karim's Britishness carries a powerful erotic charge for Nazneen. Her discovery that "when he spoke in Bengali he stammered [while] in English, he found his tongue and it gave him no trouble" particularly intrigues her (173). She understands this as a lack of confidence in the traditional community and that he instead possesses a strong sense of belonging to London. Through him, she might gain some of this confidence and ability to claim space.

Karim's role as middleman, bringing the garments for Nazneen to sew, is never seen as making him part of a system that exploits the cheap labor of Bengali housewives because her meager earnings are nonetheless hugely significant in bolstering her sense of independence. It is his life outside work, though, that has a greater effect on how she construes her place within Britain. Karim invites Nazneen to a public meeting where he hopes the Muslims of Dogwood Estate will begin to rally together against racism and in service of communal pride. The development of this group, which is soon named the Bengal Tigers, is important to much of the second half of the novel. For Sara Upstone, the activities of the Tigers and Nazneen's involvement with them provide a meaningful frame through which the whole novel can be read. Once we conceive of protest and the need to claim public space as central to Nazneen's development, Upstone argues, the full import of the novel's positive message can be understood. Upstone recognizes that the representation of protest in *Brick Lane* can often seem critical, but she insists that this is nonetheless balanced by an implication that the act of protest is an indispensible starting point: "For Ali, protest is only the *first* marker of an assertion of citizenship that must be concluded on a more quotidian, commonplace basis" (179). Other critics are far less certain that Ali retains any space for the necessity of protest, instead suggesting that the focus on Nazneen's need for individuality eviscerates any sense of the desirability of mass protest, a decision that can be particularly harmful given that "because of their subordinate position in British society, working-class British Bangladeshis are more likely to draw strength and pride from identification *as part of a group*" (Ahmed 37).

The novel offers several ways in which migrants can come to a "political" understanding of their situation within Britain. Chanu's first views of Britain speak of a stereotypical vision of the former colonial subject coming to claim the treasures of the mother country as his own: "I thought there would be a red carpet laid out for me. I was going to join the Civil Service and become Private Secretary to the Prime Minister" (26). He discovers quickly that there is little such welcome for him. Nevertheless, he continues for a while to believe that this mimicry of what he considers high English culture will eventually guarantee him success and promotion in favor of his white English colleagues: "I don't have anything to fear from Wilkie. I have a degree from Dhaka University in English Literature. Can Wilkie quote from Chaucer or Dickens or Hardy?"(29). Alongside this, though, he increasingly develops another knowledge of his situation, which is based around "the sub-section on Race, Ethnicity and Identity" of the sociology module he is studying as part of his Open University degree (29). Using the concepts made available to him though this study, Chanu becomes increasingly inclined to explain his situation through reference to structural inequality and prejudice in Britain. For Nazneen, this seems useless information that bears little relation to the actual circumstances in which they must live: "He says that racism is built into the 'system.' I don't know what 'system' means exactly" (58). Much of Nazneen's exasperation with Chanu can be seen to stem from the realization she makes that while his strategies for survival are the opposite of hers— "where she attempted to dull her mind and numb her thoughts, he argued aloud; while she wanted to look neither to the past nor to the future, he lived exclusively in both" (99)—they end in a similar place. His analyses take him nowhere: "He can see . . . He can comment, But he cannot act" (75). Nazneen's passivity mirrors that of Chanu, even as the terms of its articulation differ.

It is for this reason in particular that the activities of the Bengal Tigers seem so very attractive to Nazneen. The contrast between the static analyses Chanu offers and the dynamic activism of the community group comes particularly to the fore in the meeting to which Chanu brings the speech he has prepared, "Race and Class in UK, a Short Thesis on the White Working Class, Rate Hate, and Ways to Tackle the Issue" (344). The speech remains unspoken as instead Karim dominates the meeting, seeming to display a pragmatism that can effect real change: "He issued instructions for canvassing, targets to be met, reports to be filed, dates for the organisers to convene, plans for stewarding the march itself" (348). The ability to enact change is seen to be the key justification for political belief.

However, as with much of Nazneen's infatuation with Karim, the effectiveness of the Bengal Tigers is at least partly illusory. The big march deteriorates into infighting among various Estate gangs. Right from its conception, the ethos of the group seems weak and based on shaky concepts. The initial impetus for forming together is the racist leafleting of the Estate. The young Muslims disparage the racism of the Nationalist group responsible, the Lion Hearts: "they is getting more sophisticated. They don't say *race*, they say *culture, religion*," but then unify themselves around exactly these simplistic bases: "What are we for? We are for Muslim rights and culture . . . we are against . . . any group that opposes us" (198–99). No attempt is made seriously to define what this culture might be, but its defense is seen as a priority. Ali Ahmad sees such "rhetoric" as a failing of *Brick Lane*, arguing that "the novel is not grounded in history but seems to want to make grand pseudo-historical claims without quite knowing what they are" (Ahmad 201). This criticism appears to make the same assumption as that discussed above, which argued that Ali fails to recognize the sociopolitical determinants of these people's lives. Again it seems important to point out that the novel is resolutely focalized from inside the community, and it tries only to show the world as they might see it. Any myopia of historical or political vision is not necessarily Ali's own but that which she ascribes to her characters.

The critic who often seems most attentive to Ali's style and its implications, Jane Hiddleston, comments on the way in which "the perspective often switches from an external narrator to free indirect discourse, giving the impression that the character speaks for herself." She suggests that this allows Ali to "dramatise the unsettled relationship between the character and the narrative that gives her form" (65). Although it is not an example Hiddleston herself uses, this could be taken as a way to read an important moment in Nazneen's coming to political consciousness. Told terrible stories by Karim of the suffering of children in Palestine, "she mistook the sad weight of longing in her stomach for sorrow, and she read in the night of occupiers and orphans, of Intifada and Hamas" (201). This seems an unusually intrusive narratorial interruption, and might be read as offering evidence of the distinction between character and narrative Hiddleston finds in *Brick Lane*. However, it may not be this straightforward. The novel is extremely focalized through Nazneen and never offers information that she has not personally witnessed. The identification of self-deception could well be interpreted as Nazneen's own insight; she is frequently able simultaneously to harbor contradictory thoughts, particularly with regard to her relation to Karim, and we could read this moment as a cynicism about her own political commitment, or perhaps an awareness that the spur to social action cannot be divorced from her sexual longing for Karim, and that in both there lies the denied possibility of her agency outside of the constraints of her limited life up until this point.

Against these political conceptions of the difference of the migrant, Ali refuses to offer a facile promotion of an easy process of assimilation in which Britishness is readily adopted. The only character allowed to utter this view is Mrs. Azad. In response to Chanu's exposition of the "tragedy" of the immigrant ("the clash between Western values and our own . . . the struggle to assimilate and the need to preserve one's identity and heritage . . . the feelings of alienation engendered by a society where racism is prevalent"), she declares that he is talking "crap" and that it is the immigrants who should change, not the society (92–93). It is hard to feel that Mrs. Azad's views are endorsed in the novel as she remains a grotesque figure in her smoking and drinking and failure to socially engage, which is partly reminiscent of the Tattoo Lady. Her views inversely echo those of Mrs. Islam earlier in the book: "if you mix with all these people . . . you have to give up your culture to accept theirs" (22). Belonging in a culture is seen as an all-or-nothing choice. As much as Chanu's mimicry and sociological reductionism and Karim's naive version of anti-imperialism, these two older women offer Nazneen little in terms of practical guidance for her life. Like the signs at the doctor's surgery that "only tell you what *not* to do" (51), their assessments of the situation cannot much help alleviate Nazneen's isolation and longing for something better.

The desire to put events into some kind of explanatory framework is portrayed as close to irresistible throughout the novel. Again and again characters reach for narratives that make sense of events and fight to take control of the process of representation. At times, this battle over representation seems to replace the urge to make substantive changes, most notably when the tensions escalate between the Lion Hearts and Bengal Tigers: "On the estate there was war. The war was conducted by leaflet" (212). The struggle to tell stories to help understand events in fact comes to replace the understanding of those events. As when Nazneen watches on television the disorders that took place in Oldham in May 2001, the representation actually seems only to give a hazy idea of what is actually happening; she notices that "the roads were pocked with holes, and the houses packed together, tight as teeth" (228), but finds nothing in this that allows her to understand the confrontation between Asian youths and the police. Hiddleston notes that "the *way* in which the riots are reconstructed by the moving image is as significant in fuelling stereotypes as the violence itself" (68), and throughout the novel there is this sense that the strategies of representing the challenges of immigrant life ultimately determine its character. Increasingly Karim's espousal of Islam is seen to have little connection to how he chooses to act as seen in his excited listing of the number of hadith in different collections, reminding Nazneen of Shahana telling her how many chromosomes various creatures have without having any idea what a chromosome is. Knowledge, when divorced from a practical sense of what to do with it, is useless, and yet it becomes a fetish of a practice that seems to provide certainty but actually ducks from difficult pragmatic questions.

Late in the novel, Nazneen recalls the barber from her childhood village, Tamizuddin Mizra Haque. Despite his lowly status, he was able to command a degree of respect from his neighbors, who would always address him formally and, importantly, never contradict what he said. It was the barber's certainty, his ability to pronounce on an issue definitively that caused his fellow villagers to trust in his wisdom. Simply through acting always as if he has the correct answers, he encourages others to treat him as if this were true (314–16). Nazneen comes to realize that something very similar has taken place in her relationship with Karim. Needing some way of finding the confidence to root herself in Britain, she projected onto Karim the assured air of belonging that she lacked. During their final breakup he insists to her that he stammers as much in English as in Bengali (379). That she chose not to hear this is indicative of the investment she made in him as the representative of a way of being both Bengali and British and for finding a valid cultural space from which to develop as an individual. She comes to realize how profoundly she has misread him: "Karim did not have his place in the world. That was why he defended it" (375). At the same time, it becomes apparent that he too had constructed an ideal image of a woman within which he tried to fit her: His notion of Nazneen's being "the real thing" is little different to Chanu's of the "unspoilt village girl" (320). Nazneen's epiphany at the end of the novel is that she begins to find a way to look at the world apart from the comforting narratives of explanation: "from the very beginning to the very end, we didn't see things. What we did—we made each other up" (380). It is only when she refuses the comfort of easy explanation that she can begin to progress.

Angelia Poon suggests the novel rejects the appeal of "any revelatory hybrid truth or totalizing knowledge system for the immigrant" and instead "stresses forms of unknowing and the instability of knowledge." Ali, Poon argues, prefers "flux and at best a provisional harmony in knowledge and migrant subjectivity best symbolized by ice-skating, the sport that so mesmerizes Nazneen" (429). Although Poon summarizes well Ali's views of culture and community, the meaning of ice-skating seems to shift in the book. When Nazneen first watches it on television in the 1980s, it seems the epitome of freedom and agency. The dancer, Jane Torvill, has a "look so triumphant that you know she had conquered everything" (27). The sport becomes a metaphor for the sexual and social freedom she desires. However, when she watches a performance during the time of her affair with Karim, she is struck by "the false smiles, the made-up faces, the demented illusion of freedom chasing around their enclosure" (301–02). Again, Ali reveals some of Nazneen's barely conscious awareness that her affair may not be fulfilling her desire for agency in the way she had hoped. What can seem like a rejection of one form of restrictive knowledge can easily become a capitulation to another. At one point during her affair, Nazneen imagines taunting her dead mother for her insistence that one should accept one's fate. "Sitting next to her husband, in front of her lover," Nazneen revels in her transgression and insists that *this* is what she accepts. However, immediately after formulating the thought, her "warm feeling had begun to subside" (293). The realization that she is not exercising true autonomy but has simply swapped a role in one male vision for another disturbs her and makes her realize that this may just be another form of passive and unhelpful acceptance of fate.

Nazneen has to learn to refuse knowledge that comes from external sources and instead to trust in her own experience. A significant moment is when she rejects the newspaper story Chanu reads that declares Bangladesh to be the happiest nation in the world. Reflecting on what she knows of Hasina's experience, she cannot accept this: "It may be written down . . . [b]ut I do not believe it" (290). She is developing the confidence to decide things for herself, which necessarily involves working on a small scale, rejecting grand explanations, and progressing in small pragmatic steps. As part of this, she begins to learn to discard the idea that women are required to suffer. As a girl, she had longed "to cast off her childish baggy pants and long shirt and begin to wear this suffering that was as rich and layered and deeply coloured as the saris which enfolded Amma's troubled bones" (84). As an adult she learns to distinguish between moments of suffering, recognizing those of others as distinct from her own. It is at moments of physical pain, such as when she accidentally puts chilli in her eye (397), that she becomes most determined to act for herself. Gone is the equation of all suffering that so stifled her desire for agency. When she watches the jumpers from the World Trade Center in September 2001, she does not imaginatively project herself into their place as she had done with the woman in the Dogwood Estate, but she recognizes their predicament as separate from her own; while for a moment it seems "that hope and despair are nothing against the world," she later dreams of the men of Gouripur "doing what little they can" (305). Faced with the enormous suffering she watches on television, she can put her own situation in perspective and begin the small steps needed to assert some freedom.

The final scene of the book in which Nazneen's daughters take her ice-skating has been criticized for its seemingly absurd utopianism, particularly in its closing line: "This is England . . . you can do whatever you want" (413). However, it is important to consider that the course of the novel up to this point seems to require us not to read that statement as a confident answer applying to all situations in which migrants in England might find themselves, but as something specific to Nazneen only and at that time only. For Alistair Cormack, "a true freedom that recognizes the entirety of Nazneen's subjectivity would have to be conceived in the public realm as well as in the cloistered world of family and friendship" (713). To the contrary, the novel insists that it is precisely this small-scale assertion of freedom that is most meaningful. To extrapolate into a wider sphere of community and culture risks signing up to the types of grand knowledge claims that are so discredited elsewhere in the book. The final scene is not one of conclusion, showing that the integration of migrants in Britain is unproblematic after all, but it is more a statement of hope, a defiance of limitations and perhaps a final embrace by Nazneen of Hasina's "determination to struggle and to survive" (Dawson 137).

Chanu's friend Dr. Azad keeps a collection of snowglobes. Shaking one for Bibi, he tells her that it "is just like life . . . [t]he storm comes and everything is blurred. But all that is built on a solid foundation has only to stand fast and wait for the storm to pass" (225). Nazneen looks for a strong foundation throughout *Brick Lane* but finds repeatedly that the attractions of culture and community actually have little to offer and instead tend to instrumentalize her within narratives ultimately controlled by others. Rather, she needs to learn to trust in her "contingent hybridity" (Upstone 180), the product of everyday struggles, and focus on taking small steps without attempting to extrapolate them into solutions for all the residents of Brick Lane and Tower Hamlets.

Works Cited

Ahmad, Ali. "*Brick Lane*: A Note on the Politics of 'Good' Literary Production." *Third Text: Critical Perspectives on Contemporary Art and Culture* 18.2 (2004): 199–201.

Ahmed, Rehana. "*Brick Lane*: A Materialist Reading of the Novel and Its Reception." *Race & Class* 52.2 (2010): 25–42.

Ali, Monica. *Brick Lane*. London: Doubleday, 2003.

Brouillette, Sarah. "Literature and Gentrification on Brick Lane." *Criticism* 51.3 (2009): 425–49.

Cormack, Alistair. "Migration and the Politics of Narrative Form: Realism and the Postcolonial Subject in *Brick Lane*." *Contemporary Literature* 47.4 (2006): 695–721.

Dawson, Ashley, "The People You Don't See: Representing Informal Labour in Fortress Europe." *ARIEL: A Review of International English Literature* 40.1 (2009): 125–41.

Hiddleston, Jane. "Shapes and Shadows: (Un)veiling the Immigrant in Monica Ali's *Brick Lane*." *The Journal of Commonwealth Literature* 40.1 (2005): 57–72.

Maxey, Ruth. "'Representative' of British Asian Fiction? The Critical Reception of Monica Ali's *Brick Lane*." *British Asian Fiction: Framing the Contemporary*. Eds. Neil Murphy and Wai-Chew Sim. Amherst, NY: Cambria, 2008. 217–36.

Poon, Angelia. "To Know What's What: Forms of Migrant Knowing in Monica Ali's *Brick Lane*." *Journal of Postcolonial Writing* 45.4 (2009): 426–37.

Upstone, Sara. *British Asian Fiction: Twenty-First-Century Voices*. London and New York: Manchester UP, 2010.

Obscured by History: Language, Culture, and Conflict in Chinua Achebe's *Things Fall Apart* and Chimamanda Ngozi Adichie's *Half of a Yellow Sun*____

Jonathan Highfield

> One dips one's tongue in the ocean;
> Camps with the choir of inconstant
> Dolphins, by shallow sand banks
> Sprinkled with memories;
> Extends one's branches of coral,
> The Branches extends in the senses'
> Silence; this silence distills
> in yellow melodies.
>
> *Christopher Okigbo, "Lament of the Silent Sisters"*

The novels *Things Fall Apart* (1958) by Chinua Achebe and *Half of a Yellow Sun* (2006) by Chimamanda Ngozi Adichie examine two of the most traumatic moments in the history of the Igbo people. *Things Fall Apart* takes place in the 1890s as the British intensify their colonization efforts along the Niger River. *Half of a Yellow Sun* takes place seven decades later in newly independent Nigeria and in the breakaway republic of Biafra. Both Achebe and Adichie attempt to capture in fiction a historical event that traumatized Igbo people and shaped the history of West Africa. In *Things Fall Apart* Achebe writes of the cultural encounter between British missionaries and the Igbo, while in *Half of a Yellow Sun* Adichie writes of Biafran War and its impact on newly independent Nigeria. Both novels present language as central to the cultural conflict, and both writers attempt to create a specific time period in the works through the use of juxtaposed languages, folk sayings, and historic referents. Adichie clearly acknowledges the importance of Achebe in helping her to discover a voice that reflected the reality in which she was raised. In the introduction to the Everyman's Library edition of *The African Trilogy*, of which *Things Fall Apart* is the first volume, Adichie writes of how discovering Achebe's work in her youth became both personal and cultural discovery:

> Here was a book that was unapologetically African, that was achingly familiar, but that was, also, exotic because it detailed the life of my people a hundred years before. Because I was educated in a Nigerian system that taught me little of my pre-colonial past, because I could not, for example, imagine with any accuracy how life had been organized in my part of the world in 1890, Achebe's novels became strangely personal. (Adichie, "Introduction" ix)

Adichie has also spoken at length on how the Biafran War has been neglected in the Nigerian educational system, that Nigerians "haven't dealt with it as a collective nation" (Bolonik 37), and both novels are attempting to intervene in collective memory by engaging a history blocked in the popular consciousness.

Writing a novel dealing with contested history can be a tricky proposition. Finding the language with which to speak the history in a voice that seems to emerge from the period becomes a central part of the historical novelist's project. While a historian attempts to find the language to narrate the events of the past without prejudice, a novelist relies on the prejudices and limitations of characters to capture the nuances of a specific historical moment. When those prejudices continue to shape the present, as they do in contemporary Nigeria, the search for language can become fraught with uncertainty.

In *Half of a Yellow Sun*, Chimamanda Ngozi Adichie attempts to narrate the joys of Biafran independence and the resulting horrors as the Nigerian government launched a war to keep its territory intact. Adichie's characters use language to attempt to negotiate their way through the chaos of this time period as if the careful deployment of words can fix their place in a shifting and contested landscape. That language would be central in a novel about Biafra is not a surprise. The colonial construction of Nigeria and the emphasis on regionalism that continued to flourish after Nigeria's independence in 1960 inflated the importance of ethnicity in the region, and language has remained a flash point ever since. The over-determination of language in Nigeria is probably part of what is behind Chinua Achebe's strident defense of his decision to write in English.

While the lessons of Biafra are still contested in ideological terms, the facts of the conflict are generally agreed upon. The Biafran War (1967–1970) occurred when regions in the southeast of Nigeria decided to secede from the Nigerian state and form their own nation. In part, the disagreement sprang from the question of whether the federal, state, or the regional governments had more power, though the secession was ultimately prompted by events of 1966. In January of that year, a coup prominently led by Igbo army officers toppled the government of Abubakar Tafawa Balewa and killed several prominent northern political leaders, including the Sardauna, Ahmadu Bello, perhaps the most important Islamic religious and political leader in Nigeria. (Uzoigwe 69). In September, tens of thousands of Igbo were killed in cities across the north, and eight months later, the southeastern region declared its independence as the Republic of Biafra (Uzoigwe 97–121). The Nigerian government announced a police action to reannex the breakaway territories in July 1967 (Ojeleye 45). With the support of the United States and Great Britain, the Nigerian government imposed an air blockade that prevented most supplies, including food and medicine, from reaching Biafra (Thompson 43). The blockade was successful; food stores dried up across Biafra, and by January 1970 the war was over, with Nigeria reclaiming the territory (Jacobs 250). Casualty numbers vary, but estimates range up to three million dead, mostly Igbo and mostly of malnutrition. (Jacobs 4).

The consequences from the civil war still reverberate today. Across the Internet, in websites and chat rooms, leaders from both sides of the conflict are lionized and demonized, and entire ethnic groups are condemned for their avarice, brutality, or callousness. Any fictional treatment of Biafra must contend with readers primed for bias, anachronisms, and inaccuracies.

Adichie is not the first to write a fictional treatment of the Nigerian Civil War and life within Biafra. In "Biafra as Heritage and Symbol," John C. Hawley makes the distinction between works produced by writers with living memory of the events of 1967–1970 and writers born after the events (18). A distinction should also be made in the former category between works produced during or immediately after the events surrounding the Nigerian-Biafran war and those produced in the decades following the war, since the former have an immediacy not present in the latter, while the latter have a sense of context offered by the passage of time. *Half of a Yellow Sun* therefore follows narratives like Chinua Achebe's "Civil Peace" (1971), Elechi Amadi's *Sunset in Biafra* (1973), and Wole Soyinka's *The Man Died* (1972), written during or immediately after the civil war; novels like Cyprian Ekwensi's *Divided We Stand* (1980), Buchi Emecheta's *Destination Biafra* (1982), and Festus Iyayi's *Heroes* (1986), written after the conflict by people who lived during it; and treads the same path as Uwem Akpan's *Say You're One of Them* (2009) and Uzodinma Iweala's *Beasts of No Nation* (2006), books written by Nigerians born after the war but dealing with its legacy in their prose.

Though much of the book takes place during the war, *Half of a Yellow Sun* cannot be called a war novel. Very little of the action takes place on the front lines or among soldiers; instead, it is primarily a domestic novel focusing on the everyday as the characters try to maintain normal lives in the midst of chaos. The opening paragraph anticipates the encounter between two classes of independent Africans, the under-educated majority, for whom independence brought little in way of material improvements, and the intellectual elite, dreaming of the future:

Master was a little crazy; he had spent too many years reading books overseas, talked to himself in his office, did not always return greetings, and had too much hair. Ugwu's aunty said this in a low voice as they walked on the path. "But he is a good man," she added. "And as long as you work well, you will eat well. You will even eat meat every day." She stopped to spit; the saliva left her mouth with a sucking sound and landed on the grass. (Adichie *Half* 3)

Most of the action of *Half of a Yellow Sun* takes place among a group of mainly middle-class Igbo in the time period from the heady days of Biafran independence through the horrors of the war and its aftermath. Though the book is narrated in an omniscient style, the reader sees much of the action through the eyes of Ugwu, a village boy who becomes a professor's houseboy and protégé. The other main characters in the novel are the university professor, Odenigbo; his girlfriend, Olanna; her twin sister, Kainene; and Richard, the Englishman in love with her.

One of the important themes in the novel is the attempt by the characters to keep a sense of normality, even as the conflict works to destroy their composure and even their humanity. In an article entitled "African 'Authenticity' and the Biafran Experience," Adichie discusses her desire to look at the effects of war on a cross section of Igbo characters:

I was concerned with certain questions about what it means to be human. When you are deprived of the comforts of the life you know, when you go from eating sandwiches to eating lizards, how does this change your relationship, your sense of self, your idea of self-confidence, your relationship with the people you love? How does it change the things you value? (Adichie, "African" 51)

The use of language by the characters is a crucial part in their attempt to retain a sense of normalcy in abnormal conditions, and Adichie's careful tampering with that language reveals the fissures and strains the characters feel as they are taken out of their comfort zone and made to confront the atrocities of war. In the same essay, Adichie emphasizes the Igbo viewpoint she is writing from and how that viewpoint is influenced by the trauma inflicted upon the entire Igbo community by the war and the humiliations suffered after Biafra was dissolved:

> I was very aware, as I wrote, of the problem that often comes with being a defeated people—and the Igbo are in many ways a defeated people. It is not only that you learn to bear a collective shame, but that you sometimes go to extremes of reaction. The survivors' sense of defeat and injustice can result in their making a utopia of Biafra, when it may very well have become yet another state of tyranny. I wanted to avoid making Biafra a *utopia-in-retrospect*, which would have been disingenuous—it would have sullied the memories of all those who died. What illuminated my choices as I wrote was remembering and reliving through books and oral accounts remarkable stories of the courage of ordinary people. (Adichie, "African" 50)

Adichie manipulates the characters' voices to reflect the ways the trauma of defeat manifests itself in language. Odenigbo goes from having a towering voice in the intellectual debates at his home in Nsukka in the heady days preceding independence, to having a "silly voice" (Adichie, *Half* 197) as he ministers to Olanna after she witnesses a massacre to having "a taciturn set to his mouth" (Adichie, *Half* 404) as things in Biafra deteriorate. Similarly, the poet Okeoma, fashioned after Christopher Okigbo, who was killed during the conflict, leaves poetry behind at the start of the war but returns to writing after rediscovering his muse in Olanna; however, those poems are all lost when he is killed. The silences in the novel become signs of loss that can never be recovered. When Kainene disappears during a trip to the market, the reader is very aware of the hole left in the text by the disappearance of her voice. Kainene has been the voice of honesty and frankness throughout the book, and when she disappears it is as if no one can speak frankly. As Richard recognizes, a clarity in the book leaves with Kainene: "Darkness descended on him, and when it lifted he knew that he would never see Kainene again and that his life would always be like a candlelit room; he would see things only in shadow, only in half glimpses" (Adichie, *Half* 537). Kainene represents communication in the novel. Her ability to speak across lines of class, ethnicity, and gender only increases as things become more dire. She turns from profiteering off the war to helping those who will not survive it. The camp she works in is as much hospice as hospital, and her last act in the novel is to try to get more food to hold back death from as many as possible. With her absence, the world does seem silent, and the authority of written word takes precedence over the negotiations of communication.

Those negotiations among various languages play a great part in the novel. Most characters speak a mix of Igbo and English, and Ugwu moves back and forth between English and pidgin as he negotiates different spaces of class that he must move through in his role as houseboy in a university town. In response to a question posed in an interview about whether she struggled with how to represent language in *Half of a Yellow Sun*, Adichie responded:

> I guess so. I think most if not all of my characters are Igbo people, and it's important for me to remind my readers. I'm always negotiating both languages. But I am also writing about people, who, like me and many other Nigerians, talk both languages at the same time. My generation of Nigerians, for example, speak Igbo like Spanglish. We can't say three sentences entirely in Igbo—we usually throw in an English word. And I wanted to capture that. (qtd. in Bolonik 37)

In the early part of the book, language is playful, with characters moving effortlessly between languages: "He always responded in English to her Igbo, as if he saw her speaking Igbo to him as an insult that he had to defend himself against by insistently speaking English" (Adichie, *Half* 59). As the war approaches in the book, language becomes fraught with danger as accents become liabilities and languages become lifelines. Richard sees a man shot because "He would not say Allahu Akbar because his accent would give him away" (Adichie, *Half* 192). When caught in a mob persecuting Igbos, Olanna's cousin Arize begins speaking Yoruba, and "the crowd lost interest in them." (Adichie, *Half* 167). How and when to speak becomes crucial if one is to survive.

Along with the necessity of negotiating the African languages constructing the reality of independent Nigeria, the crucial importance of the colonial language hangs over the novel. Ugwu's mastery of English allows for his transition from houseboy to writer. When he first meets Olanna he marvels at the way she speaks English:

> Master's English was music, but what Ugwu was hearing now, from this woman, was magic. Here was a superior tongue, a luminous language, the kind of English he heard on Master's radio, rolling out with clipped precision. It reminded him of slicing a yam with a newly sharpened knife, the easy perfection in every slice. (Adichie, *Half* 28)

As Olanna becomes an increasing presence in Odenigbo's life, Ugwu relishes the opportunities to practice his English for her. After leaving Nsukka, Olanna opens a school to teach the displaced children and Ugwu becomes one of the teachers:

> [Parents] looked at Olanna, her beautiful face, her undemanding fees, and her perfect English, with awe-filled respect. They brought palm oil and yams and *garri*. A woman who traded across enemy lines brought a chicken. An army contractor brought two of his children and a carton of books—early readers, six copies of *Chike and the River*, eight simplified editions of *Pride and Prejudice*. (Adichie, *Half* 367)

The combination of texts leads to all sorts of interesting imaginative juxtapositions: Mr. Darcy scornfully watching Dick and Dora learn to hop; Dora joining Chike for his trip to Asaba and helping him foil the thieves, "Look, Chike, see the thieves. See the thieves run away. Run away, thieves!" In many ways this collection of books represents the schizophrenic consciousness of independent Nigeria and independent

Biafra, looking both toward something new and representative of diurnal reality but also attempting to cling to the cultural traditions of the British Empire. Something similar can be seen in Odenigbo's speech; even as he celebrates Patrice Lumumba for his resistance in the Congo and castigates de Gaulle for colonialism in Algeria and Hendrik Verwoerd for his apartheid regime's response to the Sharpeville riots, he utters phrases like "my good man" and "poor chap," sounding for all the world like a character out of the English humorist P. G. Wodehouse. Even during wartime in a country twice removed from British control, it is the mastery of the English language that seems paramount. Ugwu's skill with the English language provides him with a sense of self-worth and increases his attractiveness in the eyes of his next-door neighbor:

He loved the light in the older children's eyes when he explained the meaning of a word, loved the loud way Master said to Special Julius, "My wife and Ugwu are changing the face of the next generation of Biafrans with their Socratic pedagogy!" and loved, most of all, the teasing way Eberechi called him *teacher.* (Adichie, *Half* 368)

The English language becomes Ugwu's key to another life for himself, one with more opportunities than that of the village or that of a regular houseboy. In response to a question posed on Book World Live, a forum on the *Washington Post* website, Adichie explained the centrality of Ugwu to the novel:

The houseboy is the soul of the book because I sometimes think that middle-class Nigerians don't always grasp how central domestic workers are and sometimes don't see them as human beings with feelings.

Ugwu was partly inspired by Mellitus, my parents' houseboy during the war and partly by Fide, the houseboy we had when I was growing up, whom I came to love like a brother and who later died as a soldier in Sierra Leone. (qtd. in Book World Live)

Like Frederick Douglass, who transformed himself from illiterate slave to one of the most important writers and speakers of the years surrounding the US Civil War, Ugwu becomes the narrator of Biafran history within the fictional text *The World Was Silent When We Died*. Unlike Richard, a writer who ultimately finds the story untellable, Ugwu takes responsibility for ensuring the memories, both empowering and horrific, are passed on to subsequent generations. Ugwu's experiences as a soldier give him some perspectives that none of the other survivors in the novel share. Adichie suggests that his perspective offers insights into certain aspects of wartime experience that are not common to Odenigbo's university colleagues:

> I was particularly interested in class and race and gender, which I think affect everything about life in every part of the world—in some ways, the amount of humanity and dignity the world allows depends on what race and class and gender you are. (Adichie, "African" 51)

This attention to the subtleties of gender, class, and power can be seen in one of the most carefully rendered scenes in the novel. Ugwu has been forcefully conscripted into the Biafran army, and while in training at an abandoned school he discovers a copy of *Narrative of the Life of Frederick Douglass, An American Slave: Written by Himself*. The book becomes his tether to his previous life, a life where the world of books and culture was opened by Odenigbo and Olanna, and in stark contrast to the world of war and brutality where he earns the name Target Destroyer for his devastating accuracy in explosive attacks. Relaxing in a bar after battle, Ugwu finds another soldier has ripped up parts of the book to roll marijuana cigarettes. Still reeling from the loss of control of his own life, Ugwu is taunted into participating in the gang rape of a bar girl. When he looks at her after ejaculating, "She stared back at him with calm hate" (Adichie, *Half* 458). For the reader who has watched Ugwu grow up and have seen his care with Odenigbo, Olanna, and their baby, this descent into brutality signifies that anyone can be tainted by war and depravity. It also insists that many victims are unnamed and unmourned. While Ugwu feels shame because of his actions, he only truly understands the full impact of them when he returns to his village to find his sister incapacitated by the physical and psychological aftermath of a gang rape similar to the one he inflicted on the unnamed bar girl. He does not share his experiences with any other characters in the novel, and the reader does not know whether his attack on the woman in the bar or the rape of his sister makes it into the fictional book he writes. Those experiences do give him a perspective on the ability of war to strip all of the civilizing veneer from anyone.

Though Adichie is clear about not wanting to create a utopia out of Biafra, it is difficult to read Ugwu as anything but a symbol for the potential of Biafra, snuffed out by the war. The descriptions of Odenigbo's house in Nsukka, the rambling conversations, the tutoring of Ugwu all reveal a place of transformation. The previous generation of houseboys, symbolized in the novel by Harrison, had learned to imitate the recipes of the English. Ugwu, in contrast, has borrowed a title from the English, but the work itself is original and unfortunately formed by the war he survives. That *Half of a Yellow Sun* ends with Ugwu's dedication of *The World Was Silent When We Died* to Odenigbo emphasizes the loss caused by the war. What other work might Ugwu have written had the war not intervened, and how many potential writers, thinkers, and artists were prematurely silenced by death, shocked into speechlessness by the sight of atrocities, or never given the chance to develop their talents? The collection of individuals brought together by the new university at Nsukka has been permanently dispersed by the novel's end, and that dispersal does not seem to be replaced by anything but grief.

In positing a world left darker after the events in a novel, Adichie is following down the path illuminated by Chinua Achebe in his 1958 novel, *Things Fall Apart*. Through its title and epigraph, Achebe invokes the dark musings of W. B. Yeats's "The Second Coming" (1919), indicating that, as in Adichie's novel, no renewal will follow the conflagration of war. It is impossible to overstate the impact of Achebe's novel on literature in general and on African literature more specifically. Achebe, along with writers such as Es'kia Mphahlele, Wole Soyinka, Amos Tutuola, and Ngũgĩ wa Thiong'o first brought the idioms of sub-Saharan African languages alive in literature written in English. *Things Fall Apart* is in the literary canon today, taught around the world in secondary schools and universities. Faculty at Western Michigan State University created a virtual village of Umuofia, which exists on the Internet alongside Charles Dickens's London and John Steinbeck's California. High school students often read *Things Fall Apart* as a historical or anthropological text, though Achebe's well-crafted novel follows Aristotelian rules of tragedy in many ways. As Adichie does in *Half of a Yellow Sun*, Achebe attempts to capture in fiction one of the most traumatic periods in Igbo history: the cultural encounter between British missionaries and the Igbo, which will lead to the subjugation of the Igbo under British colonial rule.

Unlike the collective cast in Adichie's novel, the action in *Things Fall Apart* is driven by a single character. Set in the village of Umuofia in the 1890s the novel follows the life of Okonkwo, a powerful man with real leadership potential who loses everything because he fears that he is not manly enough, that the weaknesses of his father are in him. His struggle with himself ultimately leads to his exile just as British missionaries are entering Umuofia. When he returns, he finds he cannot rally enough support to lead an armed uprising against the British, and, in an act of petulance, commits suicide. After his death, his fellow villagers cannot even bury him because he has broken a taboo by taking his own life.

Things Fall Apart relates the story of a single man during a culture-changing event. He has embedded that man in a landscape carefully wrought to reveal the depth and complexity of Igbo society, but the novel is not primarily about that society. As Achebe has stressed, looking to Okonkwo as a cultural hero is misguided:

My friend who was an Igbo came to my house and did not understand Okonkwo's situation, a scholar from Germany came and did not understand it. But above all, Okonkwo himself did not understand it!

Okonkwo was a strong, diligent man, who tried hard, spoke the truth, amassed wealth, took titles. All of those were things the Igbo said should be done. It was not only that people spoke to him this way, they spoke to him loudly. Okonkwo heard, then acted. But there is another thing the Igbo whispers in our ears. He says that if something stands, something else stands against it; if we take up guns and knives, we should not criticize the flute and the gong and the calabash in the women's meeting, and those in Okonkwo's deepest thoughts did not hear this message that was sent in a small voice. (qtd. in Pritchett)

It is Okonkwo's failure to hear this voice, his hubris, that makes him a tragic character and gives *Things Fall Apart* its narrative tension. The reader wants Okonkwo to learn from his earlier mistakes, to grow and change as a character but Achebe presents the darker vision of a man unable to overcome his own fears.

Achebe builds the world Okonkwo inhabits through brief character sketches—the palm wine tapper who leaves his profession, the snuff maker whose product is always too damp—and folk sayings, stories, kola nut ceremonies, religious festivals, and nuanced descriptions of people inhabiting the natural world. For instance, here is a passage about the sounds of night in Okonkwo's compound:

The world was silent except for the shrill cry of insects, which was part of the night, and the sound of wooden mortar and pestle as Nwayieke pounded her foo-foo. Nwayieke lived four compounds away, and she was notorious for late cooking. Every woman in the neighborhood knew the sound of Nwayieke's mortar and pestle. It was also part of the night. (Achebe, *Things* 95)

Though it is a brief passage, it does several things. It provides a sense of the relationship of the village to the rest of the natural world with the cry of insects being part of every normal night. It provides solidarity between the women of the village, who note the sound of the pounding of mortar and pestle, and, in a novel where the world of women is denigrated by the protagonist, the scene insists on the individuality of the women in the novel. Nwayieke habitually prepares the evening meal later than everyone else and that sets her apart from the other wives in the village, even as they fulfill very similar roles in the family structure. Finally, earlier in the novel Okonkwo had beaten one of his wives for late cooking in the evening. This scene indicates to the readers that even within the norms of his own society, Okonkwo's reaction was excessive.

As in *Half of a Yellow Sun*, language in *Things Fall Apart* is contested territory. In one of the stories told by Ekwefi, Okonkwo's second wife, the trickster Tortoise names himself All-of-You to trick other guests from getting to participate in a feast (Achebe, *Things* 98). When the first missionary comes to Umuofia, he brings an Igbo translator whose dialect is so different that he cannot always be understood, and his word for "myself" is the word in the local Igbo dialect for "my buttocks" (Achebe, *Things* 144). While language misunderstandings are generally humorous in the early parts of the novel, language becomes a tool of discipline, not communication, with the arrival of the missionaries and the colonial district court. While the first missionary to Umuofia, Mr. Brown seems genuine in his desire to learn from the village elders, his school is designed to create English-speaking converts:

> Mr. Brown begged and argued and prophesied. He said that the leaders of the land in the future would be men and women who had learnt to read and write. If Umuofia failed to send her children to school, strangers would come from other places to rule them. (Achebe, *Things* 181)

While it is true that the next missionary, with his narrower view of salvation, and the District Commissioner, with his complete disregard for the belief system of the Igbo, will solidify the framework that will shackle the inhabitants of West Africa with language, both written and oral, the foundation has been laid with the elevation of those willing to become students of English. The learning of a language serves to create a new class in the region, one that will eventually have more power than the titled men of the villages.

In the penultimate scene in the novel, Okika, who is described as a great orator but one with a "trembling voice," calls for clan unity and invokes both the gods and a folktale in his speech urging that Umuofia "root out this evil" (Achebe, *Things* 203–04). Before Okika can finish, however, or his listeners can respond, his speech is interrupted by the arrival of the messengers from the District Officer's court who have come to disband the meeting. Okonkwo's rash decision to behead the head messenger ends the meeting, and as the crowd scatters, Okonkwo believes that "Umuofia would not go to war" (Achebe, *Things* 205). That realization so disturbs him that he commits suicide, an act not directed against the English invaders and their supporters but against his own village. The novel ends with the ruminations of the District Commissioner on the book he plans to write on his experiences in Africa:

> The story of the man who killed a messenger and hanged himself would make interesting reading. One could almost write a whole chapter on him. Perhaps not a whole chapter, but a reasonable paragraph at any rate. He had already chosen the title of the book, after much thought: *The Pacification of the Primitive Tribes of the Lower Niger.* (Achebe, *Things* 209)

Every page of the novel up to that point has revealed to the reader just how complex Igbo society is, so "primitive" is glaringly inaccurate, and the pacification trumpeted in the District Commissioner's proposed book does not come easily or quickly to the Lower Niger. As Philip Igbafe points out in an essay on Igbo resistance movements, secret societies proliferated along the Lower Niger in the late nineteenth and early twentieth centuries "organized on an inter-town cooperative level and dedicated to resisting European encroachment or the establishment and consolidation of British rule (Igbafe 444). That this history is largely ignored speaks to one of the central themes in Achebe's book—those who control discourse and language control whose history gets told. Okika's speech is interrupted, Okonkwo silences himself, and the reader is left with the self-satisfied voice of the colonial officer.

The ending of the novel indicates the way that the colonial control of language would shape the perception of Africa for generations. In *No Longer at Ease* (1960), Achebe writes of how the dominance of English came to shape the Nigerian consciousness:

> Nothing gave him greater pleasure than to find another Ibo-speaking student in a London bus. But when he had to speak in English with a Nigerian student from another tribe he lowered his voice. It was humiliating to have to speak to one's countryman in a foreign language, especially in the presence of the proud owners of that language. They would naturally assume that one had no language of one's own. (45)

The dominance of the language of the colonizer meant that the native languages in the region known as Nigeria did not have to develop as standardized written modes of communication and therefore would always be seen as inferior by the European colonizers. The Kenyan writer Ngũgĩ wa Thiong'o has argued that in not developing African languages into written literature means unique ways of organizing the world are being lost, and that "meeting the challenge of creating a literature . . . later opens the languages for philosophy, science, technology and all the other areas of human creative endeavours (29). Achebe has disagreed, vocally defending his decision to write in English, writing that "there is no other choice. I have been given this language and I intend to use it" ("English" 348). He continues:

I feel that the English language will be able to carry the weight of my African experience. But it will have to be a new English, still in full communion with its ancestral home, but altered to suit its new African surroundings. (349)

Achebe argues "that the culprit in Africa's language difficulties was not imperialism, as Ngũgĩ would have us believe, but the linguistic pluralism of modern African states" (*Education* 106), an argument that seems to ignore the fact that the modern African state was born out of imperialism.

Reading the translated transcript from the annual *Odenigbo Lecture* on September 4, 1999, at Owerri, Imo State, Nigeria, offers a clearer perspective into Achebe's objections to standardized African written languages. In his talk, Achebe makes the argument that the Igbo language itself is fragmented into numerous dialects, many unintelligible to each other, and that standardized Igbo is itself a colonial imposition created by an English missionary who could not himself speak Igbo (Pritchett). To emphasize his point, Achebe delivered his lecture "in a brand of dialect peculiar only to Onitsha speakers of the language and almost unintelligible to more than half the audience" (Emenyonu 436), which prompted the organizers to take the unprecedented step of printing the speech in two separate versions of Igbo and catalyzed a debate about the legitimacy of Standardized Igbo among linguistic scholars (Emenyonu 433).

It is striking that one of Adichie's main characters shares the name with the lecture series at which Achebe was invited to speak. Odenigbo means "one who writes in Igbo" (Akaji), and there is a dark irony in the naming of the character because the failure of the Biafran experiment means that the development of an Igbo written literature will not become a priority in multilingual Nigeria. Achebe's lecture raises the question whether enough similarities exist between the various Igbo dialects to forge a universally accepted written version of the language.

Reading *Half of a Yellow Sun* reveals the legacies of the work done by real versions of Achebe's missionaries and district commissioners. The massive territories they combined into resource-rich colonies and the ethnic divisions they exploited in order to control those colonies continue to define many of the independent states on the African continent. In Nigeria, English became the medium of communication across ethnic lines, and even today two of the most talented storytellers of their respective generations choose to write their stories of Igbo tragedy in English, though an English that has evolved to accommodate Igbo phrasing. In *Things Fall Apart*, Chinua Achebe tells of the moment the Igbo were incorporated into a larger political system, which took precedence over their cultural values and system of governance. Chimamanda Ngozi Adichie recounts the excitement among an educated group of Igbos as they attempt to dissolve that larger political reality in *Half of a Yellow Sun*, and the losses they incur as the revolution fails. Though written nearly fifty years apart, both novels point to the contestations around language that still reverberate in Nigeria and in regions around the globe still wrestling with how to tell the stories of colonization and its legacies.

Works Cited

Achebe, Chinua. *The Education of a British-Protected Child*. New York: Knopf, 2009.
_____. "English and the African Writer." *Transition* 75/76 (1997): 342–49.
_____. *No Longer at Ease*. London: Penguin, 2010.
_____. *Things Fall Apart*. New York: Anchor, 1994.
Adichie, Chimamanda Ngozi. "African 'Authenticity' and the Biafran Experience." *Transition* 99 (2008): 42–53.
_____. *Half of a Yellow Sun*. New York: Anchor, 2006.
_____. Introduction. *Chinua Achebe, The African Trilogy*. By Chinua Achebe. New York: Knopf, 2010. xv–xviii.
Akaji, Odo. "When Igbo Heritage Embraced the Catholic Arch Diocese: Memories from Odenigbo 2004." IgboNet, 2004. Web. 21 July 2011.
Bolonik, Kera. "Memory, Witness, and War: Chimamanda Ngozi Adichie Talks with Bookforum." *Bookforum* 14.4 (2008): 37.
"Book World Live: Chimamanda Ngozi Adichie." *The Washington Post*, June 19, 2007. Web. 21 July 2011.

Emenyonu, Ernest N. "Chinua Achebe's Vision for Writing in Indigenous Nigerian Languages: The Example of Literary Creativity in Igbo Language." *Emerging Perspectives on Chinua Achebe: Volume 2*. Eds. Ernest N. Emenyonu and Iniobong I. Uko. Trenton, NJ: Africa World Press, 2004. 433–47.

Hawley, John C. "Biafra as Heritage and Symbol: Adichie, Mbachu, and Iweala." *Research in African Literatures* 39.2 (2008): 15–26.

Igbafe, Philip A. "Western Ibo Society and Its Resistance to British Rule: The Ekumeku Movement, 1898–1911." *Journal of African History* 12.3. (1971): 441–59.

Jacobs, Dan. *The Brutality of Nations*. New York: Knopf, 1987.

Ngũgĩ wa Thiong'o. *Decolonising the Mind*. Portsmouth, NH: Heinemann, 1986.

Ojeleye, Olukunle. *The Politics of Post-War Demobilisation and Reintegration in Nigeria*. Surrey, Eng.: Ashgate, 2010.

Okigbo, Christopher. *Labyrinths*. Oxford, Eng.: Heinemann, 2011.

Pritchett, Frances W. "'Tomorrow is Uncertain: Today is Soon Enough.' By Chinua Achebe. Trans. Frances W. Pritchett." *About the Igbo Language*. Columbia U, 2006. Web. 21 July 2011.

Thompson, Joseph E. *American Policy and African Famine: The Nigeria-Biafra War, 1966–1970*. New York: Greenwood, 1990.

Uzoigwe, G. N. *Visions of Nationhood: Prelude to the Nigerian Civil War, 1960–1967*. Trenton, NJ: Africa World Press, 2009.

RESOURCES

Additional Works on Cultural Encounters_____

Drama

The Words upon the Window Pane by William Butler Yeats, 1830
Death and the King's Horseman by Wolé Soyinka, 1976
Master Harold . . . and the Boys by Athol Fugard, 1982
The Golden Age by Louis Nowra, 1985
Topdog/Underdog by Suzan-Lori Parks, 2002

Long Fiction

Don Quixote by Miguel de Cervantes, 1605–1615
Gulliver's Travels by Jonathan Swift, 1726
The Wild Irish Girl by Lady Sydney Owenson Morgan, 1806
Ivanhoe by Sir Walter Scott, 1819
The American by Henry James, 1877
The Awakening by Kate Chopin, 1899
Contending Forces by Pauline Hopkins, 1900
The Marrow of Tradition by Charles Chesnutt, 1901
Kim by Rudyard Kipling, 1901
My Ántonia by Willa Cather, 1918
Their Eyes Were Watching God by Zora Neale Hurston, 1937
Cry, the Beloved Country by Alan Paton, 1948
Pocho by José Villarreal, 1959
Eat a Bowl of Tea by Louis Chu, 1961
A House for Mr. Biswas by V. S. Naipaul, 1961
Another Country by James Baldwin, 1962
Wide Sargasso Sea by Jean Rhys, 1966
The Temptations of Big Bear by Rudy Wiebe, 1973
A Fringe of Leaves by Patrick White, 1976
When Rain Clouds Gather by Bessie Head, 1968
House Made of Dawn by N. Scott Momaday, 1968
July's People by Nadine Gordimer, 1981
Midnight's Children by Salman Rushdie, 1981
Shame by Salman Rushdie, 1983
The Bone People by Keri Hulme, 1984
Potiki by Patricia Grace, 1985
Tefuga by Peter Dickinson, 1986
The Storyteller by Mario Vargas Llosa, 1987
The Joy Luck Club by Amy Tan, 1989

Typical American by Gish Jen, 1991

Remembering Babylon by David Malouf, 1993

The White Boy Shuffle by Paul Beatty, 1996

Disgrace by J. M. Coetzee, 1999

Waiting by Ha Jin, 1999

A New World by Amit Chaudhuri, 2000

White Teeth by Zadie Smith, 2000

John Henry Days by Colson Whitehead, 2000

Family Matters by Rohinton Mistry, 2002

The Kite Runner by Khaled Hosseini, 2003

The Namesake by Jhumpa Lahiri, 2003

The Housekeeper and the Professor by Yoko Ogawa, 2003

The Time of Our Singing by Richard Powers, 2003

Small Island by Andrea Levy, 2004

The Inheritance of Loss by Kiran Desai, 2006

De Niro's Game by Rawi Hage, 2006

Mister Pip by Lloyd Jones, 2006

The Beautiful Things That Heaven Bears by Dinaw Mengestu, 2007

The White Tiger by Aravind Adiga, 2008

Netherland by Joseph O'Neill, 2008

Lush Life by Richard Price, 2008

Zeitoun by Dave Eggers, 2009

In a Strange Room by Damon Galgut, 2010

The Finkler Question by Howard Jocobson, 2010

The Surrendered by Chang-Rae Lee, 2010

Ilustrado by Miguel Syjuco, 2010

Nonfiction

The Histories by Herodotus, ca. 450 BC

Antiquities of the Jews by Flavius Josephus, ca. 80 CE

Democracy in America by Alexis de Tocqueville, 1835–1840

Incidents in the Life of a Slave Girl by Harriet Jacobs, 1861

Aké: The Years of Childhood by Wole Soyinka, 1981

I Know Why the Caged Bird Sings by Maya Angelou, 1983

Kaffir Boy by Mark Mathabane, 1986

The Enigma of Arrival by V. S. Naipaul, 1987

Don't Let's Go To The Dogs Tonight: An African Childhood by Alexandra Fuller, 2001

Reading Lolita in Tehran: A Memoir in Books by Azar Nafisi, 2003

Poetry

The Lusiads by Luis Vaz de Camoens, 1572
Selected Writings by Sor Juana Inés de la Cruz, ca. 1680
Notebook of a Return to My Native Land by Aimé Césaire, 1939
The Collected Poems of Langston Hughes by Langston Hughes, 1965
Harlem Gallery by Melvin Tolson, 1965
Immigrants in Our Own Land by Jimmy Santiago Baca, 1979
Thomas and Beulah by Rita Dove, 1986
The City in Which I Love You by Li-Young Lee, 1990
We, the Dangerous: New and Selected Poems by Janice Mirikitani, 1995
The Maw Broon Monologues by Jackie Kay, 2009

Short Fiction

Candide by Voltaire, 1759
The Beach at Falesá by Robert Louis Stevenson, 1882
Heart of Darkness by Joseph Conrad, 1902
Hadji Murad by Leo Tolstoy, 1912
Giovanni's Room by James Baldwin, 1956
The House on Mango Street by Sandra Cisneros, 1984
Love Medicine by Louise Erdrich, 1984
Interpreter of Maladies by Jhumpa Lahiri, 2000

Bibliography

Achebe, Chinua. "An Image of Africa: Racism in *Conrad's Heart of Darkness*" *Massachusetts Review* 18 (1977): 782–94.

Ahmad, Aijaz. *In Theory: Nations, Classes, Literatures.* London: Verso, 1992.

Allatson, Paul. *Latino Dreams: Transcultural Traffic and the US National Imaginary.* Amsterdam: Rodopi, 2002.

Anderson, Benedict. *Imagined Communities: Reflections on the Origin and Spread of Nationalism.* Rev. ed. London: Verso, 1991.

Anzaldúa, Gloria. *Borderlands—La Frontera: The New Mestiza.* San Francisco: Spinsters, 1987.

Appadurai, Arjun. *Modernity at Large: Cultural Dimensions of Globalization.* Minneapolis: U of Minnesota P, 1996.

Ashcroft, Bill, Gareth Griffiths, and Helen Tiffin. *The Empire Writes Back: Theory and Practice in Post-Colonial Literatures.* London: Routledge, 1989.

Baker, Houston A. *Modernism and the Harlem Renaissance.* Chicago: U of Chicago P, 1987.

Bauer, Ralph. *The Cultural Geography of Colonial American Literatures: Empire, Travel, Modernity.* Cambridge: Cambridge UP, 2003.

Bell-Villada, Gene H. *Overseas American: Growing Up Gringo in the Tropics.* Jackson: UP of Mississippi, 2005.

Bernal, Martin. *Black Athena 1: The Fabrication of Ancient Greece, 1785–1985.* New London: Free Association, 1987.

Bhabha, Homi. *The Location of Culture.* New York: Routledge, 1994.

Biddick, Kathleen. *The Shock of Medievalism.* Durham: Duke UP, 1998.

Boehmer, Elleke. *Colonial and Postcolonial Literature.* New York: Oxford UP, 2005.

Brantlinger, Patrick. *Rule of Darkness: British Literature and Imperialism, 1830–1914.* Ithaca: Cornell UP, 1990.

Calder, Alex, Jonathan Lamb, and Bridget Orr, eds. *Voyages and Beaches: Pacific Encounters, 1769–1840.* Honolulu: U of Hawai'i P, 1999.

Callahan, John F. *In The African American Grain: Call-and-Response in Twentieth-Century Black Fiction.* Urbana: U of Illinois P, 2001.

Cañizares-Esguerra, Jorge. *How to Write the History of the New World: Histories, Epistemologies, and Identities in the Eighteenth-Century Atlantic World.* Stanford: Stanford UP, 2001.

Césaire, Aimé. *Discourse on Colonialism.* New York: MRP, 1972.

Chakrabarty, Dipesh. *Provincializing Europe: Postcolonial Thought and Historical Difference.* 2nd ed. NJ: Princeton UP, 2007.

Chatterjee, Partha. *The Nation and Its Fragments: Colonial and Postcolonial Histories.* NJ: Princeton UP, 1992.

Chrisman, Laura. *Postcolonial Contraventions: Cultural Readings of Race, Imperialism, and Transnationalism*. Eng.: Manchester UP, 2003.

Christian, Barbara. *Black Women Novelists: The Development of a Tradition, 1892–1976*. Westport: Greenwood, 1980.

De Castro, Juan E. *The Spaces of Latin American Literature: Tradition, Globalization, and Cultural Production*. New York: Palgrave, 2008.

DeLoughrey, Elizabeth M. *Routes and Roots: Navigating Caribbean and Pacific Island Literatures*. Honolulu: U of Hawai'i P, 2007.

Desai, Gaurav. *Subject to Colonialism: African Self-Fashioning and the Colonial Library*. Durham, NC: Duke UP, 2001.

Diaz, Roberto Ignacio. *Unhomely Rooms: Foreign Tongues and Spanish American Literature*. Cranbury, NJ: Associated UP, 2002.

Elias, Norbert. *The Civilizing Process: Formation and Civilization*. Vol. 2. Oxford: Blackwell, 1982.

Fanon, Frantz. *Black Skin, White Masks*. Trans. Richard Philcox. New York: Grove, 2008.

Fernández Retamar, Roberto. *Caliban and Other Essays*. Trans. Edward Baker. Minneapolis: U of Minnesota P, 1989.

Gates, Henry Louis. *Figures in Black: Words, Signs, and the "Racial" Self*. New York: Oxford UP, 1989.

Geertz, Clifford. *The Interpretation of Cultures*. New York: Basic Books, 1973.

Grant, Nathan. *Masculinist Impulses: Toomer, Hurston, Black Writing, and Modernity* Columbia: U of Missouri P, 2004.

Greenblatt, Stephen, *Marvelous Possessions*: *The Wonder of the New World*. Chicago: U of Chicago P, 1992.

Hardt, Michael, and Antonio Negri. *Empire*. Cambridge: Harvard UP, 2000.

Hirsch, Steven W. *The Friendship of the Barbarians*. Hanover: UP of New England, 1985.

Kim, Elaine H. *Asian American Literature: An Introduction to the Writings and Their Social Context*. Philadelphia: Temple UP, 1982.

Korang, Kwaku Larbi. *Writing Ghana, Imagining Africa: Nation and African Modernity*. Rochester, NY: U of Rochester P, 2004.

Lazarus, Neil. *Nationalism and Cultural Practice in the Postcolonial World*. Cambridge, Eng.: Cambridge UP, 1999.

Lomnitz, Claudio. *Exits from the Labyrinth: Culture and Ideology in the Mexican National Space*. Berkeley: U of California P, 1992.

López-Calvo, Ignacio. *Latino Los Angeles in Film and Fiction: The Cultural Production of Social Anxiety*. Tucson: U of Arizona P, 2011.

Meisel, Perry, *The Myth of Popular Culture*. Oxford: Blackwell, 2010.

Memmi, Albert. *Decolonization and the Decolonized*. Minneapolis: U of Minnesota P, 2000.

Mohanty, Chandra Talpade. *Feminism Without Borders: Decolonizing Theory, Practicing Solidarity.* Durham, NC: Duke UP, 2003.

Moody, Joycelyn. *Sentimental Confessions: Spiritual Narratives of Nineteenth-Century African American Women.* Athens: U of Georgia P, 2007.

Mukherjee, Arun. *Postcolonialism: My Living.* Toronto: TSAR, 1998.

Ngai, Mae. *The Lucky Ones: One Family and the Extraordinary Invention of Chinese America.* Boston: Houghton, 2010.

Ngugi wa Thiong'o. *Decolonizing the Mind: The Politics of Language in African Literature.* London: Heinemann, 1986.

Prashad, Vijay. *The Karma of Brown Folk.* Minneapolis: U of Minnesota P, 2000.

Rampersad, Arnold, and Deborah E. McDowell. *Slavery and the Literary Imagination.* Baltimore: Johns Hopkins UP, 1989.

Richter, Daniel K. Before *the Revolution: America's Ancient Pasts.* Cambridge, MA: Belknap P of Harvard UP, 2011.

Rodó, José Enrique. *Ariel.* Trans. Margaret Sayers Peden. Austin: U of Texas P, 1988.

Said, Edward W. *Culture and Imperialism.* New York: Knopf, 1993.

_____. *Orientalism.* New York: Pantheon, 1978.

Singh, Rashna B. *Goodly Is Our Heritage: Children's Literature, Empire, and the Certitude of Character.* Lanham, MD: Scarecrow, 2004.

Smith, Vanessa. *Literary Culture and the Pacific: Nineteenth-Century Textual Encounters.* Cambridge, Eng.: Cambridge UP, 1998.

Spivak, Gayatri Chakravorty. *In Other Worlds: Essays in Cultural Politics.* New York: Methuen, 1987.

Stavans, Ilan, *Spanglish: The Makings of a New American Language.* New York: HarperCollins, 2003.

Sundquist, Eric J. *To Wake the Nations: Race in the Making of American Literature.* Cambridge, MA: Belknap P of Harvard UP, 1993.

Takaki, Ronald T. *A Different Mirror: A History of Multicultural America.* Boston: Little, Brown, 1993.

Terrell, Mary Church. *A Colored Woman in a White World.* New York: Macmillan, 1996.

Thomas, Nicholas. *Entangled Objects: Exchange, Material Culture, and Colonialism in the Pacific.* Cambridge, MA: Harvard UP, 1991.

Vaughan, Alden T. *Roots of American Racism: Essays on the Colonial Experience.* New York: Oxford UP, 1995.

Warrior, Robert. *People and the Word: Reading Native Nonfiction.* Minneapolis: U of Minnesota P, 2005

Wong, Sau-ling Cynthia. *Reading Asian American Literature: From Necessity to Extravagance.* NJ: Princeton UP, 1993.

Yao, Steven G. *Foreign Accents: Chinese-American Verse Form Exclusion to Postethnicity.* New York: Oxford UP, 2010.

Young, Robert. *Postcolonialism: A Very Short Introduction*. New York: Oxford UP, 2003.

Zolla, Elémire, *The Writer and the Shaman: A Morphology of the American Indian*. Trans. Raymond Rosenthal. New York: Harcourt, 1973.

CRITICAL
INSIGHTS

About the Editor_____

Nicholas Birns is associate teaching professor at Eugene Lang College, the New School, in New York, where he teaches courses on post–1900 American and British fiction, literary theory, Shakespeare, and the history of literary genres and traditions. He is the author of *Understanding Anthony Powell* (2004) and the coeditor of *A Companion to Australian Literature Since 1900* (2007), which was named a *CHOICE* Outstanding Academic Book of the year for 2008, and of *Vargas Llosa and Latin American Politics* (2010). His book *Theory After Theory: An Intellectual History of Literary Theory from 1950 to the Early 21st Century* appeared in 2010. His single-authored book *Encyclopedia of Literary Critics and Criticism* will be published in 2012.

Birns served as the Secretary-Treasurer of the Council of Editors of Learned Journals (CELJ) from 2007 to 2011, and has been the editor of *Antipodes: A Global Journal of Australian/New Zealand Literature* since 2001. He is also the president of the Guild of Scholars of the Episcopal Church and is a board member of the Anglican Society. Birns also holds memberships in the Authors' Guild and the National Book Critics Circle and is a senior research fellow at the Council on Hemispheric Affairs. He has contributed many articles and reviews to literature journals including the *New York Times Book Review, Arizona Quarterly, Extrapolation, Studies in Romanticism, The Australian Literary Review, Symbiosis, PAJ, Exemplaria, National Forum,* and *CLIO.* He has recently contributed essays to two *Cambridge Companion* volumes (Anthony Trollope and Mario Vargas Llosa), and is also is a frequent contributor to reference works, including two on Shakespeare (2005) and Facts on File (2011).

He has held research fellowships and/or given invited lectures at Harvard University, the Smithsonian Associates, and Syracuse University as well as at various campuses in Sweden, Australia, and Germany.

Contributors

Nicholas Birns is associate teaching professor at Eugene Lang College, the New School, in New York, where he teaches courses on post–1900 American and British fiction, literary theory, Shakespeare, and the history of literary genres and traditions. He is the author of *Understanding Anthony Powell* (2004) and the coeditor of *A Companion to Australian Literature Since 1900* (2007), which was named a *CHOICE* Outstanding Academic Book of the year for 2008, and of *Vargas Llosa and Latin American Politics* (2010). His book *Theory After Theory: An Intellectual History of Literary Theory from 1950 to the Early 21st Century* appeared in 2010. His single-authored book *Encyclopedia of Literary Critics and Criticism* will be published in 2012.

Shaobo Xie, book review editor of *ARIEL*, is an associate professor in the department of English at University of Calgary. He has published on literary theory, postcolonial studies, globalization, translation, and Chinese modernity. His major works include *Other Positions: Cultural Critique and Critical Culture*, *Thinking Through Postcoloniality* (*ARIEL* fortieth anniversary special issue, coedited with Wang Ning), *Dialogues on Cultural Studies: Interviews with Contemporary Critics* (coedited with Fengzhen Wang), and *Cultural Politics of Resistance*.

John Scheckter is professor of English at the C. W. Post Campus of Long Island University, New York. He is a founding member and past president of the American Association of Australasian Literary Studies. His writing includes *The Australian Novel, 1830–1980* and *The Isle of Pines, 1668: Henry Neville's Uncertain Utopia*. He has published numerous articles on American and postcolonial literature, autobiography, and illustrated text. He is continuing to investigate early modern imperialism and is working on a study of personal archives.

Rebecca Stuhr serves as coordinator for the humanities collections and subject specialist for history and classical studies at the University of Pennsylvania Libraries. Previously she was collection development librarian at Grinnell College and reference librarian-bibliographer for Germanic languages and literatures at the University of Kansas. With degrees from St. Olaf College and the University of California, Berkeley, Stuhr's research encompasses music performance and scholarship, ethnic American autobiography, library preservation, open access, and contemporary literature. Her publications include *Autobiographies by Americans of Color 1980–1994: An Annotated Bibliography* (1997) and its companion covering 1995–2000 (2003) and *Reading Khaled Hosseini* (2010).

Ferentz Lafarge teaches at the Georgetown Day School in Washington, DC. He holds a PhD from Yale and has taught at Eugene Lang College, the New School for Liberal Arts in New York, where he served as the director of the Race and Ethnicity

Program. He is the author of *Songs in the Key of My Life*, a memoir, and is a frequent contributor to *The Huffington Post*.

Kirilka Stavreva is professor of English and creative writing at Cornell College in Mount Vernon, Iowa, where she teaches and writes about medieval and early modern literature and drama and its performances across historical and cultural divides. Her essays on Renaissance drama and its performance, on the popular literature and gender politics of the era, as well as on critical pedagogy have appeared in book collections and journals, such as *The Journal of Medieval and Early Modern Studies*, *Borrowers and Lenders: The Journal of Shakespeare and Appropriation*, *Shakespeare Bulletin*, *Pedagogy*, and *The Journal of Popular Culture*.

Gerd Bayer is a tenured faculty member in the English department at Erlangen University, Germany, having also taught at the University of Toronto, Case Western Reserve, and the University of Wisconsin, Whitewater. The coeditor of five books, he has published a monograph on John Fowles and nature as well as essays on postmodern fiction, postcolonial studies, Holocaust studies, mockumentary film, pop culture, and early modern prose fiction. He is currently working on a monograph about narrative fiction from the English Restoration period.

Craig White, author of *Student Companion to James Fenimore Cooper* (2006), teaches American and postcolonial literature at University of Houston–Clear Lake. He has published articles on Henry James, astronomy, and literature in the antebellum United States, and the Praying Indians of Massachusetts. White earned a BA with Highest Honors in English from the University of North Carolina, an MA in English from Appalachian State University, and a PhD in English from the University of Wisconsin.

Nicole duPlessis teaches at Texas A&M University in the department of English. Her dissertation topic was "Literacy and its Discontents: Modernist Anxiety and the Literacy Fictions of Virginia Woolf, E. M. Forster, D. H. Lawrence, and Aldous Huxley." She has published articles in *Lit* and in book anthologies.

Robert Butler is a professor of English at Canisius College in Buffalo, New York, where he teaches American, African American, and modern literature. He is the author of *Native Son: The Emergence of a New Black Hero* (1995), *Contemporary African American Literature: The Open Journey* (1998), and *The Critical Response to Ralph Ellison* (2001). He has also coauthored with Jerry W. Ward Jr. *The Richard Wright Encyclopedia* (2008). His articles have appeared in journals such as *Twentieth-Century Literature*, *The Centennial Review*, *African American Review*, *MELUS*, and *CLA Journal*.

Juan E. De Castro is associate professor of literary studies at Eugene Lang College, The New School for Liberal Arts. He has published *Mario Vargas Llosa: Public Intellectual in Neoliberal Latin America* (2011); *The Spaces of Latin American Literature:*

Tradition, Globalization, and Cultural Production (2008); and *Mestizo Nations: Culture, Race, and Conformity in Latin American Literature* (2002). With Nicholas Birns he coedited *Vargas Llosa and Latin American Politics* (2010).

Jon Curley teaches in the humanities department at New Jersey Institute of Technology. His first book of poems, *New Shadows*, was published in 2009. A critical study, *Poets and Partitions: Confronting Communal Identity in Northern Ireland*, was published in 2011.

Maik Nwosu is an assistant professor of African and world literature at the University of Denver. He holds a PhD in English and textual studies from Syracuse University, New York. His research areas include African literature, African diaspora literature, postcolonial studies, world literature, semiotics, and critical theory. Nwosu's poetry collection, *The Suns of Kush*, was awarded the Association of Nigerian Authors/Cadbury Poetry Prize in 1995. His novels, *Invisible Chapters* and *Alpha Song*, received the Association of Nigerian Authors Prose Prize and the Association of Nigerian Authors/Spectrum Prose Prize in 1999 and 2002, respectively

Frank P. Fury is a full-time lecturer of English at Monmouth University in West Long Branch, New Jersey. In 2006, he earned his doctorate in English literature from Drew University in Madison, New Jersey. His areas of interest and research include modern and contemporary American literature, the short story, theater, and American cultural history. He has published articles on Ntozake Shange, Tennessee Williams, Eugene O'Neill, and William Faulkner. Additionally, in early 2010 he contributed a chapter to a collection of critical articles on the music of Bruce Springsteen

Dave Gunning teaches contemporary British and postcolonial literature at the University of Birmingham, England. He is the author of *Race and Antiracism in Black British and British Asian Literature* (2010) and currently serves as Chair of the Postcolonial Studies Association.

Jonathan Highfield is professor of English at Rhode Island School of Design. His research focuses on material culture, particularly food and foodways, in the postcolonial context. His recent scholarship includes the chapter "No Longer Praying on Borrowed Wine: Agroforesty and Food Sovereignty in Ben Okri's *The Famished Road* Triology," in *Environment at the Margins* (2011); "Driving the Devil into the Ground: Settler Myth in André Brink's *Devil's Valley*" in *Trauma, Resistance, Reconstruction in Post-1994 South African Writing* (2010); and "'Relations with Food': Agriculture, Colonialism, and Foodways in the Writing of Bessie Head," in *Postcolonial Green* (2010).

Index

acculturation
  literature and, 42, 131, 253
  societal, 41, 256, 272
Achebe, Chinua, 50, 124
  Heart of Darkness and, 124
  influence on Adichie, 262
  Things Fall Apart, 124, 262–65, 272–79
Adichie, Chimamanda Ngozi (*Half of a Yellow Sun*), 13, 262–73, 278–79
Adventures of Huckleberry Finn, The (Mark Twain), 42, 70
Afghanistan, conflict in, 53–55
African American
  identity and, 231
  literary influence, 72, 76, 158, 231, 273
  postcolonial literature and, 216, 231
  satirization of in literature, 72
  stereotypes in literature, 70, 71, 129, 164
  women's identity, 231
Ali, Monica (*Brick Lane*), 247–61
American literary influence, 70, 77, 84
anticolonialism, 199
  imperialism and, 21
  literature of the Carribean, 220
  transnationalism and, 46
  tricontinentalism and, 21
Appiah, Kwame Anthony, 32, 44, 46, 49
Ariel (*Tempest, The*), 93
Austen, Jane (*Mansfield Park*), 4, 25

Babi (*Thousand Splendid Suns, A*), 53–66
Baldwin, James, 11, 161
  Notes of a Native Son, 160
Beatty, Paul (*White Boy Shuffle, The*), 69–85
Bertram, Sir Thomas (*Mansfield Park*), 4

Bhabha, Homi K.
  cross-cultural translation and, 30
  postcolonial studies and, 23, 28–30, 32, 131
  subaltern, 129, 131
Biafran War, 262–65
Bluest Eye, The (Morrison), 69, 75–84
Breedlove, Frieda (*The Bluest Eye*), 77
Breedlove, Pecola (*The Bluest Eye*), 77
Brick Lane (Ali), 247–61
  criticism of, 248, 255, 258
  praise for, 247, 248
Brief Wondrous Life of Oscar Wao, The (Díaz), 69–75, 83–84
Bright Eyes (film), 82
Bunyan, John (*Pilgrim's Progress, The*), 108

Caliban (*Tempest, The*), 89
Caribbean, literature of the, 216
  as anticolonial, 220
Cervantes, Miguel de (*Don Quixote*), 3
Chanu (*Brick Lane*), 248
Chingachgook (*Last of the Mohicans, The*), 121, 127
Christian-Muslim interaction, 3, 89, 91
Claribel (*Tempest, The*), 90
colonial appropriation, 54, 97, 104, 114, 191
  Enlightenment literature and, 5, 111, 224
colonialism. *See also* imperialism
  Derek Walcott on, 110, 216–29
  early novel and, 114
  English Renaissance and, 98
  imperialist control and, 110, 114, 115, 127, 144, 187, 191, 192, 194, 215, 262
  isolation and, 188

colonizing
  hierarchy and, 38, 141, 190
  literature and, 4, 89, 100, 115, 150
  Mansfield Park (Austen) and, 4,
    25–26
  social construction and, 38, 145, 184
Confederacy of Dunces, A, (Toole), 70
Conrad, Joseph, 166, 178
  Heart of Darkness, 123
  postcolonial studies and, 123
control and power, 81
  colonizer, 96, 100, 113, 127, 128,
    189, 192, 199, 224
  geographical, 110
  political, 54, 194, 271
  racial, 78, 116, 168, 193, 232, 237
  spousal, 59
  technological, 115, 116, 183
Cooper, James Fenimore
  Last of the Mohicans, The, 8, 121–38
  Leatherstocking Tales, The, 121
Cullen, Countee ("Yet Do I Marvel"),
  235
cultural adaptation
  as seen in literature, 69
cultural expression. *See also* cultural
  identity
  first contact and, 103
  liberal thought and, 45, 48
  literature and, 50, 103, 111, 176, 247
  post–World War II and, 46, 207, 247
  societal norms and, 167, 184
  technology and, 47
cultural identity, 10. *See also* cultural
  expression
  confusion, 154, 188, 192, 273
  education and, 145
  nationalism, 145, 205
  politics, 11
  race, 11, 167, 176

sexuality, 11
subordination of, 180, 183
the self and, 172, 180, 274
Culture and Imperialism (Said), 22, 31,
  33

Darwin, Charles, 39
Defoe, Daniel
  childhood and early life, 109
  Robinson Crusoe, 5, 107–18, 123,
    129, 218
  travel writer, as, 112
Díaz, Junot (*Brief Wonderous Life of
  Oscar Wao, The*), 69–75, 83–84
Don Quixote (Cervantes), 3
Dostoevsky, Fyodor (*Crime and Punish-
  ment*), 166, 177–78
  Richard Wright and, 166, 177, 178
Douglas, Frederick, 271
Dr. Aziz (*Passage to India, A*), 141
Du Bois, W. E. B., 20, 21, 72, 76
Dungeons and Dragons, 69, 73, 75, 84

economic hegemony, 23
education, the colonized and, 145, 217
Ellison, Ralph (*Invisible Man*), 8, 69,
  72, 76, 84, 160, 161, 172
English Renaissance colonialism, 98
Enlightenment literature
  colonial appropriation in, 5, 111, 115
entrapment
  physical, 170, 173
  psychological, 170, 172

Fanon, Frantz, influence on Shange, 242
Fernanda (*One Hundred Years of Solitude*), 187
Fielding, Cyril (*Passage to India, A*),
  141
for colored girls . . . (Shange), 231–46

Forster, E. M.
  Howards End, 140, 141, 143, 145, 146, 151
  Passage to India, A, 140
  Room with a View, A, 140, 143, 149
  Where Angels Fear to Tread, 140, 143
Foucault, Michel
  Edward Said and, 24
  postcolonial studies and, 21, 22, 23
  poststructuralism and, 22
Friday (*Robinson Crusoe*), 111, 129

García Márquez, Gabriel, 50, 180
  One Hundred Years of Solitude, 180–93
geographical analysis
  Antonio Gramsci and, 24
  colonialist imaginative, 25
  imperialist, 24, 25
  Mansfield Park, Jane Austen, 25
  postcolonialism and, 24
Gonzalo (*Tempest, The*), 91
Gramsci, Antonio
  Edward Said and, 24, 25
  geographical hegemony, 24, 31
  postcolonial studies and, 21
Great Hunger, The (Kavanagh), 207
Greek drama, similarities to, 234, 237, 238
Greek mythology, allusions to, 211
Gus (*Native Son*), 163

Hall, Stuart, 19
Hawkeye (*Last of the Mohicans, The*), 121, 127
Heaney, Seamus, 204, 205, 209, 210, 211
Heart of Darkness (Conrad)
  postcolonial studies and, 123–31, 135, 138

Heaslop, Ronny (*Passage to India, A*), 141
hegemony, 22, 26, 98, 116
  economic, 23
Hemingway, Ernest, 40, 42, 43, 194
Hewitt, John, 208
Homeric influence, 1, 74, 223
homosexuality, 11
Hosseini, Kahled (*Thousand Splendid Suns, A*), 53–67
Howards End (Forster), 141, 143, 145, 146, 151
Hughes, Langston, 238
hybridity, postcolonial studies and, 130–35, 138

identity, African American women and, 231
imperialism, 19, 22, 51, 127. *See also* colonialism
  anticolonialism and, 21, 256
  cultural, 28, 183
  Derek Walcott on, 110, 216–29
  geographical analysis of, 25, 125
  intellectual, 22
  language and, 278
  literature in resistance to, 27, 40, 129, 140, 156, 201, 222
  literature in support of, 91, 110, 128, 140
intertextuality, 124
Invisible Man (Ellison), 8, 69, 72, 84, 160, 172

James, Henry, 9, 11, 14, 40, 162, 178

Kaufman, Gunnar (*White Boy Shuffle, The*), 70
Kavanagh, Patrick (*Great Hunger, The*), 206
Kipling, Rudyard, 9

Kurtz (*Heart of Darkness*), 127, 166

Laila (*Thousand Splendid Suns, A*), 53
language
    colonizer and, 269, 270, 271, 277
    cultural conflict and, 275
    imperialism and, 278
    response to trauma and, 262, 267,
        268
Last of the Mohicans, The (Cooper), 8,
    121–38
    postcolonial studies and, 125
Latin American
    stereotypes in literature, 70, 71
Lawrence, D. H., 7, 137
Leatherstocking Tales, The (Cooper),
    121
León, Lola de (*Brief Wondrous Life of
    Oscar Wao, The*), 70
León, Oscar de (*Brief Wondrous Life of
    Oscar Wao, The*), 69
Little Colonel, The (film)
    Bill Robinson and, 81
    Shirley Temple and, 81

Macondo, village of (*One Hundred
    Years of Solitude*), 184
MacTeer, Claudia (*Bluest Eye, The*), 77,
    80, 82
magic, 4, 92, 96, 98, 104, 194. *See also*
    witchcraft
magical realism, 181, 194, 195
Mansfield Park (Austin)
    colonizing and, 4
    geographical analysis, 25
    Said, Edward and, 26
Mariam (*Thousand Splendid Suns, A*),
    53
Marlow (*Heart of Darkness*), 126
Marx, Karl, 19, 21, 22, 24, 25, 26, 39,
    190

Mary (*Native Son*), 164
Melville, Herman (*Moby-Dick*), 37–38,
    45, 52, 225
Milton, John
    Paradise Lost, 108, 226–27
missionaries in literature, 116, 198, 262,
    273, 275, 279
Moby-Dick (Melville), 37–38, 45, 52,
    225
Montague, John, 209
Morrison, Toni (*Bluest Eye, The*), 69,
    75–84
Mrs. Moore (*Passage to India, A*), 141
Munro, Alice (*Last of the Mohicans,
    The*), 127
Munro, Cora (*Last of the Mohicans,
    The*), 127
music
    cultural encounter and, 89, 93–97,
        99, 130, 133

Naipaul, V. S., 14, 220
Nana (*Thousand Splendid Suns, A*), 58
nationalism
    literature and, 197
    poetry and, 197, 203
    response to decolonization, 197, 201,
        253
Native Son (Wright), 158
    criticism of, 159, 160
    imagery and, 164, 165, 167, 171
    James Baldwin and, 160
    narrative structure and, 168, 170
    point of view in, 166
    praise for, 158
Nazneen (*Brick Lane*), 248
non-Western peoples
    substandardization of, 111, 115, 116,
        117
Notes of a Native Son (Baldwin), 160

Okonkwo (*Things Fall Apart*), 273
Omeros (Walcott), 73, 216, 220–29
One Hundred Years of Solitude (García
    Márquez), 180–93
oppression
    colonized people and, 127, 128
    humanity in spite of, 128
Orientalism, concept of, 24, 31, 33
Orientalism (Said), 20, 23, 31, 33, 50
other, the, 25, 30, 131, 186
    filter and, 1
    language for, 1
    literature and, 2, 6, 12, 98, 140, 151,
        156, 182, 187, 204

Paradise Lost (Milton), 108, 226–27
Passage to India, A (Forster), 140
patriarchal society, rejection of, 238
Pilgrim's Progress, The (Bunyan), 108
poetry
    political commentary and, 202, 203,
        208
    public verus private, 202
    social commentary and, 200, 201
politics
    within literature, 100, 231
pop culture, in literature, 74, 83, 131
postcolonial cultural analysis, 20, 22
    Young, Robert and, 19, 20, 23
postcolonialism
    geographical analysis and, 216
    literary study and, 51, 102, 121, 216
    Young, Robert views on, 23
postcolonialism as intellectual imperial-
    ism, 22
postcolonialism versus anticolonialism,
    21
postcolonial literature, 12, 125, 126, 250
    African, 69, 216, 263, 265
    Caribbean, 221
    Latin American, 13, 69

national politics within, 14, 197, 204,
    206, 263
    transnational treatment of, 248, 250
postcolonial studies, 121, 126
    criticism of, 30, 32
    Heart of Darkness (Conrad) and, 123
    literature and, 122, 123, 221
postcolonial violence, 264
    effects of, 266
postmodernism, 32, 50, 51
Prospero (*Tempest, The*), 91, 96, 110

Quested, Adela (*Passage to India, A*), 141

racial mixing, 8, 132, 133, 135
    introduction of in literature, 9, 100
Rasheed (*Thousand Splendid Suns, A*),
    57, 61
religion in literature, 1, 108, 208
religious allegory
    Robinson Crusoe (Defoe), 108
Remedios, Renata (*One Hundred Years
    of Solitude*), 182
Renaissance Literature, 3
representation, 242, 257
Responsibilities (Yeats), 199, 232
Robinson, Bill, 81
Robinson Crusoe (Defoe), 5, 107
Romanticism, effect on cultural under-
    standing, 7
Room with a View, A (Forster), 140, 143,
    149
Rushdie, Salman, 4, 14

Said, Edward
    Antonio Gramsci and, 24, 25
    Culture and Imperialism, 22, 31, 33,
        200
    Homi K. Bhabha and, 28, 29
    Orientalism, 4, 20, 23, 31, 33, 50, 242
    postcolonial studies and, 23

self-esteem, 77
self, the, 1, 25, 131
    cultural identity and, 172, 182, 217,
        232, 233, 245
    development of, 173, 174, 175, 235,
        250, 259
    filter and, 1, 103
    language for, 1, 266
    literature and, 90, 166
Shakespeare, William (*Tempest, The*), 4,
    51, 89–104, 123
Shange, Nozake (*for colored girls . . .*),
    231–46
social interation
    class and, 90, 151, 266
    race and, 141, 151
Soyinka, Wole, 13, 16, 265, 273
Spivak, Gayatri
    postcolonial studies and, 23–24,
        26–29, 32
subaltern, 23, 27, 145

Tempest, The (Shakespeare), 4, 51,
    89–104, 123
Temple, Shirley, 75, 81
Things Fall Apart (Achebe), 124,
    262–63, 272–79
Thomas, Bigger (*Native Son*), 160
Thousand Splendid Suns, A (Hosseini),
    53–67
transnationalism, 44
    anticolonialism and, 46
transnational literature
    postcolonial, 14, 262
tricontinentalism
    anticolonialism and, 21
    Young, Robert, 20
tropicopolitanism in literature, 6
Trueblood, Jim (*Invisible Man*), 84

Twain, Mark
    *Adventures of Huckleberry Finn,
        The*, 42, 70

Uncas (*Last of the Mohicans, The*), 127
Úrsula, Amaranta (*One Hundred Years
    of Solitude*), 180

Walcott, Derek, 73, 109, 216
    early life and career, 216
    imperialism and colonialism, views
        of, 110, 216
    Junot Díaz and, 73
    Omeros, 73, 216, 220–29
    Robinson Crusoe and, 109, 218
    "True-born Englishman," 110
    Whitman, Walt and, 218
Wao, Oscar (*Brief Wondrous Life of
    Oscar Wao, The*), 69
West, Cornel, 231, 237
Where Angels Fear to Tread (Forster),
    140, 143
White Boy Shuffle, The (Beatty), 70, 71
Whitman, Walt, 7
    Walcott, Derek and, 218
witchcraft, 98, 99, 100. *See also* magic
Woolf, Virginia, 42, 43
Wright, Richard, 12, 72, 76, 158–78
    Dostoevsky, Fyodor (*Crime and
        Punishment*) and, 166, 177, 178
Yeats, W. B., 197
    early poetry, 198
    mythical images in poetry, 198, 202
    Responsibilities, 199
    "Second Coming," 272
Young, Robert
    postcolonial cultural analysis, 20
    postcolonialism and, 19, 23
    tricontinentalism, 20